Lacan and the Destiny of Literature

Continuum Literary Studies Series

Also available in the series:

Active Reading by Ben Knights and Chris Thurgar-Dawson
Beckett's Books by Matthew Feldman
British Fiction in the Sixties by Sebastian Groes
Canonizing Hypertext by Astrid Ensslin
Character and Satire in Postwar Fiction by Ian Gregson
Contemporary Fiction and Christianity by Andrew Tate
Coleridge and German Philosophy by Paul Hamilton
English Fiction in the 1930s by Chris Hopkins
Ecstasy and Understanding edited by Adrian Grafe
Fictions of Globalization by James Annesley
Joyce and Company by David Pierce
Lacan and the Destiny of Literature by Ehsan Azari
London Narratives by Lawrence Phillips
Masculinity in Fiction and Film by Brian Baker
Modernism and the Post-colonial by Peter Childs
Milton, Evil and Literary History by Claire Colebrook
Novels of the Contemporary Extreme edited by Alain-Phillipe Durand and Naomi Mandel
Recalling London by Alex Murray
Romanticism, Literature and Philosophy by Simon Swift
Seeking Meaning for Goethe's Faust by J. M. van der Laan
Sexuality and the Erotic in the Fiction of Joseph Conrad by Jeremy Hawthorn
Such Deliberate Disguises: The Art of Phillip Larkin by Richard Palmer
The Palimpsest by Sarah Dillon
The Measureless Past of Joyce, Deleuze and Derrida by Ruben Borg
Women's Fiction 1945–2000 by Deborah Philips

Lacan and the Destiny of Literature

Desire, *Jouissance* and the *Sinthome* in Shakespeare, Donne, Joyce and Ashbery

Ehsan Azari

continuum

Continuum International Publishing Group
The Tower Building 80 Maiden Lane
11 York Road Suite 704
London SE1 7NX New York NY 10038

www.continuumbooks.com

British Library Cataloguing-in-Publication Data
A catalogue record for this book is available from the British Library.

ISBN: 978-1-4411-4930-5 (Paperback)

Library of Congress Cataloging-in-Publication Data
A catalog record for this book is available from the Library of Congress.

Typeset by Newgen Imaging Systems Pvt Ltd, Chennai, India
Printed and bound in Great Britain by Biddles Ltd, King's Lynn, Norfolk

For my wife Sheila, and my children, Raghba, Manizha, Ramin and Malalay whose invaluable support and patience made the completion of this book possible!

Contents

Acknowledgements

I am grateful to Nick Mansfield, whose generous help and valuable criticism made this book possible. My heartfelt thanks also go to Ellie Ragland for her encouraging and inspiring comments on this project.

I would especially like to thank Luke Thurston for sending me his unauthorized translation of Lacan's *Seminar XXIII: Le Sinthome*, and Jack W. Stone, for his unauthorized translation of Lacan's *Seminar XXII: R.S.I.*, *'Lituraterre'*, and *L'étourdit*.

SAM (Macquarie University Students' Union Ltd) deserves all my thanks for providing me five-month free accommodation at Macquarie University Village.

Abbreviations

C	*Coriolanus*
FW	*Finnegans Wake*
H	*Hamlet*
HL	*Hotel Lautréamont*
M	*Macbeth*
MAN	*Much Ado About Nothing*
MV	*The Merchant of Venice*
S	Sonnet
SPCM	Self-Portrait in a Convex Mirror
Q	Quatrain

Introduction

In today's poststructuralist literary studies and literary criticism in the English-speaking world, Jacques Lacan has a haunting presence with his arduous and inaccessible theories. In addition to the fact that many of his seminars and texts are unavailable in English, the lack of an in-depth and detailed understanding of Lacan's later psychoanalytic theories has left the use and deployment of his theories in contemporary literary studies and criticism open to a wide-range of misinterpretations. Apart from a handful of excellent works, a close examination of much literary analysis and interpretation produced under the rubric of Lacanian literary study turns up two major drawbacks. In a diagnostic gesture, one group of critics place authors and their personae like an analysand on the couch and narrowly apply Lacanian clinical conceptions to the whole of a given textual and biographical data, reducing criticism merely to a psychiatric report on literary personae who usually suffer from one of two wholesale conditions: neurosis or psychosis. A second group seems to be more interested in critical practice marked by a superimposition of some basic Lacanian psychoanalytic tenets. As such, they seem to downgrade Lacan's thinking on literature and reduce the whole gamut of his theories to merely the mirror phase, the role of the phallus, or object *a*.

In both cases, an imbalance between an in-depth knowledge of Lacanian psychoanalytic theory and conservative literary interpretation has made Lacan's literary legacy subject to a variety of misinterpretations and misapprehensions. Such an implicit laxity vis-à-vis Lacan opens an appalling gap in the effective study and use of Lacanian literary theory and literary criticism. This dilemma compounds the dizzying obscurity of Lacan's style of speaking and writing especially as regards his theories in relation to literature and its interpretation. This situation, moreover, encourages contemporary literary critics to either avoid using Lacan altogether or to distort the key messages of his theories. Such marginalization or expulsion of the real Lacan from the literary scene has deprived contemporary literary studies of a powerful interpretative methodology that no other poststructuralist theory can offer.

What is required is a new path through the current heated literary debates in relation to Lacan and literary theory. This new methodology calls for a multi-disciplinary approach to literature that necessitates a thorough comprehension and use of the Lacanian theories that are relevant to literature and literary studies. This multi-disciplinarity can be achieved only if we set out on an intensive and all-embracing inquiry into Lacan's psychoanalytic theory as a *prima materia* for our approach to the interpretation of the literary text. Lacan's own primary concern in his literary hermeneutic has been to see a convergence between psychoanalytic thought, interpretation and literary discourse. In Lacan, psychoanalysis supports literature, as both shares the same object of study. This implies that literature is concerned with the illustration and dramatization of human subjectivity whereas psychoanalysis strives to reveal the moments that determine and constitute such subjectivity. Simply put, psychoanalysis stages the theoretical *mise-en acte* of what literature shows. In this context, I argue that Lacan transcends Derrida's deconstruction in relation to literary interpretation, because his psychoanalytic knowledge is equipped to deconstruct deconstruction by examining and re-examining the debris that the deconstructive approach produces out of a literary text. For example, when deconstruction reached finitude in dealing with an avant-garde literary discourse such as James Joyce's, Lacan moves beyond and unfolds the causes and rationality behind the irrationality, internal contradictions and heterogeneity in a literary text.

The paramount aim of this book is a genealogical exploration of Lacan's psychoanalytic theory, especially those concepts that we are going to use for the analysis of a selection of various literary texts. To this end, I have divided this study into two parts: the first is devoted entirely to an in-depth exposure of Lacanian psychoanalytic and literary theory; and the second attempts to present a practical Lacanian literary criticism. As such, I invert Freud and Lacan's insistence on the *universitas litterarum* (literary university), as a requisite for the training of psychoanalysts through literature. A literary critic must have a profound understanding of the skills necessary to master both literature and psychoanalysis. When interpreting a text a critic has to have one eye on Lacan's theory and another on the texture of a literary work at the same time. This approach to literature calls for an in-depth study of Lacanian psychoanalytic theory as *a priori* to any literary investigation. As such, we will be able to balance psychoanalytic knowledge with critical analysis in our research. For only thorough knowledge this can equip us to appraise literary discourses in a way appropriate to Lacan. Lacanian theory is never far from literature itself. Every one of Lacan's conceptualizations and theorizations concerning desire, the subject, *jouissance*, the *sinthome*, writing, and so on have been articulated and developed in terms of rhetorical and tropic configuration, as well as through a densely literary use of language. Many key Lacanian concepts have been articulated through the mediation of, or in direct dialogue with, literature. This, no doubt, reflects Lacan's emphasis on the ascendancy of literature over psychoanalysis, and its leading role in the articulation of psychoanalytic theory. Lacan's approach to literature diverts from the predetermined Freudian applied psychoanalysis and psychobiography. On the contrary, Lacan's textual reading varies from text to text and develops a critical process where both literary dramatization and psychoanalytic truth flow side by side. This is the major difference between Lacan's literature and literary theory and the literary interpretation of orthodox psychoanalysis. There are frequent moments in literature where the poetics of literary language brings to the surface multi-layered sediments of major psychoanalytic truths. Lacan situates himself in a theoretical and critical vantage point from which he passionately focuses on generative moments in literary discourse. This exemplifies the central relationship between psychoanalytic theory and literature.

Furthermore, the first short part of this study turns to what I consider to be a supplement to Lacanian literary theory, a *technē* in the Aristotelian sense and a *priori*. As *technē*, it provides us with skills and an understanding of Lacan's puzzling concepts, and as *a priori*, it allows us to experience Lacan's interpretive methodology for the exegesis of a broad selection of literary texts. It is not simply a brief glossary of Lacanian psychoanalytic epistemology, which nowadays has become fashionable in theoretically based critical investigations in literary and cultural studies. As part of Lacanian literary theory, the first theoretical part spells out what literature means and how a literary text includes and excludes human subjectivity. These primary reasons explain to a greater extent the axiology of dividing this study into two parts: an extensive and detailed description and interpretation of Lacan himself, and the larger part dedicated to Lacanian literary criticism in praxis.

Such a structural and thematic division that, for some readers, might look inconvenient is also related to the advent of theory in literary study. The birth of theory marks the frontier between traditional and modern literary criticism. A criticism based on value-judgement which considered a critic to be a judge of whether a literary text is good or bad or whether it is up to the highest literary standard, ruled criticism from the time of Aristotle. The critic from Greek *krites* (judge) essentially was the one whose business was to pass evaluative judgements on literature. The primary attention was focused on the canonization of literature on the grounds of a set of empirical regulations. Theory has emerged as a meta-language, with the exploitation of Saussurian linguistics. Paul de Man in his influential essay 'Resistance to Theory', stresses the difficulties of a tropic system in language and he is keen to recommend its exclusion from criticism, whereas tropes mark the starting point in Lacanian literary criticism.

The necessity of a theory-based criticism in Anglo-American literary study was stressed by practitioners of literary criticism. Jonathan Culler in his two books, *Structuralist Poetics: Structuralism Linguistics and the Study of Literature* and *The Pursuit of Signs: Semiotics, Literature, Deconstruction*, attempts to justify the existence of a complete conceptual framework before embarking on the critique of a literary text. As de Man suggested, Russian formalism, by applying linguistics to a literary text and then structuralism underlined the need for modern literary theory as *a priori* for understanding literature. Such a need in its cross-disciplinarity and inter-disciplinarity was extensively developed by the Frankfurt School in the 1940s and 1950s. This school largely promoted the interaction of theories and their application for explaining literary, social, philosophical and cultural discourses.

It is nonetheless important to define the limits of our probe into Lacan and literature. Poststructuralist literary criticism in English seems to remain deprived of access to some of the important concepts in the final phase of Lacan's life that have long been in currency in other European languages especially French and Spanish. This problem adds to the already proverbial inaccessibility of the Lacanian text. Although, as I said above, a number of influential books have recently been published on Lacan and literature in English, critics and students of literature may well still be disappointed when they see that these too have left obscure key questions in Lacan's theories that are important for literary studies. In such a confused state of affairs, I wish to approach late Lacan with the utmost caution and care. It is impossible to write about Lacan without taking risks. Since Lacan's thinking on literature and criticism is dispersed across his vast corpus of seminars and texts, I have attempted to piece together his literary and critical insights and reconstructed them as far as I could in order to have them form a consistent body of knowledge.

Similarly, I propose to combine the key points of Lacan's essay '*Lituraterre*', with the theory of the *sinthome* in order to reinforce and empower our interpretative and exegetical techniques. To single out the significance of *lituraterre* in Lacanian literary criticism, I argue that we will be able to gauge the constituents of a literary text more effectively, if we combine both *lituraterre* with the *sinthome* for literary practice. This is because this combination enables us to get into the micro-fractions of a literary text. Moreover, the critical technics devised in this essay offers a topological reading of literature. To this end, following Lacan, I use the pun *lituraterre* with multiple references, as a verb to allow the indexing and analysis of the textual structure of a literary discourse, in a synergy that creates a new technical means for poststructuralist reading and literary inquiry. I pick out the concepts of *littoral*, for example, from the above essay in order to analyse postmodern poetics. The *littoral* appears through certain deformations and ruptures in the organization of language, which lead to a break-up in the semantic, phonemic and morphological articulation of the text. Such ruptures are exemplary within avant-garde writing in which the imaginary becomes dysfunctional and the symbolic conflates with the real. Similarly, I argue that it is appropriate to connect the conceptualization of Lacan's *jouissance de la femme* with mystical *jouissance*, thus detaching it from the gender imperative, for Lacan sees it as intrinsically asexual. I also underscore Lacan's great discovery of feminine *jouissance* or a mystical cosmic ecstasy as the *jouissance* of the Other experienced through the mystic body. This assertion could be controversial in Anglo-American thinking where the inscription of mystical discourse is mostly addressed in theology or, at best is flirted with in New Age thinking.

As said, the first part of the book functions as a preliminary to the interpretation of literature. Instead of mixing the clinical and the literary Lacan, this part opens lines of negotiation between these two fields by undertaking a detailed study of those of Lacan's psychoanalytic concepts that are crucial for the reading and analysis of various literary works presented in the second part of this book. The first two chapters examine desire as the Lacanian *cogito*, so central is it to his early psychoanalytic teachings. After spelling out the genealogy of desire and its importance for the subject's inauguration in the symbolic register, the first and second chapters seek the roots of Lacan's concept with an emphasis on the importance of language as the carrier of the subject's unconscious desire.

The first chapter outlines the onto-genesis of desire, its cause and symbols such as the object *a* and the phallus. The essential argument here is that these two objects stand in the web of desire as interchangeable objects for the lost and primordial object. The second chapter looks at desire in relation to gender difference as well as the influence of the latter upon the economy of desire. The discussion then moves to a response to the criticism of Lacan's theory of feminine desire by poststructuralist feminists, Irigaray and Cixous. Irigaray attacks Lacan on account of his earlier emphasis on the phallus as the only signifier that determines both masculine and feminine desires. My argument also addresses the limits of Lacan's earlier phallocentrism in relation to Irigaray's theory of feminine desire, which is altered by later Lacan, especially with the development of his theory of feminine *jouissance*. This chapter also investigates Irigaray and Cixous' definition of feminine desire in terms of a desire for the same. It also disputes Cixous' emphasis on woman's writing as the only way to liberate feminine desire, for writing, as Lacan postulates, with its existential relationship with the subject's body and unconscious, essentially touches the real and remains beyond the phallic economy. Here, Lacan's theory of writing (*écriture*) confirms the French feminists' argument that a woman can find her true self by way of writing which can inscribe something that ex-ists. However *écriture* for Lacan is beyond any gender imperatives. In her own fiction, however, Cixous uses the same old language, and seems unable to bring a new phonetic and semantic structure to her language.

The third chapter extends the discussion beyond the finitude of desire in light of the late teachings of Lacan in which desire loses its central position. This chapter considers the Lacanian theory of feminine *jouissance* as a by-product of the many centuries suppression of mystic *jouissance* in Western culture. This feminization of *jouissance* is also related to the idealization of women, of which courtly love in the Middle Ages was a vivid example. This chapter provides an overview of the moments in and through which desire begins to dissolve. *Le Sinthome* is a centred concept that arose in the final phase of Lacan's teaching through a one-year seminar on James Joyce. This seminar develops a remarkably fertile Lacanian theory on literature and the arts. Issues related to Lacan's theory of literature are further evaluated in which literature first appears as a symptom. In this seminar, Lacan rejects the definition of literature as the mere mimesis of the unconscious. Emphasis is laid on a theory of *écriture* as an effect of language and a means of play with the real and the unconscious, for as he says, '[w]riting as jouissance', and 'writing as the bone of which language would be the flesh' (Lacan, cited in Marini, 1992, 228). In other words, the *sinthome* is a signifying formation beyond analysis. The argument then proceeds to a discussion of Lacan's theory of the *sinthome* as a redefinition of the symptom in terms of a crucial signifier that holds the three registers together. Foreclosure of the Name-of-the-Father from phallic signification lies at the root cause of the emergence of the *sinthome*, but always as an art, a *suppléance* of the author or an artist for avoiding psychosis.

The fourth chapter functions as a bridge between Lacanian theory and its theoretical use for the appraisal of a literature. This chapter vigorously argues for the importance of the literary Lacan. It attempts to untangle the very complex Lacanian theory of the letter, writing, and its relation to the real.

After an exhaustive study of Lacan's theories of desire and beyond, his relation to literary studies, and his principles of literary theory and literary criticism, Chapter 5 leads us to the Shakespearean theatre of desire. I have selected *Hamlet, Coriolanus, Macbeth* and *The Merchant of Venice* in reference to the structure of desire, for as a collection of texts they offer exemplary patterns of the operation of desire. They also provide fertile situations in which masculine and feminine desires are played out in an imaginary illusion in which desire is always displaced. *Hamlet* has masculine desire as its context, whereas *Macbeth* offers multiple forms of feminine desire. The limits of Freud's comments on both plays are also addressed. *The Merchant of Venice* circles around desire in relation to object *a* and the phallus, while *Coriolanus* oscillates between the phallic mother and desire under a feminine masquerade. These factors have governed my selection of Shakespearean texts. For example, the *Hamlet* section attempts to explain the most difficult points that have been mostly left untouched in Anglo-American literary studies. This section is also intended to answer the question: why is *Hamlet* a tragedy of desire?

The sixth chapter addresses mystical *jouissance* in the poetry of John Donne. This chapter scrutinizes Donne's celebrated 'Divine Poems' and 'Love Lyrics' with reference to Lacan's theory of desire, love and *jouissance*. Donne's poetics display these concepts in its eroticized melancholy, mystical love and ecstasy. I argue that the identification of Donne's poetry as metaphysical is an example of the repression of mystical literary discourse in Western culture. To this end, the chapter also engages with the traditional criticism of Donne. In the light of Lacan's theory of *Le Sinthome*, the seventh chapter concentrates on Joyce's *Finnegans Wake*. Selecting chapter four of the second book of the novel, 'Four Old Sailors', the discussion spells out the rationale behind the Joycean subversion of language in its semantic, syntactical and phonetic systems with an emphasis on Joyce's littering of the letter and its meaning. The overall aim of this chapter is to engage Lacan with Joyce's textual devices (something that he himself theorizes in *Le Sinthome*) – wordplay, puns, polysemy, fragmentation of the signifier and the letter, audio-visual witticism, alliteration, antonomasia and so on – and their relation to the object *a* and the phallus. The chapter bears out the fact that Lacan's critique of Joyce grounds itself on the overall system of his language usage not by way of the message he wants to communicate. We will attempt to show in Joyce's text that literature is first experienced as a symptom; a signifying practice and an index of the real. If we accept Barthes's definition of literature as the locus of the real, then Lacan would be the one who can tell us what the real is:

> From ancient times to the efforts of our avant-garde, literature has been concerned to represent something. What? I will put it crudely: the real. The real is not representable, and it is because men ceaselessly try to represent it by words that there is a history of literature. that real is not representable, but only demonstrable . . . with Lacan, as the impossible, that which is unattainable and escapes discourse. (Barthes, 1993b, 465)

Finally, the eighth and last chapter explores the *littoral* as a terrain in John Ashbery's poetry which separates unconscious knowledge from *jouissance*. This chapter's theoretical background is based on a combination of Lacan's theories of *le sinthome* and *lituraterre*, showing the different textual construction of the *sinthome* in comparison with the *Wake*. My attempt is to perform a Lacanian autopsy on poetic discourse to show the textual ruptures that the poet wants to cover by different linguistic methods, intertextuality and ambiguity. These poetic and non-poetic devices are discussed as part of the poet's *sinthome*. The chapter embarks on a textually focused analysis of Ashbery's long poem, 'Self-Portrait in a Convex Mirror', and his collection of poems, *Hotel Lautréamont*. The emphasis in the long poem is mainly on the imaginary relation of the subject with the Other, and the pre-verbal identification of the subject and desire; and in the collection of poems, it is on the cut in the signifying process in the symbolic register or *littoral* as the symptom and signature of the poet. We call this an imagist relation for here in the long poem as in the mirror phase, every link with the Other is established on the basis of an imaginary bond between the ego and ideal-ego.

The last two chapters of this study attempt to inscribe, disseminate and foster Lacanian literary criticism in reference to the theoretical foundation laid in his final teachings. The choice of Joyce and Ashbery here is because they fit etiological thought in final Lacan. That which reveals itself in literature as dismantling of the language system constitutes a unique symptom of an author and his way of joyful play with his or her own unconscious. The symptom finds its signifying structure in writing. This is what Lacan envisioned long before

Le Sinthome, as he writes in *Écrits*: '[if] symptoms can be read, it is because they themselves are already inscribed in a writing process' (Lacan, 2006, 371).

The reversal of the psychoanalytic dictum – *universitas litterarum* – as I noted at the outset, means engaging in negotiations between two separate fields: psychoanalysis and literature, which will lead us to master a methodology of reading, models of application and nodes of implication between these realms. Besides developing knowledge which can be applied in multiple interpretive contexts, we can obtain tools by which we can find out what constitutes the subject matter of a critical literary enquiry. As we will see, one outcome of the theoretical part emerges as new ways of experimenting with psychoanalytic literary criticism in action in the second part of the study. Our interrogation of different concepts ultimately will result in a synergy whose productivity will be seen when Lacan's topological account of literature in his famous essay *lituraterre* and the *sinthome* will enable us to discover the internal dynamisms of Joyce and Ashbery's texts.

The last word on dealing with Lacan. There is a downside to every academic daring to write on Lacan and especially the use of his clinical and theoretical works for literary theory and criticism. Every time I describe or interpret Lacan's obscure points or argue with him, I wish to write in a parenthesis: *[if I am right!]*. Having included these parentheses in what follows will undoubtedly make this book structurally look like Beckett and Pinter's texts full of *silences* and *pauses*. Therefore, I will humbly remove this phrase from my discussion. Probably Lacan himself was aware of such difficulties in the use of his text when he wrote in the preface to Anika Lemaire's thesis: '[M]y *Écrits* are unsuitable for a thesis, particularly an academic thesis: they are antithetical by nature: one either takes what they formulate or one leaves them' (Lacan, cited in Lemaire, 1991, vii). The best approach is to simply try and explain Lacan's discourse. As he himself says in *Encore*, '[y]ou are not obliged to understand my writings. If you don't understand them, so much the better – that will give you the opportunity to explain them' (Lacan, 1998a, 34). Sometimes we come across debates in which Lacan is supplanted by other poststructuralist thinkers, especially Derrida, Kristeva and Barthes. Since Lacan is very difficult to follow, some critics have chosen to go for easier options by adopting alternative concepts, some of which were originally developed by Lacan, thus concealing their paternity. In the end, my aim here is to clarify Lacan's ideas in order to show how useful they are to literary studies.

Chapter 1

Desire, the Lacanian *Cogito*

The term desire, an iconic conception in the Western metaphysical tradition, has acquired new shades of meaning and force with Lacan. This amorphous notion in Lacanian epistemology does not bring to mind a concept or a set of concepts corresponding to an empirical observation or theoretical assumption. This implies that working out a fixed and stable definition for desire is problematic. As Lacan says, when giving a definition to 'nothingness', it is never simply nothing but more never-here. The same goes for desire, which by its nature gives rise to its own elision and impossibility. Being an alienating articulation, desire is often misconstrued. It morphs into another desire and as Lacan insists the analytical experience '[s]hows us that *not to want to desire* and *to desire* are the same thing' [*emphasis added*] (Lacan, 1979a, 235). Since desire as a concept liquidates itself and is non-conceptual, the only way to decipher desire, like a dream, is interpretation. Keeping this paradox in view, I will in this chapter start off by untangling the concept of desire and then attempt to investigate its object cause and its signifier as parts of the absolute conditions for its operation.

During the heyday of the structuralism of the nineteen-sixties, Lacan summarized his theoretical position about desire in Seminar XI: *The Four Fundamental Concepts of Psychoanalysis* (1964), where he argues, '[D]esire, in fact, is interpretation itself' (Lacan, 1979a, 176). Lacan works out an all-embracing interpretation of desire by way of a theory that dismisses phenomenology and the Western metaphysical conceptual tradition. Lacan precisely manages to articulate the inarticulable nature of desire in his theoretical discourse. This was the primary reason Althusser admired Lacan so much, writing in 1966, '*outside of Lacan, there is at present no one*' [*original emphasis*] (Althusser, 1996, 49). According to Althusser, Lacan built up a theoretical system that was able to generate notions and ideas that were '[c]apable of accounting for the *total set* of facts and of the field of analytic practice' (49).

Lacan promulgates interpretation as a key theoretical methodology for the understanding of desire and its causal relationship with the subject. He reiterates in *Écrits* that psychoanalysis has discovered the function of desire in a way that unfolds its relation with the history of the subject, by developing a certain hermeneutics and revealing desire's structural elements. As a body of knowledge and praxis, psychoanalysis provides an interpretative insight and authority through which we can observe desire as experienced, and its modes of expression in a subjective configuration.

Lacan began his Promethean journey to unfold the centuries-old riddle of desire by first exploring the Freudian theory of *Wunsch* (wish), the Hegelian concept of *Begierde* (desire), Heidegger's theory of Being and *Dasein,* and Saussure's and Jakobson's structuralist linguistics. He even borrowed the framework for the dialectic of desire, and the desire of the analyst, from Socrates and Plato. Lacan constructed an epistemological mosaic out of these fundamental postulates that, as we have pointed out earlier, makes it impossible to subsume desire into a single conceptual category. As an index of heterogeneity and heterodoxy, desire is first and foremost alienated and unconscious, and instead of belonging to the desiring subject, it belongs to the Other as the locus of signifiers. When correcting a statement of two of his pupils towards the end of *The Four Fundamental Concepts,* Lacan wrote, '[w]*e would say rather that desire is the non-representative representative*' [*original emphasis*] (Lacan, 1979a, 218). Desire is non-representative because it represents not need but something else, of which need is only the trace. It is, in fact, representative of nothing, for it is alienated from need and demand, and is related to the subject's loss of being and the Other's ex-sistence. Yet, with all its alienation, it is considered a representative, since it is illustrative of an infinite unconscious longing for possessing and enjoying the primordial object of satisfaction. What is this loss? The originary loss is the loss of an object, *Das Ding* (the *Thing,* the primordial object or Other), that which remains inarticulable in the signifier. The desired object is a substitute for this *Thing,* and thus represents the loss that gives rise to desire.

Lacan works out his theory of desire in terms of two other correlative elements, need and demand. Pure biological need has to be articulated in a demand by the mediation of the signifier that comes from the Other. The object of need loses its significance when it enters the signifier, for demand essentially is a demand for love. Due to repression, the demand cannot articulate the original object that desire seeks a substitute for. This leaves a gap between demand and desire, for desire is *of* and *for* something impossible. Desire is thus that part of the demand that remains tenaciously persistent once the biological need ends in satisfaction. From this point of satisfaction, the demand cannot hold on to desire anymore because desire has an excessive and unspeakable aim. A gap opens between the symbolic and the imaginary, and in fact, between the imaginary and the real. It is part of the condition for desire that a subject must allow for the articulation of his organic needs in the signifier.

> Desire is an effect in the subject of the condition – which is imposed on him by the existence of discourse – that his need passes through the defiles of the signifier

> . . . and, as I intimated above, by opening up the dialectic of transference, we must establish the notion of the Other with a capital O as being the locus of speech's deployment (the other scene, *ein anderer Schauplatz*, of which Freud speaks in the *Traumdeutung*). (Lacan, 2002, 252)

Desire is desire of/for the Other. What does this mean? Originally inspired by Hegel, the Lacanian Other is located in the symbolic as the locus where speech and the demand of the subject come from. This is the site where signifiers emerge with a subject's desire and that is, in the meantime, the constitutive locus of the unconscious. Lacan says in this context that the unconscious is the '*discours de L'Autre*' (discourse of the Other) (Lacan, 2002, 183). This Other is also, like the subject, barred and marked by a lack. Therefore, the subject desires what the Other desires, and the subject becomes a thing that locates himself and his desire in the place of the object of the Other's desire, through the mediation of identification. In other words, the signifier of the subject comes from the locus of the Other that thus carries the subject's desire. The subject addresses his desire to the Other for the Other itself and its experience is the experience of desire for the subject. This means that, as Lacan says, '[i]t is qua Other that man desires (this is what provides the true scope of human passion)' (Lacan, 2002, 300). It is in this context that Lacan claims that the unconscious is the discourse of the Other. The Other is here the subject of unconscious discourse. Since desire is not the subject's own desire, the subject is unaware what to desire, for due to repression in the unconscious the subject remains ignorant of his own desire. The subject, however, knows the direction of his demand and the object he wants, but remains ignorant of where his desire is located, and where it functions. Because the demand comes from the Other and the desire is of the Other:

> For it is clear that here man's continued nescience of his desire is not so much nescience of what he demands, which may after all be isolated, as nescience of whence he desires. This is where my formulation that the unconscious is (the) discourse about the Other [*discours de l'Autre*] fits in, in which the *de* should be understood in the sense of the Latin *de* (objective determination): *de Alio in oratione* (you complete it: *tua res agitur*). (Lacan, 2002, 300)

At this point, we need to point to the correlation of the subject's desires and the Other. The fundamental question here is how can the desire of the subject be the desire of the Other while both are radically alienated and separated from one another forever? A magic object comes to the help of the subject which Lacan calls the object *a*. In Lacan's psychoanalysis, this object is the cause of desire, and comes from the separation of a part from the maternal body, dividing the subject by way of the signifier. This object links the subject to the Other from which the subject is separated by the wall of language. As a residue, the object *a* is always attached to the Other. The object *a* can hold the place of the desired object as long as it is linked to the Other. The subject's desire is in fact produced by its alienation in the signifier and his division that finds recognition in the Other's desire. Lacan shows that the subject and his desire are determined by a discourse that begins to emerge in the Other. The subject only can reach the Other through the mediation of the object *a*.

Why, as we have hinted above, is desire always a desire for something else? The demand that conveys desire locates itself in a metonymy that is, '[e]ternally extending toward the *desire for something else*' (Lacan, 2002, 158). In this sense, desire is opposed to an individual's will and even his demand despite the fact that it remains concealed in a demand. Once the demand is achieved and we obtain the object, or to put it more precisely, objec*t a*, we no longer need it. When Ophelia is within the reach of Hamlet, he sends her to a convent to become a nun, because she ceases from this point on to be the object of his desire. There is a correlation between the object and lack. When the object is within reach, we do not desire it. In other words, we don't wish to have something that is already in our possession. This makes desire slip from one object to another, and the object that we are about to possess, has to be rejected. Such refusal allows fixation to move onto another object. For Lacan, Don Juan seeks the 'thing' from bed to bed and never finds it. This is what Lacan means when he says desire always shies away from demand partly because desire is inarticulable in a demand. As Lacan says, '[d]esire is also excavated in the [area] shy of demand' (253). This suggests that desire functions as a motor of demands, and thus escapes capture.

As the consequence of the loss and trauma of castration, desire, in a way, begins with a deprivation or death. Subsequently desire becomes a desire for death, placing the subject, as Lacan says, between two deaths. The first death, as we stated earlier, occurs with the symbolic (the beginning of the history of the subject with the entry into language) which brings desire to life, and then ends with the final literal death that terminates it. From this viewpoint, one might say that desire begins with a cry, the cry that puts pure need into a signifier, and is silenced with death as Hamlet's last words, 'the rest is silence', (*H*, V-ii, 395) suggest. Desire remains unnamable and always reproduces itself in different guises, because Lacan's desire essentially aims at its own re-appropriation and reproduction. The subject is unable to give its own desire a name, for the subject doesn't know the name of unconscious desire. Here desire functions the way a drive does by seeking its goal, but it has no aim. Once desire is temporarily quenched, it immediately slides into another desire. The endless chain of objects, with the help of fantasy, co-ordinates the operation of desire in an open system of deferral. In any case, in order to sustain itself, desire must produce the lack that causes it. An hysteric subject would love lack even more than desire itself, and the obsessional would sustain his love with the re-creation of the trauma that gave birth to desire. Lack signifies the loss that gives birth to desire.

When we said metaphorically that desire begins with a cry, this implied that the status of an emerging desire is a non-verbal form in the imaginary. This is because desire has its origin in the imaginary. As the child first rehearses fragmented trans-linguistic signifiers, he, in fact, is rehearsing the presence and absence of the mother, as Freud's *fort/da* game demonstrates. This exemplary game is the password for desire, because the infant loses his imaginary habitat and begins to stage a game with the fragmented signifiers through which a signification of the absence and presence of the mother is played out. This game also identifies the locus of signifiers and pre-verbal communication – the first Other or m(Other). Thus, the child's desire is the other's desire to which it is attached. This other with small (o) is the specular image that determines the desire of the imaginary. The child's real preoccupation is with the signifier, for it alone can give him some sort of access to the imaginary object of satisfaction. Thus, the symbolic register only offers an elusive conduit to the signified by virtue of the signifier that signifies nothing, and this very signifier comes to function as the signified.

By playing this game, the child knows that his desire is the Other's desire, the Other that he identifies with. Whenever we use the other with a small (o), it implies that the desire of the imaginary is at work, and when we deal with desire in the symbolic, this place has to be taken by the Other. This shows that desire begins with wordless equivocation, sounds, grimaces, colours, phonemes, morphemes and so on that Lacan identifies as *lalangue* (Lacan's neologism that combines the article *la* and the noun *langue* together). Since according to Lacan, *lalangue* emerges as the effect of the unconscious and the organic body, then we can assert that desire itself in a broader perspective is a result of the interaction of the organic body with the unconscious. The important thing to note is that *lalangue* emerges from the Other, but as Other or what Lacan calls the One that is in touch with *jouissance*. For, '[*l*]*alangue* is where jouissance is deposited and where it is held in reserve; it is the place where the residues of signification accumulate as a kind of alluvium produced in the flow of speech' (Dravers, 2002, 144).

These primitive articulations that gradually progress into signifiers and words bring about a split between the child and the mother, for the child's needs need to be passed through language. Hence, *lalangue* is located anterior to the accession to language and in fact opens up the space for the unconscious and the body to bestow upon the subject a possibility of making his first attempts to speak, and accordingly to desire a desire that is not his own. This *lalangue* is irreducibly in contact with the real of the flesh, though it is related to the imaginary, but its function and structure are symbolic. The *lalangue* has a meaning but it is an unconscious meaning, far different from a linguistic meaning.

The meaning of *lalangue*, however, is not a meaning in an ordinary sense of the word but an unconscious meaning, the knowledge of the unconscious, which remains non-knowledge for the subject. As Lacan remarks, '[t]he signifying inventory of *lalangue* supplies only the cipher of meaning' (Lacan, 1990, 9). Our exposition of the pre-linguistic references of desire indicates that desire could be related to the psychosomatic field, but it is a need that functions as an inverted desire. This need operates in the guise of a desire that is capable of carrying out a desiring operation, which means that whatever happens in the field of soma has its psychical equivalent. As Lacan noted, '[I]f we speak of the psycho-somatic, it is insofar as desire must intervene in it' (Lacan, 1979a, 228). The place where we can detect a somatic link to desire is a transitional space before the accession of the subject to language. Furthermore, language, as we pointed out earlier, is the killing of the thing. Its unique gift is in mediating human desire by way of its symbolic and poetic possibilities. Without this endowment, man would never have been able to desire. This also means that by mediating desire, language is a site of the confluence of need and demand.

In addition, Lacan defines desire in its relation to need and demand in mathematical terms as the difference that is produced from the subtraction of need from demand. Demand has a double function; on the one hand, it articulates within itself a need, and on the other, it carries a demand for love. This so-called mathematical operation ought to be read metaphorically, because there remains much residue that a subtraction may produce. Let us put Lacan's formula as [$D — N = d$], where D stands for demand, N for need and d for desire. Such an operation of subtraction cannot take place, as the members of the subtraction are not of the same denomination. Mathematical logic suggests that the subtraction of [$D — N = d$], will only be possible when D is larger in quantity than the sum total of N and d or at least the same as N. What this equation testifies to is the fact that such a subtraction would never give a concrete result, because the aim of need has shifted from the original object. Primary repression is also alienated from need. Therefore, it cannot be fully '[a]rticulated in demand too; it nevertheless appears in an offshoot that presents itself in man's desire' (Lacan, 2002, 275). For the same reason, demand is also not singular, for demand as Lacan says, '[i]tself bears on something other than the satisfactions it calls for. It is demand for a presence or an absence' (276). In short, it implies that there is always an x associated with D and a y with N, and Lacan's subtraction has to be written as: $Dx — Ny = d\ (xy)$. This last formula shows that none of the components of desire including desire itself has a pure substance.

By altering Lacan's equation, we will do justice to the relationship between need, demand and desire. What is at stake here is a remainder falling from each component of the triad. What is that remainder? On the part of demand, it is addressed to the Other that is barred, and thus the demand for love is alienated, as the Other cannot answer the subject's demand for love. As we have just mentioned, need is an alienated need, for it cannot be fully articulated in demand, for demand cannot offer the real thing that need wants. Nor can we imagine a satisfaction for need, for the original object of satisfaction is already lost. Simply put, need has an object, either the first object of satisfaction or its substitute. It belongs to the register of the imaginary and the real – as instinctual impulse; it has a real object independent of the subject, whereas, demand belongs to speech and is addressed to an interlocutor, therefore, it is subject to dependency, and a demand for love. One remainder of need shakes off the primary repression that demand cannot accommodate, and, as Lacan insists, this remainder '[a]ppears in an offshoot that presents itself in man as desire' (Lacan, 2002, 275–276).

Desire is interlinked diachronically to the primary repression that produces lack. This diachrony, within Hegel's philosophy, relates man and human desire to one another as historical. The remainder that causes desire is the object *a*, left over from the original object of love which is inarticulable in language but which causes desire and, with the help of fantasy, sets the stage for desire. Desire may not be reducible to either need or demand, but resides in the fissure between the two. This fissure indicates a narrow split where the remainders of both reside.

> Desire begins to take shape in the margin in which demand rips away from need, this margin being the one that demand – whose appeal can be unconditional only with respect to the Other – opens up in the guise of the possible gap need may give rise to here, because it has no universal satisfaction (this is called 'anxiety'). A margin which as linear as it may be, allows its vertiginous character to appear, provided it is not trampled by the elephantine feet of the Other's whimsy. (Lacan, 2002, 299)

In the exceptional moments of a symptom, the demands stop their slippage when desire shows a fixation on a particular object. The dialectical relationship between demand and desire enables desire to build up a bipolar relationship with need and demand. It is on the side of need insofar as within it, need attains its object, and it is on the side of demand insofar as it facilitates its engagement with the Other. This engagement, however, is a tyrannical one for the Other covets the subject in the latter's every move. Through a similar dialectical process, need submits itself to the signifiers of demand. As Lacan argues in his unpublished *Théorie du symbolisme* the signifier represses desire when it articulates need. Repression, in return, causes desire to be misconstrued. Nevertheless, desire in its dialectical relationship with the Other, qualifies the subject to ask the Other for recognition, because the Other is the location from where the subject is seen. This appeal always remains unanswered, for the Other is barred with lack itself.

All psychoanalytic categories are dialectical, and desire cannot stay outside this rule. The relation of the subject and the Other is influenced by the Hegelian master/slave dialectic. This dialectic also structures desire but unlike the Hegelian dialectic, it doesn't culminate in a synthesis, because the existence of the unconscious fends this off. Without a dialectical structure in language, the subject would fall into psychosis or schizophrenia. As such, the subject would treat and use words as things, a failure of signification where the unconscious overtakes conscious discourse. Similarly, the chain of signifiers would have no *points de caption* – the anchoring points in a signifying chain that allow for the production of some sort of meaning retroactively – and there would be no differentiation between binary oppositions in the discourse of the subject; his desire too would lose its dialectical structure. It is worth recalling briefly the key sources of Lacan as a way of further grasping the truth about the theory of desire and its correlates.

After being introduced to desire, the subject loses his being with his entry into the symbolic. In other words, when the signifier is introduced by preexisting language into the subject's universe, the signifier in turn introduces the thing into an empty space of loss. This empty space introduces in the subject the loss through which he begins to desire, that thus identifies the lack in being of the subject. This means that desire is essentially a desire for being, for by virtue of such a mediation of desire, the subject wants to recover his lost being. The entrance to the symbolic bestows upon the subject a status of an existence that remains being-less. The subject is thus an effect of the signifier and exists only in language as the symbolic function for desire. Since the Other is the locus of speech and language, the subject fades away and begins to exist somewhere within as well as beneath the signifying chain of discourse.

A pure and simple form of desire for Lacan is the desire for death. Death brings to an end the subject's discontinuity-in-being so that desire-for-death is produced as an effect. Lacan postulates this by taking into account Heidegger's being-unto-death, Freud's beyond of the pleasure principle as well as his absolute return of a living organism to its original state of stillness. Freud also posits in his clinical practice that the repetitiveness of the symptom implies an inertia that points to a state of non-being or an inorganic state. In this way, Lacan saw death as a 'logical end' to desire, the precedent of which is set by the symbol or signifier as the killing of the thing. As Lacan says, '[T]he symbol first manifests itself as the killing of the thing, and this death results in the endless perpetuation of the subject's desire' (Lacan, 2002, 101).

Desire and the law have bipolar but negative correlative functions. They are like enemies: what desire wants to accomplish, the law inhibits and desire for its part transgresses the injunctions of the law that allow for a symbolic integration of subjectivity. The super-ego with its own tyrannical law requires the subject to transgress the symbolic law which by mediation of the Oedipus complex regulates social and cultural interaction. The law of the super-ego, thus, bypasses the law of desire and commands the subject to go after what desire inhibits.

In this sense, the super-ego is both the promoter and destruction of the symbolic law. Simply put, the symbolic law that comes from Levi-Strauss into Lacanian psychoanalysis is the over-riding regulator of all inter-human relations in a given culture and finds itself at odds with the super-ego that always prompts a subject of desire to enjoy what is prohibited by the symbolic law. In this context, the super-ego has a dual and perverse function vis-à-vis desire. When the super-ego is on the side of the law it is also on the side of desire, and when it is on the side of its own tyrannical law, it is on the side of *jouissance.*

These qualities make desire essentially ethical, because it calls for the prohibition of primitive *jouissance,* and it is on the side of the Law as desire inaugurates a lack. It is the Name-of-the-Father that builds a structure by linking desire and the Law. The Law exhibits the Kantian moral law that we see illustrated in *Hamlet.* As Moustapha Safouan writes, '[d]esire has only two faces; with one face it is the law with the other it is transgression' (Safouan, 2004, 75). Desire operates between two threats, namely, castration and lack. In this sense, desire is desire for death, for desire is compelled by castration to identify with the signifier, which brings death to what it signifies, and is itself a signifier of nothing but death. That is why Lacan called Antigone the heroine of a pure desire. He also refers to Empedocles, the legendary Greek pre-Socratic poet, philosopher, and mystic who committed suicide after he claimed he could ascend to an original purity with the divine. Lacan writes that '[E]mpedocles, by throwing himself into Mount Etna, leaves forever present in the memory of men the symbolic act of his being-toward-death' (Lacan, 2002, 101). Besides, Lacan's signifier and the idea that the very emergence of words heralds death comes from both Heidegger and Hegel, for according to them, speech was the death of being.

Freud's theory of wish and libido anticipate Lacan's theory of desire. In his early seminars, Lacan considers desire close to the Freudian libido, especially to its forcefulness and the fact that it is a quantity but cultivates a qualitative effect. As Lacan says, '[d]esire, a function central to all human experience, is the desire for nothing nameable. And at the same time this desire lies at the origin of every variety of animation' (Lacan, 1991a, 223). Lacan's theory, although influenced by many sources, was mainly developed within the matrix of Freudian theory, for as Lacan says, '*Desidero* is the Freudian *cogito*' (Lacan, 1979a, 154). Lacan's postulation of desire, however, is different from Freud's in many ways. The fundamental discrepancy is that Freud's *Wunsch* appears as *Wunscherfüllung* (fulfilled wish) in dreams or in symptoms, but Lacan's desire arises and ends unfulfilled. An unconscious wish for Freud, as Laplanche and Pontalis state, was the '[r]estoration of signs which are bound to the earliest experiences of satisfaction; this restoration operates according to the laws of the primary process' (Laplanche and Pontalis, 1973, 481). Thus, what for Freud was a site of the satisfaction of desire, for Lacan was a mark of its postponement. Freud considered wishes in their multiplicity to have a titanic power, whereas Lacan saw desire as single and channelled through a metonymic chain. At this stage of our discussion of desire, it is necessary to discuss the objects that condition desire in its operation. In what follows we will take up this issue with the object *a* and the phallus as signifiers which functions as landmarks and pathfinders for desire.

The cause and symbol of desire

Does desire have an object? There are two answers to this question. The first is *no,* because the archaic object of desire to which the subject was originally symbiotically attached, is lost and does not exist anymore. The second answer is *yes,* for desire has a thousand and one objects, though they are mere substitutes and fictional. All these objects come under the umbrella of object *a.* The phallus is another type of object involved in desire that functions as a symbol or marker of desire. The object *a,* signifies the phallus and exists in a place that is marked by the lack of *jouissance.* The phallus is the transcendental signifier in Lacanian epistemology that, on the one hand, makes every signification in the symbolic register possible, and escapes the signifying chain, leaving it incomplete, on the other. With the paternal metaphor and the symbolic law, the phallus becomes the signifier of lack and consequently the signifier of desire. The phallus is thus an image of an object whereas the object *a* is an object that causes desire. The former object exists in the imaginary and becomes a signifier in the symbolic, whereas the latter remains always real and substantial. Considered this way, object *a* as a fallout of pre-Oedipal lack precedes the phallus as a signifier of the post-Oedipal lack instituted by the Name-of-the-Father. These double lacks problematize desire in its articulation. Both object *a,* and the phallus are correlative with one another. Insofar as fantasy functions as a mediation for desire, each represents lack and has an effect on the other. The phallus is the signifier of the subject's alienation in discourse. The phallus functions in the symbolic as a signifier of lack, lack that is the absolute condition for desire. The object *a* in earlier Lacan is a substitute for the *jouissance* of the lost phallus. Desire operates only with the help of these two omnipotent components, object *a,* and the phallus. The phallus (as missing signifier), serves as the signifier of lack in the subject as well as the Other, and the object *a* tries to fill these gaps. The logic behind this is the fact that they operate in a dialectical relationship with one another. In the game of desire, the phallus functions as a signpost of lack, and the object *a,* on the contrary, signals an overcoming of that lack. Let us explore these two signifiers.

1. The object *a*

As an object cause of desire, the object *a* invites an unconscious fantasy to come forward to stage desire. This object locates desire within itself and sustains it in the symbolic. Lacan, in his seminar on *Hamlet,* compares the object *a* with Ophelia in relation to Hamlet's desire to which we will return in coming chapters. At the root of the operation that produces this object and the signifier is castration which brings about the loss of the imaginary phallus and detaches an object *a.* This detachment means object *a* is a remainder of the primordial object. Lacan explores the status of the object *a* in different ways in his teaching. In *The Four Fundamental Concepts,* he observes it as an outcome of two operations, namely, alienation and separation. A subject constitutes itself by losing its symbiotic bond with the primordial object, by way of its entry into language. The castration complex causes the subject to sacrifice his *jouissance,* of which the phallus is a signifier, as an exchange in the economy of desire. The object *a* is the object that desire seeks. This status is primarily given to the object *a* because of its organic ties with *The Thing,* the original object of desire, which makes it possible for the subject to build up a relationship with this object in the symbolic. The object *a* thus supports desire by running both behind and in front of it. It is in the front, for desire pursues it, and when it is behind, as an unmoved-mover, it pushes desire forward. As Lacan says, '[t]he object a, *from behind desire, imprints, imposes, and directs the itinerary of desire*' [*original emphasis*] (Lacan, cited in Harari, 2001, 68).

Lacan defines the object *a* in terms of Plato's *agalma,* a treasure hidden in a worthless chest. This object does not have a value in itself. However, it draws its value from the role it plays in the operation of desire. Its first and foremost role is to sustain desire by virtue of an effect that re-establishes a link with the lost object. It thus occupies and fills that place that the subject has lost access to. This filling is elusive, and leaves desire unsatisfied. This object plays its role by way of the mediation of fantasy that often occupies the place of an imaginary demand. Since it is not articulable in the symbolic, with a metaphoric structure, object *a* plays the role of substitute. That is why this object is called by Lacan *objet petit a,* a substitute for the French 'autre', the small part for the whole. This implies that object *a* builds a link between the subject and the Other, because the subject is separated from the Other by the unconscious. The subject's desire is directed to this object rather than the Other, which is an impossible object. In this context, object *a* is the surplus of *jouissance.* Taken from the imaginary, this object builds links with the real object of desire. It takes and leaves a plethora of objects, in order to fit the fantasy. For, as Nasio argues, '[t]he function of fantasy is to fix and define the subject's desire which is why human desire has the property of being coordinated not to the real object, but to the fantasy' (Nasio, 1998, 55–57).

The itinerary of desire begins with the barred Other (A or O) that casts aside a leftover, object *a.* Thus desire is only to be mediated by fantasy. Lacan tries to explain this process in an algorithm, $<> *a,* which means the barred subject desires object *a.* The lozenge (<>) means here 'desire of'. This bears out that object *a* arises both in front of and behind desire. The trajectory will be in mathematical form as:

$$\text{Ø [barred Other]} \rightarrow \boldsymbol{a} \rightarrow \mathbf{d} \rightarrow \$ <> \boldsymbol{a}$$

As the above formula shows, desire together with the signifier arise from the locus of the Other (A or O), and the object *a* pins itself to this Other in order to function as an object cause of desire. The object *a* as we have said above, invites fantasy to stage desire's drama, the fantasy that Lacan formulates as *$<>a.*

The desiring subject attaches himself to the object *a,* as the latter ascribes itself to the Other. Such an attachment is shown by Molière in *The Miser,* when we see old Harpagon's obsession with keeping the fortune he has buried in the garden. This fortune functions in Harpagon's desire as an object *a.* Even when he marries young Rosina, he idolizes her as an object, not as a wife, as he remains wholly indifferent to Rosina's sexual appeal. Lacan argues that the *jouissance* Harpagon derives from money is, in fact, the surplus *jouissance* of object *a.* When he loses his strongbox, his cries and mourning show his love for the object *a.* His hoarding is part of his 'perverse desire', that, according to Lacan, shows Harpagon as a master fetishist keeping this object of fantasy in order to preserve his object cause of desire.

Why and how can object *a* be the cause of desire? It would be problematic if we took this cause in a philosophical sense, since it is psychical and located in the line that splits the symbolic from the real. The cause of the subject is located in his entry into the symbolic. Thus language itself causes this split. Similarly, object *a* is a leftover of the split between the subject and the Other, on the border between the real and the symbolic. The cause of desire is the cause of the split of the subject as well. As Lacan writes, '[F]or every speaking being, the cause of its desire is, in terms of structure, strictly equivalent, so to speak, to its bending, that is, to what I have called its division as a subject' (Lacan, 1998a, 127). This is the reason why Lacan wrote this object *a,* the small part of the big A, as a mathematical sign that functions like a symbol for a quantity as well as an operation. Lacan draws on this mathematical sign as a formalization that allows it to be a signifier that has an effect other than that of meaning. This quality enables the object *a* to acquire other significations than that which meaning can endow. Therefore, it is an object which is constituted by its qualities of contingency and desirability. This is a status that evolves beyond symbolization. This object is desirable because it is received from the matrix of the Other and has the power to build a relation with the subject, for it functions like '[a]n insect on the Moebius-Strip', (Marini, 1992, 189). Lacan reiterates the importance of the object *a* in *Seminar XII: The Real, The Symbolic, and The Imaginary* (RSI) (1974–1975). In relation to the Other, it has the same position as the signifier of the phallus.

In relation to the mother, the object *a* represents, in part, her body as the Other by actualizing the process of pre-Oedipal desire in the symbolic. If we see the breast as the original object *a*, this object is detached from the maternal body, not from her self. This attachment to the maternal body allows the imaginary dimension to come into play in the process of desire. It indicates that the object *a* is closely linked with bodily erogenous zones formed by a cut, a cut that signifies separation of the child from his mother. This explains why Lacan puts emphasis on the object *a* as a body-part, as he puts it figuratively, '*I love you, but, because inexplicably I love in you more than you – the Object petit a – I mutilate you*' [*original emphasis*] (Lacan, 1979a, 268).

The object *a* emerges as part of the inaugural constitution of the subject when the pre-linguistic symbiotic knot is severed by the imaginary articulation of the maternal body in the shape of an alter ego, or specular image, in the mirror phase. As such, object *a* retains its captivating and seductive imaginary power in the symbolic. It functions as an index for all the desirable objects in the world. In *The Four Fundamental Concepts*, Lacan notes that for a better understanding of the function of object *a*, we need to look at his theoretical vocabulary for a definition of the gaze. The gaze is structured like an object *a* before the advent of the signifying process, for it is essentially an object in relation to the Other. It is not on the side of the subject but like object *a* on the side of the Other. As opposed to the look, the gaze is instead the object of a looking back. For Lacan, the gaze is one of the objects *a* that fill the gap in the subject after its division by the signifier.

> The *petit a* never crosses this gap. Recollect what we learned about the gaze, the most characteristic term for apprehending the proper function of the object *a*. This *a* is presented precisely, in the field of the mirage of the narcissistic function of desire, as the object that cannot be swallowed, as it were, which remains stuck in the gullet of the signifier. (Lacan, 1979a, 270)

As only an imaginary fragment of the maternal body, the object *a* represents a temporary surplus *jouissance*. Within such a framework, it is not the aim, but a means of activating and causing desire. As pointed out at the outset, desire emerges out of a lack that, even if it is nothing, is still functional and needs an object to fill it. The object *a*, and the phallus allow a subject to play out and preserve his desire by fantasy in a metonymic chain. This cut makes this object a residue of the division of the subject by the signifier in the sphere of the Other. The object *a* doesn't lend itself to symbolization, but appears as an imaginary substitute for the Other, in many shapes and forms, in order to support desire and its subject. A woman often takes a position that is on the side of the object *a*, and the phallus, on the other hand, is on the side of the man. As an object that causes and locates desire within itself, object *a* orients a subject towards his desire. It functions alternatively as a signifier in relation to desire like the phallus. It also functions as an object when the latter functions as a symbol for the operation of desire. This gives the phallus a privileged status. This shows the enigmatic status of the phallic function that organizes sexual orientations by requiring a choice.

2. The phallus

Lacan defines his most controversial concept, the phallus, as a crypto-marker of desire that stands for the lack within which desire emerges. This marker, in order to become a signifier in the symbolic, upon which all signification rests, passes through Lacan's triadic registers in the Oedipus complex. Lacan identifies three structural moments, correlative to the Oedipal phase through which the phallus becomes a signifier in the symbolic register. The first moment is when the still ungendered child assumes the mother has the phallus. Therefore, he desires to be her phallus, and thus the object of her desire. The child identifies with both the mother and her object of desire. This causes a split in desire, for the desire of the child dislocates itself by occupying the Other's desire. This moment is named by Lacan *frustration*, which develops because the imaginary father imposes on the child an abstinence from his narcissistic desire so that he can be the phallus for the mother's desire. The second moment brings about a second type of lack, the lack of the real of the symbolic phallus. The role of the imaginary father who is the bearer and possessor of the phallus and the signifier of the Other's desire is rejected. This is a traumatic moment when the child realizes the mother does not have the phallus. This moment is thus responsible for generating many symptoms, including *Penisneid* on the part of a girl. This lack of having, on the part of the Other, on which the child's desire is fixated becomes the source of many symptoms. In an imaginary and theatrical network, the child loses his imaginary tie by losing the real phallus. This moment is *privation*, which is the meaning of not having the phallus. This is the beginning of the mother/child dialectic of desire. The third moment, *castration*, strips away the child's *jouissance* as a payoff for gaining access to desire. In this way, the subject accepts castration and consequently signs up for a desire that guarantees him a degree of normalization in the symbolic order. The drama of the Oedipus complex ends with the arrival of the phallic father who brings his law and punishes the child with castration. The lack in this moment is the symbolic loss of the imaginary phallus. Lacan claims that in view of this logic, a boy and a girl both develop multiple unconscious desires, or to put it in other words, their response to the phallus varies, when it comes to the articulation of the phallus in the symbolic order. This turns the phallus into a determining position of power in relation to desire, as well as in relation to the discourse that the phallus makes possible by this role.

When Lacan says that the phallus is an imaginary effect, he does not mean that by entering into the symbolic order it cannot sustain its imaginary function.

In the post-mirror phase, the phallus veils the lack in the symbolic order which opens up a field of signification for the body in language. The boundless potential of the signifying system of language empowers a subject to signify the materiality of the imaginary in the symbolic register. Structurally speaking, there is little difference between the imaginary and the symbolic, for the imaginary as the field of images has to be symbolized in the second field of the symbolic in signifiers and words. The logic of this argument suggests that desire too sustains its imaginary correlation within the symbolic. Thus being symbolic, desire cannot lose its imaginary connections with the past. The imaginary dimension of desire is related to a broader relationship of the subject in the mirror phase, where the subject takes the other, the specular image, as the object of his desire. Fantasy enacts this imaginary fixation on the past.

The correlation of the imaginary with the symbolic, nonetheless, may be disrupted by a failure of the imaginary phallus to enter into the symbolic phallus. This may disrupt the function of the symbolic signification of the real phallus. This is because, as we said earlier, it is the phallic signifier that makes signification possible. This implies that the foreclosure of the phallic signifier results in the appearance of the real phallus in the symbolic order. For Lacan, Freud's case study 'Little Hans' is an example of the symbolic abolition of the phallus. Little Hans fails to acknowledge castration and the turning of the phallus into a signifier and thus he remains outside the symbolic order. This makes him bound to the maternal body and the real phallus. Fear of castration prohibits him from repressing his primordial desire, leading him to develop a phobia of the street as other sadomasochistic impulses Freud writes about in detail in his case histories. This statement continually causes him to suffer psychotic experiences. In short, the above three moments distinguish the phallus in three different modes, which Lacan calls the real phallus, the imaginary phallus and the symbolic phallus. The first one is the biological masculine organ that play its role in the Oedipal triangle. The second denotes the imaginary function of the phallus. The child inscribes himself as the object of the mother's desire by being an imaginary phallus. The third is the symbolic phallus which, with the interference of castration at the post-Oedipal phase, serves as a signifier of lack and thus desire.

In his seminar on *Hamlet*, Lacan's theoretical development of the economy of the phallus suggests that the phallus is an object of exchange between different desiring subjects. Lacan argues that the universal reality of the phallus enables a subject to have desire by means of a substitutive self-representation, in such a way that the phallus provides conditions for the subject that can compensate for the lack of being, the lack of the primordial object and castration. In this way, Lacan assigns a crossover role for the phallus. As an imaginary object and as a master signifier, it is identified with the empty set or zero, and functions in the signifying chain as a signified for all other signifiers. Lacan was keen to call the phallus in 'Rome Discourse', with the Sanskrit *laksana*, which has a double meaning of 'the phallus' and 'an emblem, symbol, or sign'. At the centre of the economy of desire is the phallus, which, as the signifier, is brought forward by the entry of the father and his law into the Oedipal triangle, imposing an unconditional castration. In other words, the phallus, by definition, calls for different attitudes from a man and a woman vis-à-vis the lack, of which it is a signifier. The lack for a girl is real because of her anatomy. A boy shares separation from the maternal body with a girl, but with regard to the lack imposed by castration, he feels this lack through a threat of losing the phallus.

In conclusion, desire is indeed the *cogito* of Lacan's earlier works. From the beginning of his career, until at least the mid-1960s, desire was the centre of Lacan's theoretical concern. Whatever he said or wrote up until this point was related directly or indirectly to desire. Lacan's methodology for a conceptualization of desire was based on the logic of a multiple and non-totalizable interpretation. The logical outcome of this approach makes desire precisely impossible and inarticulable. This suggests that there would always be something left over from any articulation of desire. Yet, desire is the only possible way for the subject to recover his lost being by means of a fantasy and with the mediation of an *object a.* Desire is born and sustained by a lack constituted by castration and the loss of the primitive object of satisfaction. Lacan's suggestion that desire must be taken literally, has to be read metaphorically (though this may sound odd), because desire can be mapped out only by a critical and literary scrutiny as the term 'interpretation' suggests. Lacan himself tell us this:

> Since the point is to take desire, and since it can only be taken literally [*á la lettre*], since it is the letter's snare that determines, nay overdetermines, its place as a heavenly bird, how can we fail to require the bird catcher to first be a man of letters?
>
> Who among us has attempted to articulate the importance of the 'literary' element in Freud's work. (Lacan, 2002, 264)

Lacan has re-articulated and completed the long circle of meditation on desire in Western thought. In his theoretical discourse, Lacan unraveled the traditional philosophical approach, the cosmological structure of metaphysics, as well as the onto-biological, and instinctual procedure of Freud. Lacan, for instance, demystified Hegel's assumption that the slave/master struggle was for 'prestige'. Lacan argued that Hegel was unaware of the helpless and premature status of man in birth. Lacan has relocated this dialectics between the subject and the Other to whom the subject remains tied. In short, Lacan translates Hegelian 'prestige' into a wholeness that the subject's desire sets as its goal. This very idea brings us to the question whether desire is gendered or not? The next section attempts to answer this.

Chapter 2

Desire and Sexual Difference

Lacan's approach to sexual difference should not be judged by 'The Significance of the Phallus', as some feminists do, where the Freudian universality of the masculine libido is justified. This paper, originally delivered in 1958 in Germany sparked anger among French feminists. Here the phallus is a master signifier and a universal masculine emblem that governs language. Despite Lacan's claim that the phallus is not the real object of desire but only a signifier, and since it is the product of castration, a signifier of lack, it still functions as a determinant of sexual fate for members of both sexes. For, according to Lacan, the phallus is a signifier that functions as a regulator of every signification in discourse. Since the phallus is the signifier of desire, one might argue that desire is essentially masculine, or at least measured in terms of masculinity. The subject's relation to the signifier is marked by the phallus. '[T]he phallus is the privileged signifier of this mark in which the role [part] as Logos is wedded to the advent of desire' (Lacan, 2002, 277). The historical status of the phallus, its generative power, anatomical reality and its social significance in human culture, are parts of the argument Lacan presents to justify his theory of the phallus. However, with the formula of sexuation and the theory of feminine *jouissance,* Lacan seems to back away from his radical position on feminine desire and allows for it to be remodeled. His phallicization of gender ends when he places feminine *jouissance,* and the desire for it, beyond the phallus.

Before discussing Lacan's theory of the phallus as seen by leading French feminist theoreticians, let us see how the phallic signifier as an agency determines the choice of desire for members of both sexes in terms of *being* and *having* the phallus. Lacan calls this determining power of castration, the phallic function. However, the phallic function is unable to define a woman's desire as such, because there is no signifier to represent a woman in the symbolic order. This makes her predisposed to the supremacy of the masculine signifier by which she has to orientate her own desire. This shows that feminine desire, as it is constructed in the symbolic by a masculine signifier, is false. A woman's response to this false desire is masquerade. This alienates a woman from her own self, body and desire. For a woman to desire, she must follow the order of a masculine desire and function as only a support to the operation of masculine desire by accepting a desire that is not her own.

In order to comprehend the phallic function and its role in the determination of desire, it is necessary to focus on Lacan's formula of sexuation developed in *Encore.* Although there are some differences with his earlier theorization with regard to sexual difference in his formulas of sexuation, Lacan has preserved the centrality of the phallic signifier to some extent.

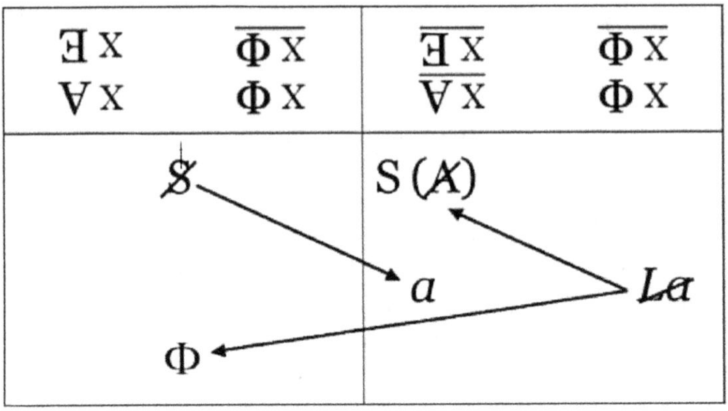

Source: Lacan, 1998a, 78

As the diagram shows, he defines masculine and feminine sexuality as a choice between different types of *jouissance.* Lacan's diagram has two sides, one for the masculine and the other for the feminine, where the horizontal and vertical lines function in the table as bars marking boundaries for the sexes. On the left (masculine) side we have the barred subject ($) and symbolic phallus (Φ). On the right (feminine side), we have the signifier of a lack in the Other, object *a,* and the barred ~~*The*~~ (woman), designating the absence of woman in the symbolic S(Ⱥ) order.

On the top of these two sides, Lacan wrote two pairs of formulas grounded on symbolic logic. He describes his four formulas in this way: the first pair Ax stands for the universal quantifier or universal proposition, and the second pair Ex, as the existential quantifier or proposition. On the male side, we have a negative existential proposition written on the top: $\exists x \bullet \overline{\Phi x}$. This formula reads: there is one x that is not subject to the phallic function. This x comes from the example of the leader of the herd in Freud's *Totem and Taboo* who has access to all female members of the herd. Beneath, is an affirmative universal proposition: $\forall x \bullet \overline{\Phi x}$ that reads: all men are subject to the phallic function. The formula $\exists x \bullet \overline{\Phi x}$. is what Lacan defines as, 'the father function – whereby we find via negation, the proposition Φx, which grounds the operative (*exercise*) of what makes up for the sexual relationship with castration' (Lacan, 1998a, 79). On the feminine side, Lacan characterizes both in negative terms: On the $\overline{\exists x} \bullet \overline{\Phi x}$ top means that there is no x or speaking being that is not subject to the phallic function, and beneath, a negative universal proposition $\overline{\forall x} \bullet \overline{\Phi x}$ means that the phallic function is valid for not-all or the not-whole woman. The negative is shown by an arrow (or line) on top, and the affirmative, without an arrow.

What is at stake in this diagram? What exactly does Lacan want to say? The lower two sides of the table privilege the feminine position in the field of desire, for she is in direct relation with the signifier of the barred Other $S(\not{A})$, as well as the symbolic phallus Φ, whereas the masculine can have only an indirect access to object *a*. The trans-phallic feminine side indicates that a woman can enjoy both the symbolic phallus and the barred Other, shown in the table by pointed arrows. These arrows explain all that we need to know about what sexuation means in Lacan's epistemology. When a woman is linked to the phallus and the barred Other, at the core of this relation lies access to two kinds of phallic and the 'ineffable' *jouissance* of the Other. A man, on the contrary, is unable to do so, unless he changes his sexual orientation by placing himself on the feminine side of the table. Man has access only to phallic *jouissance,* which is limited, and even as Lacan insists, may prevent a man from fully achieving *jouissance,* because it is only the enjoyment of the organ. As Bruce Fink notes, sexuation has nothing to do with sexual difference, gender or sexual orientation. It is simply a choice of *jouissance* beyond anatomical determinants:

> The discussion of these two jouissances [phallic, and of the Other] brings us to the subject of what Lacan calls 'sexuation.' It should be recalled that sexuation is not biological sex: what Lacan calls masculine structure and feminine structure do not have to do with one's biological organs but rather with the kind of jouissance that one is able to obtain. (Fink, 2002a, 36)

Desire always remains outside anatomical existence. This elevates the phallic function to a dominant status in the determination of one's desire, but this function isn't linked to the relation with gender and its normativity. This, however, means that masculine and feminine spaces in a given culture are not grounded on biological determinants, but on a choice of *jouissance.* This choice, according to Lacan, implies that members of both sexes are free to adopt one or the other position in the field of desire in relation to the phallus. It is necessary then that we discuss masculine and feminine desires in more detail.

Masculine desire: $\Phi(a)$

It is a complex process to identify and differentiate masculine and feminine desire, for they cannot be accounted for by anatomical differences, but must be seen as an unconscious position in relation to desire. Therefore, when we say masculine or feminine desire, it does not necessarily imply a man's desire proper, or a woman's desire proper. Instead of anatomical determinants, the symbolic significance of sexuality accounts for a choice vis-à-vis desire. Since, unlike a woman, a man has the symbolic phallus, he can situate himself in a position that can play the role of the symbolic phallus for the Other, but before he can make such a claim, he must yield himself to the law of castration. This shows that masculine desire is located in the symbolic order of culture, not as traditional psychology claims, in biological determinants. The symbolic register replaces the imaginary phallus by structuring the mother/child nexus around a symbolic phallus, always charged with signification insofar as it is the signifier of the Other's desire. Lacan draws on the Hegelian concept of *Aufhebung* (synthesis) as an essential factor that raises the status of an imaginary object (the phallus) to a signifier in the symbolic, a signifier of the Other's desire.

This symbolic phallus designates a fundamental lack in the subject because of its status as being a signifier of the Other, and a signifier for lack, the lack that produces masculine desire in an infinite metonymic structure. So the status of wholeness that Lacan attributes to a man for having the phallus doesn't give him an advantage in actual terms, because, first, the phallus always appears as a lack; and second, this lack is marked by castration. For that reason, in having the phallus, a man's desire can never escape castration. As Salecl says:

> For men, the way they desire (which is crucial also for the relation that they form with object a on the side of their partner) is conditioned by the fact that castration marked them by a lack, which also means that their phallic function has been negated. (Salecl, 2000, 304–305)

The formula that Lacan, according to Jacques-Alain Miller, worked out for masculine desire $[\Phi(a)]$, outlines that masculine desire contains two elements, namely the symbolic phallus Φ and the object *a*, where the first 'signifies that there is a will to *jouissance* that necessitates fantasy' (Miller, cited in Salecl, 2000, 24). As this formula suggests, the will for *jouissance*, must be directed towards an object *a*. Thus, as Lacan says, masculine desire is eccentric, one might say that it is like shifting sands, changing direction from one object to another, or to put it in other words, masculine desire is more predisposed to infidelity than feminine desire. In this context, Lacan identifies masculine desire as driven by polymorphous perversion. Miller reshapes Lacan's formula of fantasy $[\$<>\Phi(a)]$, and argues that the two formulas indicate that man realizes his desire always with the phallic function or castration, and when he desires a woman, it can give him access to the barred Other, as a woman acts out the Other's desire for him:

> What these two formulas indicate is that at the moment when a man discovers the course of his desire, the Φ function becomes more insistent, while as the course of his desire for a woman begins to come into action, he is lucky

> to reach A, in other words to realize that the Other does not exist. (Miller, 2000, 24)

From what we have discussed in this section, it is very clear that Miller adds nothing to Lacan's argument about masculine desire, because access to the signifier of the barred Other in the symbolic for a man is available only through a woman, and a masculine desire is often determined by the phallic function. This is precisely conveyed by Lacan's formula of masculine desire [$\Phi(a)$], where a masculine subject holds the place of the phallus in relation to object *a*, the object of drive. This dependence of desire on object *a*, in itself demonstrates our claim about desire and its association with anatomical factors. It is because as the remnant of the maternal body, the object *a* has materiality *per se.* Due to this fact which Lacan emphasizes in *Seminar XX: Encore* (1972–1973), the object *a*, to which love is addressed, is the semblance of being, being-there – *Dasein* in the Heideggarian sense.

> Love itself, as I stressed last time, is addressed to the semblance. And if it is true that the Other is only reached if it attaches itself (*qu'à s'accoler*), as I said last time, to *a*, the cause of desire, then love is also addressed to the semblance of being. That there-being is not nothing. It is attributed to (*supposé à*) that object that is *a*. (Lacan, 1998a, 92)

Partly by its connection with the real and partly with the mediation of fantasy, masculine desire is caused and activated by the object *a*, that unlike the situation for a feminine subject, is outside the morphology of his body. Masculine desire remains within the boundaries of the phallic function, and consequently gains access to phallic *jouissance* by way of fantasy in which a woman functions as an object *a*.

In order to differentiate the ways men and women desire or to draw a modality upon which we can imagine the two paths of desire, we need to look at desire at the extremes of its operation. Lacan himself initiated this method. In the case of male and female homosexuals, for example Schreber and Dora, we can find the similarities and differences between masculine and feminine desires. In *Seminar III: The Psychoses* (1955–1956), Lacan relates Schreber's symptom to a failure in the paternal metaphor. In other words, there was a failure to substitute one signifier for another, or substitute the Name-of-the-Father for the desire of the mother. Here, Lacan recounts Schreber's delusions as an unconscious attempt to produce a feminine position, and his megalomania as a response to primordial narcissism: '[t]he megalomania represents that by which the narcissistic fear expresses itself' (Lacan, 1993, 312).

From this point of view, we may well identify a masculine desire, which is repressed by the law of the father, and consequently cannot satisfy fully a man's sexual needs, for a woman is unable to offer the phallus as an exchange in a love relationship. Lacan sees this as a reason why the male subject is so promiscuous when it comes to sexual desire. A male subject would seek the satisfaction of his unsatisfied desire by shifting from one woman to another. Besides, a female homosexual will dephallicize herself by entering the male structure, and a male homosexual will, on the contrary, adopt the feminine structure.

This, as we have pointed out above, doesn't mean that there exist specific models for masculine and feminine desires in relation to biological or anatomical determinants. Gendered desire, according to Lacan, is an unconscious sexual position that can be held by either man or woman. This desiring position functions with the phallus as its signifier, and an object *a* as the cause and the support of the fantasy that stages that desire.

Feminine desire: A(φ)

We have just insisted that Lacan is not concerned with a feminine and masculine subject in terms of a biological understanding of anatomy. He refers to them as speaking beings with feminine or masculine attributes that are brought forth by language. The symbolic fails to articulate a woman, for she lacks the signifier there, and is related to the signifier of the Other's desire only on the condition that she is castrated in relation to masculine desire. The lack of her own signifier leaves her outside the symbolic. Since, as Lacan's diagram of sexuation illustrates, she is located on the side of the Other, she appears as an object *a*, the goddess who is an adjunct to man's desire. As such, her desire is always neutral, for she plays out a castrated desire. In order to desire, a woman, must join the economy of phallic desire dominated by masculine discourse. As such, she exists in the symbolic to facilitate masculine desire. In *Encore,* Lacan develops his theory of femininity with the premise of a unique trans-phallic-*jouissance* that is only available to women and mystics alike. One may argue that a man is not qualified to experience this *jouissance* unless he takes a feminine position or becomes a practizing mystic. This privileges a woman as she has access to both, namely phallic *jouissance,* and feminine *jouissance*; and even both at the same time. The multiplicity of feminine *jouissance* appropriates different desires. This makes a woman doubly privileged since her desire is not one but plenty. In what follows, we will bring to light the conditions that make feminine desire polysexual followed by a focus on Irigaray's, and Cixous' responses to Lacanian theory.

In earlier Lacan, in light of the logic of the Oedipus complex, speaking beings, regardless of their sexual differences, have to inscribe themselves in the prevailing masculine-oriented symbolic world of language. In this process, a female subject would be held back and restrained in her passage through the Oedipal stage because of her anatomical difference and its psychological implication in the pre-existing social order.

Desire is grounded in lack, and this lack for a female subject turns out to be a double lack, namely the lack of the Other (separation from the primordial object of love) and the lack of the phallus. Therefore, we would have to see feminine desire as a desire aimed in two directions. First, a woman will have a desire to be the phallus for a masculine desire in order to be normal in culture. This would reduce her merely to an object of a male's desire. Second, a woman would disclaim her own desire by placing herself on the masculine side of desire by being a phallic woman. Both paradigms of feminine desire relocate her desire in the phallic economy. However, feminine *jouissance* will be beyond desire, because it is outside the phallic economy. Here we reach an aporia where Lacanian theory seems to turn around against itself. There are four possibilities in the Lacanian theory of feminine *jouissance*. Lacan doesn't specify any kind of feminine desire in relation to feminine *jouissance*, but we may well argue that there must be a specific desire for a woman to transgress to attain her non-phallic *jouissance*. Without undermining her own desire, a woman cannot experience this *jouissance*. On the opposite side of the argument, when a woman has access to an overwhelming *jouissance* of her own, she doesn't need to have a desire in the first place. For, from Lacan, we know that desire is a defence against *jouissance*. This contradicts the whole of Lacan's phallic economy, for a woman inherently is free from the repression of phallic discourse. By taking the third avenue, we might bring to the fore Lacan's theory of love in which he provides this gnomic formula: '[O]nly love can make *jouissance* condescend to desire' (Lacan, cited in Braunstein, 2003, 114). If love is something that conjoins desire and *jouissance*, this love has to be a divine one, for only mystics and women can experience it. Finally, we may well argue that feminine *jouissance* is a defence against desire and castration, for this peculiar feminine *qua* mystic experience enables one to have ultimate enjoyment beyond the phallic economy. As such, a feminine *jouissance* has to be a woman's masquerade, not her lack of the phallus. It is in light of this argument that Irigaray in *Speculum of the Other Woman* calls this feminine *qua* mystic *jouissance* a way of surrendering masculinity. As Sellers says,

> Irigaray suggests that at the heart of the mystical experience is a surrendering of the self as (masculine) subject. She believes this experience of self-loss – relinquishing of 'self-identity-as-same' – together with the visions and outpourings it entails, offer women a context in which to break free from the prison within which the (masculine) subject must define himself. (Sellers, 1991, 137)

Feminine sexuality in Lacan sometimes seems a theoretical paradox. His early teaching suggests that a girl experiences castration, its effect and the resulting split earlier than her male counterpart, when she discovers her anatomical difference from a boy. Castration thus makes a girl believe that she has been castrated once and for all. This disclosure grounds her sexual identification on a masculine signifier, the object of her desire that she lacks, a void which she is now conscious of. Thus, a woman constitutes her sexual identification prior to a male subject. Unlike a male subject, this lack of the phallus makes it impossible for her to transfer the object of primordial love, the maternal body, onto the possession of the phallus. The knowledge of all this gives rise to a primary alienation within the female self, which inaugurates the structuring of her desire with the advent of castration and its prohibiting law.

This means that sexed-beings inevitably respond differently to castration. A male subject will remain unconsciously under the threat of castration as a punishment, and a female subject would unconsciously know that her punishment of castration is already accomplished. In this way, castration would logically strengthen the dyadic link between the girl and the m(Other). She develops in the unconscious what Lacan calls a desire for pre-Oedipal symbiotic oneness. However, the outcome for a male subject would lead to a desire for power and domination in the symbolic order. The symbolic castration institutes two positions within masculine and feminine bodies, namely, castrated woman and phallic man. These positions are constructed within a pre-existing phallocentric culture.

The phallus is the symbol of a normative heterosexual desire. The phallic law excludes woman as being neither universal nor an exception to the law. In this context, Lacan has surprised all by his controversial statement that woman doesn't exist. The rejection of her own body and desire is a price she pays in order to live with a masculine regulated desire. Given the option of *having* or *being* the phallus, Jacques-Alain Miller, following Lacan, divides women in relation to their desire into two categorical models. Those who are on the side of *having* the phallus are distinguished as phallic women, and those with a position of *being* the phallus as *true woman.* The phallic woman would behave as though she has the phallus. With masquerade, on the other hand, the woman internalizes a void in her subjectivity, and accepts the model of a feminine desire that the phallicized symbolic order of culture has designed for her. As such, a phallic woman's desire, at the level of the ego, will exhibit personality traits of an undaunted man, but in the unconscious, she will still retain a repressed feminine desire. This makes the essential structure of her desire feminine despite her cultural and social behaviour as a man. Is this construct imposed on woman an inverted transvestism? Of course, I use transvestism metaphorically here, for once a woman performs a desire that is not her own, she is not herself but someone else.

> The pastiche woman, however, hides her lack of having and pretends to be the possessor who lacks nothing and no one. She remains a woman and shows this through her savagery in protecting that which is hers – a savagery marked by hubris, or excess . . . pastiche woman denounces men as being

> castrated and often completes herself in this way with a man, in whose shadow she remains. (Miller, 2000, 21)

The *true woman* on the side of *being* the phallus, accepts the feminine paradigm of phallic desire in the culture. Lacan's formula of feminine desire [A(φ)] puts a female in a position to see the imaginary phallus as the cause and object of her desire, a position that in masculine desire is occupied by the object *a*. Thus, for a woman's desire, the essential question is of either *having* or *being* the phallus. The not-*having*, and the lack that is brought about by an absence of the signifier for her desire in the symbolic makes a woman doubly alienated, which subsequently makes her inaccessible to herself, her desire and her body. The double lack we mentioned above gives rise to this doubleness of feminine desire. The phallic signifier on the side of masculine desire spares the man the double lack that causes conflict between a woman and her own desire. Lacan sees no limit to such feminine submission where a woman is giving and sacrificing everything she has for man.

> Hence the universal of what women desire is sheer madness: all women are mad, they say. That's precisely why they are not-all, that is to say not-at-all-mad-about-the-whole [*folles-du-tout*]; accommodating rather; to the point where there is no limit to the concessions made by any woman for a man: of her body, her soul, her possessions. (Lacan, 1990, 40)

Borrowed from Joan Rivère, Lacan's *masquerade* is more of a mask used by woman to shield against the castrating power of the phallus. With *masquerade*, a woman acts out her femininity by accepting phallic desire and paradoxically she sustains her own desire by rejecting it. Furthermore, she plays a game that allows her to enter the symbolic order.

A woman's denial of her submission to castration leads her to manifest symptoms. Following Freud, Lacan singles out hysteria as a feminine epidemic within the European aristocracy at the time of Freud. Lacan relies on the Freudian claim that hysteria is a clinical model of a feminine 'unfulfilled wish', and in the Lacanian sense, an unfulfilled desire. Lacan's observations reveal that hysteria was a key feminine symptom playing out a female subject's rejection of the phallic function inscribed in the symbolic. An hysteric's resistance is related to a fixation in imaginary identification, and in fact, it is a defiance of masculine supremacy in the symbolic. Hysterics of both sexes express their desire through bodily symptoms, representing a deep conflict in sexual identity. An hysteric's desire is always loaded with conflict: '[t]he hysteric maintains the primacy of subjective division, the contradiction between conscious and unconscious, and thus the conflictual, or self-contradictory nature of desire itself' (Fink, 1998, 35). Nonetheless, hysteria has always been identified with femininity as woman's psychosomatic payoff for conflict in gender identity. The Freudian concept of *Somatisches Entgegenkommen* (somatic compliance) can help us see such conflict in operation. This concept shows how an hysteric body provides a specific organ (different for each individual) to mediate the symbolic expression of desire in non-verbal bodily communication. In other words, a hysteric body collapses the difference between psychical or somatic symptoms, which thus '[a]ffords the unconscious mental processes a physical outlet' (Laplanche and Pontalis, 1973, 423).

Another typical example in psychoanalytic literature was Dora, Cixous' heroine. Like Freud, Lacan too showed keen interest in the case of this young Viennese girl. He found Dora to be caught in an intricate web of romance where the relation with the object of love was the core of her symptom. Lacan saw in Dora a clear case of hysteria, where her identification with her mother shows the structure of her desire. At the conscious level, Dora projects this object of love onto Frau K, Dora's father's mistress. She identifies with Herr K, and takes on his desire for Frau K, his wife. She sustains the Other's desire insofar as she is not its object. Dora's object of desire is the object of her father's desire, and Lacan makes this a model for feminine homosexual desire, in which the hysteric subject sustains the Other's desire. This model illustrates how in feminine homosexuality, the subject identifies with the father and the object of his desire.

The important thing Lacan marks in Freud's approach was the way, as an analyst, he ignored the operation of his own desire in the course of treatment. Dora and Antigone offer two distinct models of feminine desire. While Dora displays her desire in its sexual dimension, Antigone, on the contrary, demonstrates hers in a fight for power with patriarchal supremacy. Despite the contrary positions, they both seek in the course of their desire to accomplish the same goal, the defence of feminine desire. Dora uses *masquerade* to act out her desire while Antigone appears as the queen of phallic women. Dora rejects the position of being an object of exchange between her father and K., as Lacan argues.

On the other hand, towards the end of the play, we see a drastic change in Antigone's desire, when she passionately desires her own death, or as she calls it her 'bridal dower', in the way a mystic would. Lacan identifies her desire as a desire for the m(Other), exactly the desire that is beyond the phallus. What happens to her desire? The text alludes to the fact that the desire of the mother is the origin of everything. For Lacan, Antigone's desire is an example of pure desire because it is genuinely for death and nothing else, as she says in the play:

> Going to my rest, where death shall take me
> Alive across the silent river.

No wedding-day; no marriage-music:
Death will be all my bridal dower.

(*Antigone*, 148)

We always arrive at a paradox when we want to provide an ontological picture of bodily *jouissance*, the ultimate pleasure and excessive suffering that Lacan calls *jouissance* beyond the phallus, a kind of ascetic experience described as mystical, bodily or feminine *jouissance*. Such an experience situates a subject beyond desire, for it occurs in the ecstasies of body and mind, the casting out of the phallic law. In *Encore*, Lacan argues his theoretical position that feminine *jouissance* is the *jouissance* of the Other that cannot be articulated in language and is, in fact, the experience of the real or non-existence. As Lacan says, '[T]here is a *jouissance* that is hers about which she herself perhaps knows nothing if not that she experiences it – that much she knows. She knows it, of course, when it comes (*arrive*). It doesn't happen (*arrive*) to all of them' (Lacan, 1998a, 74). Besides, a woman's language is different to man's. She can talk authentically only with another woman, for the symbolic order is entirely contaminated by the phallic law. A woman doesn't have a signifying representation in the symbolic, she keeps her desire to herself because she doesn't have a language of her own. As Lacan postulates in *Encore*, a woman is not whole, therefore she has a 'supplementary', *jouissance* that the phallic function is unable to designate as he says, 'You will notice that I said "supplementary." If I had said "complementary" what a mess we'd be in! We would fall back into the whole' (73).

A careful reading of *Encore* reveals that Lacan identifies different varieties of this *jouissance*. One version is the *jouissance* of the Other, '[t]he Other I said to be symbolised by the body' (Lacan, 1998a, 39). The same *jouissance* then becomes God's *jouissance* and also the narcissistic *jouissance* of the body. As Lacan remarks, '[t]he Supreme Being's *jouissance*, that is God's. To put it plainly, by loving God, we love ourselves, and by first loving ourselves – "well-ordered charity," as it is put – we pay the appropriate homage to God' (70–71).

As indicated thus far, for Lacan, the woman and the mystic have the privilege of having access to the experience of surplus enjoyment, but why are they not aware of it? In order to find an answer, we need to have a look at the Lacanian concept of knowledge and particularly symbolic knowledge (*savoir*) to find out why women mystics don't know what they sometimes experience. This unconscious knowledge is non-existent in the symbolic. Thus, it was once a reality but is now gone forever. This surplus *jouissance* belongs to the real that remains beyond articulation in the signifying chain of language. As such, it has to be hidden from the knowledge of the subject, for it is outside of consciousness. The real that contains this *jouissance* only appears in hallucination, delusion or trance that mystics are often talking about as the ecstasy of their immersion in divinity. Lacan was forever an admirer of mystic literature to which he related his own text. He himself made a pun on his name, 'Jacques-ulation' to identify himself with 'mystical jaculations':

> These mystical jaculations are neither idle chatter nor empty verbiage; they provide, all in all, some of the best reading one can find – at the bottom of the page, drop a footnote, 'Add to that list Jacques Lacan's *Écrits*, because it's of the same order.' (Lacan, 1998a, 76)

Slavoj Žižek is cognizant of such a paradox concerning feminine *jouissance*. He reduces this *jouissance* to Lacan's idealization of the Other and woman as the object of love, while keeping silent about the mystical dimension of the Lacanian concept. For him, this feminine *jouissance,* or a return to the blissful state of pre-Oedipal *jouissance,* seems illusory. He writes, '[t]he pre-symbolic "eternally Feminine" is a retroactive patriarchal fantasy' (Žižek, 1994, 107). Žižek does not accept that Lacan surpassed Freudian phallocentrism. As we have said, Lacan was able to prove the particularity of woman's *jouissance* and give it a parallel in the world of mystical desire and all-embracing bodily *jouissance.* Žižek denies that this feminine *jouissance* that Lacan painstakingly tries to figure out in *Encore,* is removed from the phallic function of the symbolic. He writes, 'Lacan does talk about feminine *jouissance* eluding the phallic domain, he conceives of it as an ineffable "dark continent" separated from (the male) discourse by a frontier impossible to trespass' (107).

From what we have said, it is arguable that the Lacanian theory of desire reveals everything that poststructuralist feminist theorists claim about feminine desire. Lacan has made a great contribution in postulating femininity in its entirety, as he says in *Encore* that *jouissance* beyond the phallus '[w]ould give another consistency to the woman's liberation movement' (Lacan, 1998a, 74). His phallocentrism in his earlier teaching, however, may be conceived of as an insight into a historical truth about Western phallocentric culture, not a universal truth about sexual difference in itself. As we have spelt out, much of the controversy centres on Lacan's 'The Signification of the Phallus', where the phallus is given a transcendental agency in making sense of every signification in the symbolic register. We will discuss in brief the most important points of Hélène Cixous and Luce Irigaray's criticism of Lacan's approach to feminine sexuality, as a coda to this chapter. The problem with these feminists, however, is that both consider feminine desire in reductionist terms, as only sexual desire, or a desire whose object is merely sexual pleasure, whereas in Lacanian theory, desire is much more than that. Both Irigaray and Cixous seem aligned in their criticism of Lacan, and see feminine desire in an infinite multiplicity often in a fight to free itself from the prison of phallic discourse. We may well locate three major points in their theory of feminine desire. First, a woman's desire is often foreign to herself, because a feminine voice and language are excluded from the dominant phallic discourse. In the symbolic order, woman doesn't exist as a desiring subject, but rather as a desired object, reducing her to a neutral object of exchange in the phallic economy of desire. Second, for a woman to set her autonomous desire free, she has to create her own writing beyond the existing phallic signifying system. Third, a woman's desire is amorphous and may be located in all parts of her body. This desire can only be channelled by cutting across gender beyond the masculine configuration of the subject and his desire. Lacan agrees with them that a woman's desire cannot be symbolized, simply because of the lack of her own signifier in the symbolic order. This lack requires her to go through the Oedipus Complex as a masculine subject by virtue of her identification with the father. This is because only masculinity has its inscription as universal in the symbolic. Cixous, in 'The Laugh of the Medusa', stipulates *écriture féminine* (feminine writing) as a way through which a woman can repulse the phallic law by having access to her genuine desire. By her own kind of writing, she can put her body and desire in the letter, as Cixous says:

> It [writing] will give her back her goods, her pleasures, her organs, her immense bodily territories which have been kept under seal; it will tear her away from the superegoised structure in which she has always occupied the place reserved for the guilty (guilty of everything, guilty at every turn: for having desire). (Cixous, 1997, 351)

Here Cixous refers to castration and its signifier as a dogma that has been passed to Lacan by Freud. She refers to Lacan and his controversial paper 'The Signification of the Phallus', by stating that the phallus is a marker that a man wants in order to assert his defence against the law of castration. By carrying this lack of *not having* the phallus, a woman exists only to realize his desire, the way Hegel's master would have his desire recognized by the slave. A desire based on lack is also absurd for Cixous, for it deprives woman of her boundless desire, because a woman wouldn't be able to give what she lacks. For a woman, desire is essentially 'the desire-that-gives' (361). As such, Cixous mixes up drives and *jouissance* with desire.

From Cixous' writings, we can see that she postulates a poly-sexual feminine desire and sees the realization of such a cosmic feminine desire in bisexuality. Woman's desire, according to her, is not centred in a few erotogenic zones that come into psychoanalytic literature as the outcome of an age-old imaginary masculine fantasy. She agrees that a woman's desire is a 'loving-desire'. Cixous' statement, '[I] want all of me with all of him,' (Cixous, 1997, 360) says all a woman can say about her *jouissance*. The rest should be left to the body in its paroxysm outside language. Since she says that a woman's desire bursts from every part of her body, and only a man who is himself all, can satisfy this feminine desire. Cixous, like Irigaray, sees a fundamental bisexuality in both woman as well as man as that which can make such a desire a reality. In 'Sorties', she reiterates her theoretical position by saying that feminine desire is subject to being appropriated by phallic discourse. The language that is governed by the phallic signifier functions as a vehicle for masculine desire to obliterate the feminine. Like Irigaray, Cixous raises the issue of difference within the operation of desire. As Sellers says, '[l]anguage, she [Cixous] concludes, has become the "Empire of the Selfsame"; and she urges women to "break into" language, exploding the law of its discourse to make language "fly"' (Sellers, 1991, 251).

Cixous argues that feminine writing is the only way that woman can have access to her original desire, for this would free her body from being an object of the other's desire. Feminine writing would also allow bodily drives to express themselves freely. This brings Cixous close to late Lacan who conceptualized writing in terms of *sinthome*, and *jouissance*. For Lacan, however, writing in this sense was not gendered, but rather a peculiar way of reaching out to one's unconscious enjoyment in the real. In Cixous' universe, writing seems rather utopian, because she doesn't prescribe a new language beyond the phallic signifier. However, late Lacan, as we will see later, is similar by postulating his theory of writing as being in the register of real.

Similarly, Irigaray's first aim is to free feminine desire from those attributes that are superimposed by an economy of desire that is grounded in masculine paradigm. Thus, feminine desire must be only in reference to itself, analysed within her own world. For her, the primacy of the phallus is nothing but a masculine fantasy that centres feminine desire on a single organ that Lacan elaborated in terms of phallic *jouissance*. Irigaray's defence of bisexuality comes as a defence against a desire defined by the phallic law. She postulates two categories of bisexuality. The first represents a complete being, rejecting the fear of castration and veiling sexual difference. This complete being means that once phallic law is transgressed, feminine desire would reach its totality, and its satisfaction. The second identifies a woman with one who retains within herself the existence of two sexes. She thus implies that feminine desire does not have a centre like that of a man. She calls for woman's liberation, first by freeing her own desire from a guilty desire, as her desire is often violated and denied historically.

For Irigaray, feminine desire in Western culture is generated by a masculine visual fantasy, as a man always desires by looking. Irigaray, however, accepts Lacan's notion of a woman's attachment to the Other and her autoeroticism as a part of what the Other demands from being the subject. As she writes in 'This Sex Which is Not One', 'the woman always remains several, but she is kept from being dispersed because the Other is already within herself and is autoerotically familiar to her. This is not to say that she appropriates the other for herself, that she reduces it to her own property' (Irigaray, 1997, 367). The Other that a woman has within herself is the mother, the originary object of desire that here Irigaray writes with a lower case (o). Lacan does the same in his diagram of sexuation, where the Other is on the side of the woman. Irigaray also criticizes Lacan for not adding feminine fluidity to his long list of the objects *a*. Feminine fluidity for her was the fluidity of a woman's desire, as Susan Sellers writes, 'In "the Mechanics of Fluids", Irigaray develops her insistence that the "fluidity" of women's sexuality may undermine the masculine schema' (Sellers, 1991, 115).

According to Irigaray, feminine desire means her sexual pleasure can be achieved when she is free from the burdens of either *having* or *being* the phallus. Therefore, a woman's desire must be the realization of her autoeroticism and bisexuality. She even takes a step farther than Cixous when she sees woman's orgasm not as a single culminating point like that of a man. One thing that is important to note here is that in the Cixous-Irigarayan reading of Lacan, Rivière's masquerade is extended to both sexes. For Lacan sees some masculine cultural attributes, such as parades and medals, as cultural exhibitions of a masculine masquerade. While the veil is a woman's mask, by the same token, all a man displays as his bravery is his mask of the lack of the phallus and the castration upon which desire is based. Irigaray, nonetheless, endorses Lacan's theory of woman's *jouissance* being incompatible with the phallic function. However, she criticizes Lacan's formulas of sexual difference and sees them as a result of a masculine bodily fantasy. She comments: '[t]his linguistic home that man has managed to substitute even for his dwelling in a body, whether his own body or another's has used a woman as a construct arguing with the phallus' (Irigaray, cited in Campbell, 2000, 129).

Irigaray seems cognizant of the limit and paradox of the Lacanian theory of feminine *jouissance*, for it arguably leaves the question of a distinct definition of feminine desire unanswered. This *jouissance* that Lacan connects with mystic ecstasy, remains beyond language, outside conscious awareness and consequently beyond desire. Desire has been identified as a defence against falling into *jouissance*. If, for a woman, this *jouissance* is actually available, what happens to her desire then? Irigaray's answer is that this *jouissance* is a kind of defence against normative phallic desire. Calling mysticism mysterious and hysterical, she '[s]uggests that at the heart of the mystical experience is a surrendering of the self as (masculine) subject. She believes this experience of self-loss – the relinquishing of "self-identity-as-same" – together with the vision and outpourings it entails, offers women a context in which to break free from the prison within which the (masculine) subject must define himself' (Sellers, 1991, 137). Irigaray prescribes writing as a vehicle for escape from phallic desire.

Neither Lacan nor Irigaray justify their definition of feminine *jouissance* in its relation to feminine desire. Lacan never answers this crucial question, and Irigaray is simply using Lacan against Lacan. For, as we said above, Lacan knew that feminine *jouissance* is beyond desire and a flight from language and phallic discourse. Cixous and Irigaray thus try to appropriate and define feminine desire in terms of desire for the same. Nevertheless, unlike Butler, they do not critique heterosexuality. For them feminine desire was only represented as fragmentary in the Lacanian symbolic register. They criticize Lacan for his argument that *being* and *having* the phallus is the governing law that determines desire for both sexes. Cixous condemns Lacan as a priest who preaches the familiar phallic law of a masculine-dominated culture, as well as masculine fantasies about women.

Chapter 3

Beyond Desire: Love, Mystic *Jouissance* and *The Sinthome*

Desire begins losing its place as a centripetal force within Lacan's theories in the mid-1960s. This theoretical matrix was effaced in Lacan's thinking with his seminar on James Joyce. In this chapter, we will discuss how Lacan closes the door on the past and takes new turn in his theoretical conceptualization. Then we will attempt to show moments when desire is suspended with a focus on Lacan's theory of love, *jouissance* and what Lacan designates as enigmatic mystical ecstasies. We will also examine the unique place of desire in fantasy when it comes into relation with love and even *jouissance*. From there, we will proceed to the concept of *sinthome* that marks a radical shift in Lacan's teaching, where the negativity of desire seems to be replaced by the more positive enjoyment of one's unconscious. We will attempt to highlight *sinthome* as a theoretical landmark in Lacan's thinking within which language changes its role from mediation to abutting directly on the drives and *jouissance*.

My purpose, however, is not to claim that, in the face of Lacan's new findings, his theory of desire has become irrelevant or out of date. Nor do I wish to argue that the concepts dealt with in this chapter are simply an advanced version of Lacan's earlier theories. On the contrary, my aim, in the upcoming chapters, is to show that all of Lacan's theories that have been discussed in this study have had an immense importance in literary studies and psychoanalytic textual interpretation. Desire, *jouissance* and *sinthome*, thus, imply different theoretical concepts, each important in its own right in relation to literature. To take an example, Lacan's desire is crucial for the understanding of classical tragedies. His theories of love and *jouissance* give us a rigorous interpretative principle to deconstruct poetry, and finally, his *sinthome* offers a far-reaching critique of modern and postmodern literature.

When Lacan abandoned structural linguistics and embarked on theories of the drives and topology, his focus of attention also shifted from desire. In his colloquium, 'Technique and Casuistry', delivered in January 1964 in Rome, Lacan signals for the first time the limits of desire. Commenting on this colloquium, he states in a brief essay, 'On Freud's "Trieb" and the Psychoanalyst's Desire,' that desire often tarries under the threat of the pleasure principle.

The pleasure principle supports but places limits on desire by means of repetition compulsion and by saving it from the threat of *jouissance.* Taking on Freud's theory of libido which reduces it to male desire, Lacan writes that the libido is a quantifiable energy but is far from being a sexual instinct in which, '[o]nly certain *quanta* of constancy are recognized therein' (Lacan, 2006, 723). Lacan argues that the sexual 'coloring'of the libido that Freud emphatically insisted on, is the '[c]olor of emptiness: suspended in the light of a gap' (ibid.). This gap is left open by the pleasure principle in which desire encounters its limit and frustration, because the pleasure principle never allows for the satisfaction of desire. This shows the limiting power the pleasure principle has upon desire, because of which the latter reaches a dead end. This makes desire submissive to the prohibition that comes about with the law.

Lacan goes further when he designates a disjunction between desire and *jouissance,* when he maintains that desire begins to disfigure itself as soon as it gets closer to *jouissance.* This disfiguring of desire is described by Lacan as a '[m]isadventure of desire at the hedge of jouissance' (724). In a brilliant allusion to a lizard's 'self-mutilation', 'its tail being jettisoned when in distress' (ibid.), Lacan affirms that desire too mutilates itself when it approaches the *jouissance* that the pleasure principle wants to prohibit. It is the fact that desire is often in an inverse relation to the pleasure principle that confirms the domination of signifiers in the symbolic register. In the above essay, Lacan also shows a disjunction and conflict between desire and the drive. As an unconscious force for prohibition, desire often takes refuge in the house of the law, where the drive is always striving to transgress the pleasure principle by aiming at *jouissance.* This is because the symbolic is the realm of desire whereas the drives belong to the realm of the real as well as imaginary. As Lacan writes, '[t]his occurs because the drive divides the subject and desire, the latter sustaining itself only in the relation it misrecognizes between that division and an object which causes it' (724). Lacan, moreover, attempts to explain desire in its relation, and its pervasive conflict with and opposition to both the drives and *jouissance.* Lacan reverses his earlier theoretical postulate concerning desire as being a driving force '[a]t the origin of every variety of animation' (Lacan, 1991a, 223), by asserting that the drives are of greater importance than desire.

As such, Lacan repositions desire in his theories in two major ways. First, he disputes his earlier position regarding an antinomic polarity between desire and the law, by arguing that desire is often subservient to the law. Desire obeys and supports the law to the extent that it fulfils the same functions as the law does, because desire, in a final analysis, means the insistence of the lack. When the law produces lack by its prohibiting power, or castration, desire persists in lack, as the latter is an absolute condition within the terrain of the law. From this explanation, we may argue that a repressed desire is on the side of the law as much as the law is on the side of desire. How can desire be essentially a transgression of the law as Lacan emphasizes in *The Ethic of Psychoanalysis* and on the side of the law at the same time? In a footnote to his essay, Miller interprets this as a common feature in Lacanian epistemology. Miller grounds his argument here on Lacan's topological theory of which the moebius strip is an example.

> The notion of one thing being on 'the same side as' or 'the opposite side from' another is very common in Lacan's work and is not always easy to translate effectively. When it refers to a diagram, the sides are often graphic and visible. Hence, one might say that 'desire is aligned with the law'. (Miller, 1996, 427)

On the other hand, *jouissance* may not be threatened by the provisions of the law as much as desire for the law subsequently causes the liquidation of desire in its own space. The law regulates desire and places restrictions on it. However, in late Lacan, *jouissance* can happen beyond the law and the phallus, which seems not to be restricted by either the law or desire. *Jouissance* for its part is restricted by language, as in earlier Lacan the word was the murder of the thing.

Such are the endless vicissitudes, trickery and paradoxes of desire. As in fantasy, according to Lacan, the subject under cover of desire misrecognizes his division caused by the object *a*. By such a misrecognition, desire helps the subject to identify with the object *a*. The latter, on its part, links the subject with the originary object, for it always represents an exit from the symbolic network, being in touch with the real. This real, as Lacan writes, '[c]reates [*fait*] desire by reproducing therein the relationship of the subject to the lost object' (Lacan, 2006, 724). As such, fantasy is an illusory configuration of a scenario in which desire and its objects come into play behind an imaginary wall that divides reality from its perception in consciousness.

> Identifications are determined by desire without satisfying the drive. This occurs because the drive divides the subject and desire, the latter sustaining itself only in the relation it misrecognizes between the division and an object, which causes it. Such is the structure of fantasy (724).

In addition, fantasy, especially when it involves love, provides for an idealization of the lover and his identification with the object cause of desire. This identification lies beyond desire, as love often causes the suspension of desire in an elusive unification with the idyllic woman in courtly love, and the divine in mystical love. From what we have argued above, we may well conclude that both desire and its beyond represent themselves in a fantasy, for insofar as desire leaves the drive unsatisfied, it visits frustration on *jouissance*, and when it acts out a bond of love it takes the subject beyond desire by means of love and the object *a*.

Lacan takes a further step concerning his disaffection with the idea of desire when in *The Four Fundamental Concepts;* he excludes desire from the four pillars of his teaching, namely, the unconscious, repetition, transference and the drive, blaming traditional psychology and Freud for attributing infinitude and indestructibility to desire:

> If, in the register of a traditional psychology, stress is laid on the uncontrollable, infinite character of human desire – seeing in it the mark of some divine slipper that has left its imprint on it – what analytic experience enables us to declare is rather the limited function of desire. Desire, more than any other point in the range of human possibility, meets its limits somewhere. (Lacan, 1979a, 30–31)

It is appropriate here to ask where that 'somewhere' where desire comes at its limit, and what does Lacan mean by a 'limited function' of desire? The answer to the first question lies in the reproductive function of desire that carries lack, the experience of the past, into the future. The answer to the second question, however, lies in love and *jouissance* where the subject is experiencing its primordial oneness with the lost object, even though this oneness is elusive. Freud, according to Lacan, misunderstood such a compulsive function in the light of which he interpreted desire as something infinite and indestructible. Lacan questions the consistency of the term 'indestructibility', with regard to desire, based on the logical time of psychoanalysis. In his theory of temporality, he suggests that the inconsistency of any logical articulation is bound to a logical time, not a chronological time of the clock. In Lacanian psychoanalysis, logical time bears on the temporality of any logical articulation. Freud's definition of desire as eternal and indestructible, according to Lacan, was an outcome of a misunderstanding about these two types of time. Lacan thus distances himself from Freud when desire no longer functions as a transcendental signifier in the former's discourse.

Following Lacan, we may well uphold the idea that when there is love at play, desire disappears. Love, especially mystical love, is a site in which a misapprehension of recovering the lost object to which love is addressed takes place. In other words, in transference, the subject takes the place of the object, because of the configuration of primordial love. Here lies the fundamental opposition between love and desire. When one desires something, one tries to deprive oneself of that object. Lacan argues that by virtue of an unconscious impulse a subject who desires will be unconsciously '[e]nunciating the sentence, "I ask you to refuse what I offer you", I could only motivate it by "that's not it" that I took up again last time' (Lacan, 1998a,126). The opposite is true for love, as it always creates the illusion of fusion with the object. Lacan offers various definitions of love in his seminars. In Seminar X: *On Anxiety* (1962–1963), he depicts love as a sublimation of desire that opens up a possibility through which *jouissance*, '[c]ondescends to desire' (Harari, 2001, 80). Here the desire in question is the unsatisfied desire of the hysteric subject that, by its reproduction as unsatisfied itself dissolves into a *jouissance*. This is a *jouissance* which Lacan calls the *jouissance* of suffering. This reproduction marks the lack through which desire insists, and anxiety emerges in the replacement of the object with some other object. Such symmetry between desire and *jouissance* becomes possible by way of anxiety, as anxiety reveals itself as a failure in desire, a failure not caused by the lack of a substitute for the object but by the replacement by this substitute of the original lost object. This means that anxiety by definition is a result of the incompatibility of the substitute object with the primordial object, as when immersed in anxiety; a subject unconsciously knows that the desired object is not the one he once had access to. In this context, Lacan argues that desire settles anxiety to some degree.

Desire always dwells in the lack-in-being in order to reproduce itself, while love and *jouissance* attempt to fill the void created by this lack-in-being. This fixation on lack by virtue of desiring appropriates a metonymic structure that slips from one signifier to another, or substitutes one object *a* for another. In the meantime, this draws a distinction between desire and love, as desire reproduces itself by keeping up the desiring operation, while love, on the contrary halts this operation by way of a fixation on the object that replicates the absolute lost object. Love, by offering a fusion with the object, separates the subject from its own desire. It is always possible for love to emerge in the space of desire, while the latter allows for a reconfiguration of the demand for love, and a demand for recognition. This implies that love provides a short circuit for desire and in some ways rescues a subject from the overwhelming trial of desire. Unlike desire, love may reach its impossible goal, and this very feature raises love beyond the boundary of desire. In the Lacanian theory of love, the conflation of two desires in love means the conflation of two different and asymmetrical discourses. This means that the lover and the beloved do not demand the same thing.

Lacan in his latter teaching defines love as a supplement that makes the existence of the sexual relationship possible, for in love a kind of paradoxical relationship tends to be established between two unconscious knowledges. This means that each partner in love is unconsciously related to the Other to which both desire and love are addressed. In modern French thinking, this notion of love finds its articulation in different ways by Bataille and Badiou. Bataille misinterprets Lacan's theory of love when he conceives love as a coincidence of two desires for the same object. For him, desire is purer when it has become more and more carnally addressed. Thus, Bataille reduces love to a hedonistic passion, sexual excesses and a pornographic lust in which two desires intersect.

> The object of sensual desire is by nature another desire. The desire of the senses is the desire, if not to destroy oneself, at least to be consumed and to

> lose oneself without reservation . . . Love in its essence is so clearly the coincidence of two desires that there is nothing more meaningful in love, even in the purest love. (Bataille, 1986, 265)

For Badiou love, on the other hand, means essentially an 'experience', 'to be taken in its most general sense, presentation as such, the situation' (Badiou, 2000a, 266). By this experience two sexed positions 'man' and 'woman' retroactively present themselves as disjunctive. In Lacanian fashion, Badiou argues that the experience for both positions is different for '[t]he disjunction is not observable and cannot itself be made the object of an experience or of direct knowledge [*savoir*]' (267). Since the knowledge is unconscious knowledge or *savoir*, therefore, it cannot be known to either of the above positions. This spells out Lacan's important argument that the sexual relationship remains beyond any social bond or symbolization, because it is inherently deceptive, being only experienced by two speaking beings. By contrast, love allows for such a bond which is neither natural nor godly, but simply a human creation in order to make the existence of sexual relationship (which is essentially non-existence), possible.

Lacan hints at courtly love as a symbolic manifestation of the non-existence of the sexual relationship. For in courtly love, the being of a woman is cherished rather than a sexual relation with her. The imaginary dimension of love allows the subject to re-articulate this grand illusion to everything from the love of angels, to sexual love, and love of God.

Lacan, in *Encore* re-articulates and redefines this persistent proposition: *il n'y a pas de rapport sexuel*: there is no such thing as a sexual relationship. This relation may be constructed by love, as a supplement. Love makes this non-existent sexual relationship possible by establishing a bond between two beings. Lacan conceives of this feature of love as something that wants to be said or written. The writing at issue here obviously illustrates Lacan's usual gargantuan appetite for paradoxes. As he states at the end of *Encore*:

> The displacement of the negation from the 'stops not being written', to the 'doesn't stop being written', in other words, from contingency to necessity – there lies the point of suspension to which all love is attached.
>
> All love, subsisting only on the basis of the 'stops not being written', tends to make the negation shift to the 'doesn't stop being written', doesn't stop, won't stop. (Lacan, 1998a, 145)

There is a confluence of psychoanalysis, Aristotle's philosophy, and logic in the above paradoxical passage that seems odd at first glance. By revising Aristotle's categories, of the possible, the impossible, the contingent and the necessary, Lacan adds writing or being written as, a new category or a mode of being.

By removing the metaphysical from Aristotle's categories, Lacan argues that possible and impossible, and consequently contingency and necessity should not be taken into account as binary oppositions, but interchangeable modes of existence. Therefore, for Lacan ' "[t]o stop not being written", is not a formulation proffered haphazardly. I associated it with contingency, whereas I delighted in [characterizing] the necessary as that which "doesn't stop being written", for the necessary is not the real' (Lacan, 1998a, 144). Lacan, in the meantime, defines the non-existence of the sexual relationship as something which 'doesn't stop not being written' (144).

What does Lacan really mean by the non-existence of the sexual relationship? Lacan himself answers this in his *Seimnar XIX . . . Our Pire* (1972–1973), '[w]hen I say that there is no sexual relation, I put forward very precisely a truth concerning speaking being sex does not define any relation' (Lacan, cited in Marini, 1992, 230). The sexual relation is non-existent, because as Lacan argues in his formulas of sexuation, there is no signifier for sexual difference in the symbolic, and phallic *jouissance* is like Freudian libido, universal for both man and woman. Further, according to Lacan, woman is *not all*, which means not represented by a universal signifier. However, love creates an illusion of the existence of the sexual relationship, because with the mediation of the object *a* and the phallus, two speaking beings can fall into a relationship. With the mediation of the body and its *jouissance*, mystic love builds such a relation too. Love functions to compensate for the lack that comes about with the non-existence of the sexual relationship. As such, Lacan insists that love wants to locate itself in a space where two 'unconscious knowledges', come into a kind of relation. Love between two subjects is experienced in the gap that is formed within the intersection of the two conditions of 'contingency', (what is not yet written but is on the verge of being written, and 'necessity',) that which (always can be written). This means that love transposes from a situation of not being written to a new situation of being written:

> What was new here was the desire to ground this proposition *in logic*. For the purpose, Lacan contested and revised Aristotle's categories, *the possible, the impossible, the contingent, the necessary,* and he added *the impotence* [*l'impuissance*] to write the sexual relation, which made all discourse a 'broken discourse'. (Marini, 1992, 230)

At stake here is the real that neither can be spoken nor written in the symbolic articulation of language, as Lacan puts it, '[t]here is no existence of the sexual relationship in the act of speaking' (Lacan,1998a,144–145). This impossibility itself allows for a possibility of an encounter with the real. The contingency of this encounter occurs in the symbolic by means that stay always beyond the symbolic in the form of a *tuche* – the chance encounter with the real, such as the symptom or an affect which inscribe themselves in the symbolic order in terms of a trauma. In other words, the interchangeability between contingency and necessity means that the first of the above statements should be negated in order to take the form of 'doesn't stop being written'. Love occupies an intermediary ground between the two statements as Lacan writes, '[a]ll love, subsisting only on the basis of the "stops not being written", tends to make the negation shift to the "doesn't stop being written", doesn't stop, won't stop' (Lacan, 1998a, 145).

It is appropriate at this point of our discussion to answer the crucial question why Lacan has chosen to explain his theory of love in terms of writing or being written? Writing in late Lacan should not be understood as writing in its ordinary meaning. Lacan places writing in a much higher register than speech, for writing supports and touches the real. This privilege makes writing something that is unspeakable and unsymbolizable that remains outside the symbolic or something that ex-ists. Lacan argues that this unspeakable and unknowable thing can be written but only in algebraic symbols, such as the Borromean knots or a discourse that was created by James Joyce. Thus, writing in the Lacanian sense doesn't necessarily mean a writing that could be readable or meaningful. For example, the object cause of desire is written as '*a*', the symbolic phallus as 'Φ', phallic *jouissance* as 'jφ', the real phallus as 'Π', as a non-word discourse. Lacan in a very dense and difficult chapter of *Encore*, 'The Function of the Written', ponders this topic. The first thing to be emphasized about the concept of writing or the written is that it has to be taken as equivalent to unconscious knowledge that remains always impossible to understand. He argues that the 'written' is similar to the bar that separates the signifier from the signified, as he states, '[t]he bar, like everything involving what is written, is based only on the following – what is written is not to be understood' (Lacan, 1998a, 34). Thus, for Lacan, whatever is written is an effect of discourse and that aspect of language that is 'conditioned by discourse' (35).

In *Encore*, Lacan postulates the antithesis between the love linked with sexual rapport, and a new form of love that remains asexual. This is true and heavenly love that Lacan wants to spell out in terms of *jouissance de femme* that we discussed in previous chapters. Lacan also says that mystics also, like women, experience this kind of *jouissance* without knowing anything about it. From Lacan's account, we find that some women, but all mystics whether male or female, experience this *jouissance* in their ecstatic raptures, the effect of which is no doubt mystical love. Therefore, we can call this *jouissance* a mystical *jouissance* instead. Perhaps Lacan was so preoccupied by the logic of his formula of sexuation and his earlier theoretical configuration that he termed this *jouissance* a female *jouissance,* and superimposed effeminacy on mysticism. Žižek seems uncertain when explaining feminine *jouissance.* He sees it as the idealization of woman by Lacan. In his essay, 'Otto Weininger, or, "Woman doesn't exist," he is keen to keep this kind of *jouissance* only for women and nothing else, as he says that feminine *jouissance* is an ineffable "dark continent" separated from (the male) discourse by a frontier impossible to trespass' (Žižek, 1994,107). Romantic love remains beyond desire, but the former trespasses on the defensive frontier of desire, insofar as the latter was a barrier to *jouissance* in Lacan's consideration. Mystical love, on the contrary, is asexual and bears on the Other's *jouissance* which inscribes itself, as mystic literary discourse shows, on the subject's body. Divine love is experienced in the psychosomatic ecstasies of the body. Mystic love in Lacanian thinking is different from the 'act of love' (sexual intercourse), as Lacan insists in *Encore*. The 'act of love' is addressed to an object *a* in desire within the phallic economy, whereas, mystical love is 'poetry': 'However, what he approaches is the cause of his desire that I have designated as object *a* that is the act of love. To make love *(faire l'amour)*, the very expression indicates, is poetry. However, there is a world between poetry and the act' (Lacan, 1998a, 72).

Mystical love or the *jouissance* of the Other ex-ists, because it cannot be articulated by unconscious knowledge, for it stays beyond the articulation of the signifier. We find the effect of this love in speaking about it, the other side of the mystic narrative that we will explore in upcoming chapters. The mystico-theological discourses of all religions are unthinkable without a strong propensity to speak about love. This speaking of/about love produces a *jouissance*. This is exactly what Barthes says in *A Lover's Discourse*:

> On the road from Phalerum, a bored traveller catches sight of another man walking ahead of him, catches up and asks him to tell about the banquet given by Agathon. Such is the genesis of the theory of love: an accident, boredom, a desire to talk, or if you will, a gossip lasting a little over a mile. (Barthes, 1993b, 429)

Thus talking about love is in itself a desire. The poetry that Lacan talks about mediates the effect of the Other's *jouissance* by bridging the gaps in the flow of the signifying stream in mystical discourse. The insistence and excesses of speaking about love itself reveal the poet's symptom. We will see this when we are dealing with poetry in coming chapters. Because of an interaction between love and desire, the object to which mystic love is addressed has to be changed into a being, a Supreme Being. The rise of this Supreme Being as a holy object of love brings us to the transcendental space of mysticism. On this account, the love of a Supreme Being will require the annihilation of a narcissistic self-love, and the transcendence of the object of love. Sadomasochism and the death drive come into play within mystical poetry, showing the association of love with desire, where the ultimate goal, as in Antigone's case, is self-annihilation, ironically life in death. This pivotal feature of love, together with desire, takes us back to our discussion of feminine *jouissance*, a brief account of which we have presented in previous chapters.

Such a combination of love and desire opens a transcendental space for playing out the drama of love. Where desire reproduces itself as paradise lost in a metonymic structure, love creates an illusion of paradise found in a metaphoric structure. Therefore, the metonymy of desire would yield itself to the metaphor of love. This transcendental space is the space of the real, unknowable, unthinkable and inassimilable to signification. Mystical poetry bears evidence of such a confluence of love and desire where raptures of bodily *jouissance* conjoin with ecstatic erotica, divine love and death. As Lacan says, '[t]he real itself is three, that is *jouissance*, body, and death. As long as they are knotty only by the unverified deadlock of sex' (Lacan, 2002, 102). This unbridled love is what the mystic poet claims is a hypnotized state of being in love which is a threshold to the Other's *jouissance.* Mystical songs are thus love letters that are addressed to the Other. Following Lacan, Barthes calls a mystic an amorous subject, one who would, like Schreber, serenade himself as both the lover and the beloved of God, in an existential rapture of ecstasy. This is the mystic way of overcoming primordial loss and living out the illusion of a communion with the object of primordial love. There is no place for sex in such transcendental moments for mystics. As Lacan says, '[a]s long as the soul souloves the soul (*l' âme, âme l' âme*), sex is not counted' (Lacan, 1998, 84). This Lacanian 'soulove', is to love as a verb for mystics. A mystic body thus is yearning for a kind of hysterical trance that denies both the self and lack. In mysticism, it is the Other, the divine that yearns for the love exchange. As Verhaeghe says,

> Lacan recognises the same process in mystics: they too testify to a non-limited, totally invasive enjoyment that colonises the whole body, a *jouissance* that comes from God. In *seminar XX*, Lacan calls this an 'other *jouissance* and finds it in women as well'. (Verhaeghe, 2001, 89)

Where does this mystic link between feminine jouissance and mysticism come from in Lacan's theory in *Encore?* Deborah Luepnitz writes that the whole idea of mysticism – to which Lacan attributes his *Écrits* as well – comes from Simone de Beauvoir. De Beauvoir devoted one chapter of *The Second Sex* to mystical love, where feminine love seems to be incommensurate with its counterpart, mystic love. Unlike Lacan, de Beauvoir deems mystic love as the sole property of a woman, claiming there is a 'legion' of women who feel such love or, in Lacanian terms, feminine *jouissance.* We shall see that for Lacan, in his love of a woman, man's object of love attains a transcendental position like that of God (Courtly Love according to Lacan is a vivid example of this); and for de Beauvoir it is the woman who seeks God in a man, in her object of love. As she writes: '[L]ove has been assigned to woman as her supreme vocation, and when she directs towards a man, she is seeking God in him' (Beauvoir, 1988, 679). It seems that Lacan and de Beauvoir reverse the roles of man and woman in the love-bond. For Lacan, it is often men who beg women to tell them exactly what they experience in their *jouissance*, whereas for de Beauvoir, it is women who beg men, as she writes, '[w]oman is habituated to living on her knees; ordinarily she expects her salvation to come down from the heaven where the males sit enthroned' (779). Lacan attempts to reverse and twist this around by saying, '[t]he plausibility of what I am claiming here – namely, the woman knows nothing of this jouissance – is underscored by the fact that all the time people have been begging them, begging them on their hands and knees' (Lacan, 1998a, 75).

The symmetrical configuration of love and *jouissance* is further developed by Lacan in *Encore* while keeping an ontological reference to desire. By making references to theology, the neo-Platonic universalization of the signifier, and Oneness while discussing love, Lacan suggests that the essential goal in love and desire is the One. In a love game, both lovers demand this One in an imaginary exchange:

> Love is impotent though mutual, because it is not aware it is but the desire to be One, which leads us to the impossibility of establishing the relation between 'them two' (*la relation d'aux*). The relationship between them-two-what? – them two sexes. (Lacan, 1998, 6)

Here Lacan lays emphasis, on the one hand, on the One as the Other, and rehearses his persistent idea of the lack of any sexual rapport. This longing for becoming One, and castration make the sexual rapport structurally impossible. As such, in mysticism, the body enjoys itself fully as it is pushed beyond the limits of castration and the lack through which desire insists. The limit of the pleasure principle, which essentially is the phallic principle, remains outside mystic love. Thus in mystic love, desire coalesces with love, for both are addressed and invested in the same One, in which the law of algebra breaks down, for in love of the One (1+1=1). This means that in mystic love, the lover wants to be loved by God to the extent of dissolution of the lover in God.

After briefly examining theories of love and *jouissance* in Lacan's oeuvre, let us now turn to his theory of the *sinthome*. A radical shift and re-orientation of Lacan's theories culminates in his *Seminar XXIII: Le Sinthome* (1975–1976), where the symptom, in its new definition, functions as the place of the Name-of-the-Father, by holding together the three Lacanian registers. The Name-of-the-Father was responsible for sustaining the structure of desire within the structure of the law. In *Le Sinthome,* Lacan insists that it is the naming father that makes the son develop a name for himself or herself, as the paternal name is foreclosed from the symbolic. In other words, Lacan here lays much emphasis on *sinthome* as a fixation on enjoying one's unconscious that consequently fills the gap between desire and *jouissance*, and bridges the void of the foreclosure between them. Desire, as such, has a very marginal significance after this seminar, even though it continues to be referred to throughout Lacan's works.

To give an example, in *Encore*, Lacan still holds on to the essential definition of desire as both an interpretation and a structure born in the symbolic register. Even in *Le Sinthome*, Lacan posits analytical practice as the locus in which desire shows the objectivity at its origin. As he says, 'we do not believe in the object, but we observe desire. From this observation of desire, we infer that the cause is objectal [objectivée]' (Lacan, 1975–1976, n. p.).

The *Sinthome* also breaks with topology and begins to discuss a very difficult set of knots and knotting by virtue of which Lacan claims that he is expressing what isn't expressible in an ordinary scientific discourse. He declares the new turn in his teaching as a blockage that at times occurs along the path of the desire for knowledge, as he writes, '[t]he desire for knowledge encounters obstacles. As an embodiment of this obstacle I have invented the knot' (Lacan, 1975–1976, n. p.). This seminar outlines a radical distinction and antinomy between desire and the *sinthome*. Desire insists on appropriating and re-appropriating the fundamental gap in being, whereas *sinthome* brings up all the joys of the unconscious with the mediation of literature and art. This means that the subject identifies through his symptom, and *sinthome* becomes a cure and a blessing in which the drives and their immediate goals come into a play within which the subject and his or her unconscious are the main players. This identification with one's symptom enables the subject to create his own way of enjoying the unconscious. From our past discussion, we know that identification takes place with the object of desire, the other in the imaginary and the Other in the symbolic. This identification between the *sinthome* and the real of the drives and *jouissance* enables a subject to venture beyond the phallic and symbolic signification. This identification further helps the subject to write and enjoy his own symptom. Such a network of writing, like Joyce's text, designates a signifying formation that remains beyond analysis. Lacan makes a brief foray into his theory of *sinthome* in *Encore* when he sees writing as inscribable in the register of the real. Lacan turns to Joyce's text to illustrate the *sinthome* in practice:

> However, you could read Joyce, for example. You will see therein how language is perfected when it knows how to play with writing . . . What happens in Joyce's work? The signifier stuffs (*vient truffer*) the signified. It is because the signifiers fit together, combine, and concertina – read *Finnegans Wake* – that something is produced by way of meaning (*comme signifié*) that may seem enigmatic, but is clearly what is closest to what we analysts, thanks to analytic discourse, have to read – slips of the tongue (*lapsus*). (Lacan, 1998a, 36)

Like desire, it is difficult to find a clear definition for *sinthome*. Finding a way to enjoy the core of one's unconscious is what identifies the *sinthome*, something that always remains a self-creation, beyond analysis. Since the *sinthome* has art as its bedrock, the enjoyment stems from the literary and art productions that provide an access to the core of the unconscious, not its repressed portion.

We will return to this aspect of *sinthome* in the next chapter when we are dealing with literary Lacan. These objects of sublimation in fact identify the space of *sinthome* as a locus of the drives.

Lacan uses the multipun *sinthome*, the old spelling in French of the word symptôm. This symptom, however, is different from that discussed in the earlier teaching of Lacan; instead, it is considered not as a metaphor or a coded message, but as a pure form of the real beyond the symbolic register. This is a paradoxical mix of Greek, *sin* (English) and *homme* (French). This word further evokes multiple meanings, such as, sin, *Synth-homme* (artificial self-creation as well as saint man), *sinthomaquinas* (St Thomas Aquinas), symptom, to name but a few. The *jouissance* experienced in *sinthome* is described as an opaque *jouissance. Sinthome* shares its opacity with feminine *jouissance.* The symptom in this new context implies no more a message encoded for someone, but a means for a headlong plunge into the real without any mediation by desire, or love. Lacan also relates *sinthome* to Aquinas referring to Joyce's citation of his works in the *Portrait of the Artist as a Young Man* especially of the notion of *claritas,* something ineffable like the divine illumination in mysticism. Lacan notes that Joyce substitutes *claritas* for 'splendor of being', something in which Lacan shows little interest.

In addition, Lacan defines *sinthome,* in topological terms, as the fourth ring in the Borromean Knot, which he renames the Borromean chain [*chaînoeud*].

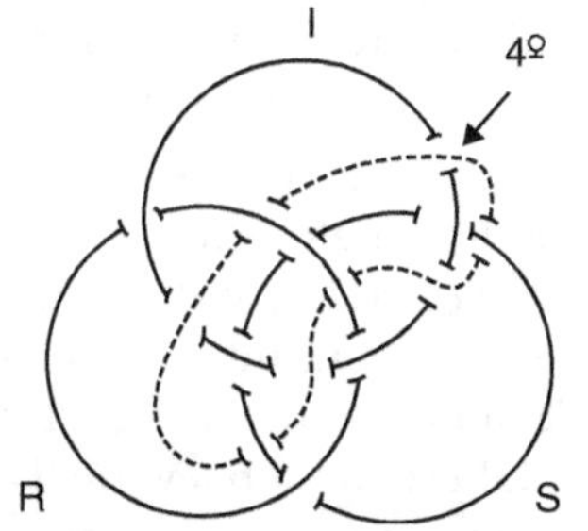

Source: Harari, 2002, 61

This ring, by holding the three registers together, supports the subject and saves him from falling into psychosis, for a structure like psychosis, initiated by the foreclosure of the Name-of-the-Father unties the three rings of the knot. As the fourth knot, like love, the *sinthome* makes the sexual relationship possible to write. As Lacan says in *Le Sinthome*:

> That what I have defined for the first time as a *sinthome,* is what permits the keeping together of the Symbolic, the Real and the Imaginary. (. . .) On the

> level of the *sinthome*, there is a relationship. (. . .) there is only a relationship where there is a *sinthome*. (Lacan cited in Verhaeghe, 2001, 144–145)

The *sinthome* – the fourth ring – tries to hold the rings together, and therefore the creator of the work of art experiences the real of the unconscious, the experience that consolidates his/her identification with his/her own symptom. This identification is with the real of the drives beyond phallic signification. As Verhaeghe says,

> Lacan presents us with the idea of a certain kind of identification, based on a decision of the subject. Instead of the usual identification, i.e. the identification with the Other, this time the identification concerns the real part of the drive beyond its phallic signification. Lacan terms this as the identification with the *sinthome*. (Verhaeghe, 2001, 144)

With the collapse of the symbolic, signifiers cannot co-exist in a signifying chain and suture themselves to the real of the body and drives. Žižek defines *sinthome* as a psychosomatic issue and highlights Kafka's short story, 'A Country Doctor', as an example of pure *sinthome* illustrated in terms of a bodily wound:

> In so far as the *sinthome* is a certain signifier which is not enchained in a network but immediately filled, penetrated with enjoyment, its status is by definition 'psychosomatic', that of a terrifying bodily mark which is merely a mute attestation bearing witness to a disgusting enjoyment, without representing anything or anyone. (Žižek, 1989, 76)

The topology of lack and the hole helps this process, first, for lack in earlier Lacan was a locus that gave rise to desire, and the hole, in late Lacan, is essentially a hole in the real that the *sinthome* intends to fill. Second, looking at the lack and the hole in a text can offer a definition of desire and *sinthome*. Lack implies a spatial absence, and therefore it obeys the laws of space and supports desire. As Miller says in his essay 'Lacan's Later Teaching', lack allows for '[t]he combinatory rules of language' (Miller, 2003,17). These combinatory rules naturally call for a metonymy and a substitute for the objects that will inescapably lead to desire. As opposed to lack, the hole doesn't accept these rules in language, for it doesn't come under the law of space. Therefore it remains, as Miller argues, in the place of the Other, a hole. This is the hole that supports *jouissance* and is being filled by the *sinthome*, which identifies in-decipherable voids and holes in the real that come into inscription in a synthomatic writing:

> It is in relationship to the hole that there is ex-sistence, which is the correct position for the remainder, the correct position of the real – that is to say, the

> exclusion of the sense [meaning]. Lacan's later teaching tends, in effect, to define the real by the exclusion of sense. This puts everything that is interpretation in question and produces as a consequence a cleansing of thought. (Miller, 2003, 17)

The point that concerns us most here is the consequence for literary criticism of this conceptual division in relation to desire in Lacan's final teachings. According to Miller, in final Lacan, we have to understand these shifts of attention as the 'dénouement' of his earlier theories. It may be true and useful for psychoanalysis and analytical practice *per se.* However, whatever the shifts in Lacanian theory, each stage of his theories is equally important for literary studies. *Le Sinthome* demonstrates that for Lacan, literature was not foreign territory. Unlike Derrida's assertion that Lacan wasn't interested much in literature, his literary studies are of crucial importance for the understanding of literature and art. He takes literature as his guide in his seminar on Joyce that illustrates the indebtedness of psychoanalysis to literature. Literature plays the role of intermediary for most of Lacan's psychoanalytic discoveries, the last of which was an explanation of literature as symptom.

Joyce's novel *Finnegans Wake* offered him a representational expression of the real of *jouissance* that he had postulated in his theory of *sinthome.*

This real of *jouissance* that identification with the *sinthome* makes possible, is a 'somewhere', like the one we have mentioned at the outset of this chapter, where Lacan anticipated the dissolution of desire in *The Four Fundamental Concepts.* Feminine *jouissance,* that we showed is synonymous with mystic *jouissance,* reveals ecstasies that are within and projected by the mystics onto the divine. At the heart of this beyond-desire lies a total disappearance of the self and the emergence of the Other that suspends a subject's desire. Looked at closely, mystic love has a sinthomatic structure, because the mystics find ecstasy as a way of losing the core of their selves in the Other. Besides mystical love, the *sinthome* as the endgame of Lacanian psychoanalysis takes the boundary of human subjectivity beyond desire. This beyond-desire reveals a new field in psychoanalysis that places the symptom at the centre of the structure of a subject insofar as the subject identifies with the symptom. If we restrict this identification only to Joyce's text or Lacan's style, it would be a mistake, for as Lacan suggests, *sinthome* is in the first place the individual's enjoyment of his unconscious, in which choice is determined by the ego of the individual. Everyone enjoys and suffers in his own way. Individual choice implies finding what to do with one's unconscious as well as one's symptom. Joyce's text provided a fertile ground for Lacan's final theoretical discoveries that assert that literature and art emerge as symptoms that shield, first of all, the artist from his/her truth. As an analyst, Lacan claims that he was the one who discovered the truth behind the encrypted artifice of Joyce's symptom. The cause of *sinthome* for Lacan was the lack of the signifier of the Name-of-the-Father in a subject's symbolic universe. The artist that makes a name for himself/herself, exhibits a desire to compensate for this lack.

Lacan's theory of desire and beyond is thus grounded upon an equal significance of each element of its conceptual space. The conceptual space opens before us three premises for literature: literature as desire, literature as love and *jouissance* and literature as symptom. Canonical literature, especially Shakespeare, offers an exciting illustration as well as interpretation of the Lacanian theory of desire. Mystical literary discourse on its part, puts a premium on *jouissance* and love. Moreover, modern literary discourses, especially James Joyce's, presents us with a sinthomatic literary resource that bears on the crux of the Lacanian theoretical achievement in relation to *sinthome.* Our theoretical exploration enables us to make an in-depth inquiry into literature in terms of desire and beyond. Before we can trace the above theoretical premises in literary texts, which is indeed, the principal aim of this study, let us see how he outlines the parameters of his literary criticism, and how he analyses literary texts.

Chapter 4

Lacan, Literary Theory and Criticism

We have arrived at a point of departure from the first part of the book, which was devoted to recounting a genealogical scheme of Lacan's psychoanalytic theory concerning desire and what was beyond and external to it. I wish to discuss three major topics in this transitional chapter to the next part of the book, which is aimed at practical Lacanian inquiry into a set of exemplary literary texts. First, I will look at Lacan's sustained interest and critical approach to literature, and his major influence on various schools of poststructuralist literary studies. This section also intends to show how Lacan's early exposure of the unconscious in terms of the signifier and linguistic structure, brought psychoanalysis to the centre stage of poststructuralist literary studies. Second, we will throw light on the Lacanian theory of writing that has been largely overlooked in Anglo-American literary studies. This will prepare a way for identifying literature as writing and the *sinthome* that Lacan developed in the final phase of his teachings.

The emphasis in this section will be put on responding to the following problems: What exactly is Lacan's theory of writing? And what can it add to our understanding of the anatomy and the interpretation of a literary text? This will lead us to our third goal: demonstrating how the fundamental tenets of the Lacanian theory of writing and literature bestow upon literary study an innovative interpretative power. From there, I will briefly consider Lacan's immense influence on a number of important contemporary literary critics. In short, the overall objective in this chapter is to argue that literary Lacan exists and is more important than clinical Lacan when it comes to literature and literary theory.

Lacan's literature

Is Lacan as relevant to and important for literature as literature was for him? Let us start off with Derrida and Jacques-Alain Miller's adverse reflections on this issue. Derrida makes two assertions in his critical essay, 'The Purveyor of Truth', that 'Lacan has never been directly and systematically interested in the so-called literary text' (Derrida, 1988, 176); and 'Lacan never asks what distinguishes one literary fiction from another' (178). Lacan's lifelong engagement with literature, however, proves the contrary. Besides, it is important to ask why Derrida should make such statements especially in 1975, when Lacan was making a historical commitment to literary theory by way of a one-year-long seminar on James Joyce. This seminar reflects Lacan's profound interest and fascination with Joyce's text and how the impact of Joyce brought a radical theoretical shift in his entire teachings. Lacan's critical interpretation in this seminar has not been limited to a focus on the author alone, but encompassed generic and stylistic features, art and language-use in the Joycean text.

The same goes for Miller's claim in his paper 'Lacan Clinician', (delivered to professors of English at the University of Ottawa, 10 May 1984). He claims that '[t]here isn't any literary criticism in Lacan, just as there isn't any anthropology in Freud' (Miller, 1999, 23). In this polemical paper, nevertheless, Miller leaves Lacan's literary importance and his theories on literature to literary critics themselves to find out and justify. Given this misinterpretation, it is true that when Roudinesco wrote: '[i]n 1965, Miller's discourse radicalized Lacan's. In theory, that discourse pretended to be strictly Lacanian, but in practice, it brought to Lacanianism the pressure of a combatant militarism' (Roudinesco, 1997, 196).

Contrary to the claims of Derrida and Miller, Lacan dedicated a considerable amount of time in his fifty-year career to a close and ingenious study and interpretation of modern and canonical Western literature. From Plato to Shakespeare and from Chekhov to Marguerite Duras, his literary study covered all literary genres, and his diverse critical approaches concentrated on the aesthetic and textual determinants of scores of literary texts. Besides an object of literary and critical analysis, literature for Lacan was a primary source for developing, verifying and illustrating his own psychoanalytic discoveries. The role of the literary in Lacan is thus enormous. His own writing style bears witness to our claim. It thus doesn't seem coincidental that he begins his major theoretical seminars using literary texts, by Shakespeare, Poe, Gide, James Joyce, Greek classical authors and so on.

Even though Lacan develops a variety of models of critical inquiry into literature, his crucial notion of literature as a signifying practice that functions as a ground for both literary and critical discourses remains consistently the same. Critical discourse within literature *per se* operates as a site for standing and speaking the truth about psychoanalytic concepts such as desire, love, *jouissance* and so on. In this sense, literature reveals the determining psychoanalytical elements behind the production of a literary text. The experience of the literary for Lacan was a precondition for positing, crystallizing, and displaying psychoanalytical concepts. A close reading of the vast body of the Lacanian text on literature reveals that an author, a poet, an artist and a psychoanalytic critic all play the same signifying game. As Bowie says:

> What we have in Lacan is, of course, a theory that reaches out towards poets. Analysts and poets are part of the collaborative textual enterprise; both groups are concerned with the irreducibility, the uncontainability, the unstoppability of the signifying process. (Bowie, 1987, 147–148)

After Lacan, we have a different understanding of literature, for he has changed the very idea of literature and poetry, considered largely since Plato as modes of imitation. The advent of the subject in the signifier, and the diachronicity of signification in the signifying chain – as an effect of desire – allowed for his description of literary discourse as fantasy and as an artifact that exhibits the subject's inbuilt alienation, and works to fill the gap of the subject's division in the symbolic universe of language. For Lacan, a creator of a literary text, therefore, knows to posit desire in language without needing to master psychoanalysis; and a poet knows far better than any one else about the representational expression of desire in language. His theory of the subject and desire, in fact, is inseparable from literary and cultural theory. It is not because Lacan bases his theory in linguistic processes but in the poetic nature of desire, that it is relevant to both psychoanalyst and poet alike. Since the subject's desire lies in a metaphoric process that arises from the intersection of the imaginary and the symbolic, a poet with his preoccupation with the imaginary can show us all the processes of desire. For example, referring to John Donne, Lacan wrote in *Seminar VI: Desire and Its Interpretation* (1959–1960):

> It may be appropriate to ask poets what they know of desire. In fact, the poet attests to a deep relationship between desire and language, at the same time he demonstrates – to what extent the poetical relationship to desire is always difficult since it involves depiction of its own object: thus the so-called metaphysical poetry (see 'The Ecstasy' of John Donne) evokes desire better than does figurative poetry, which seeks to represent it. (Lacan, cited in García, 1990, 51)

Lacan challenged the traditional Freudian insistence on literature as the expression of the unconscious. Freud argued for the deduction of textual knowledge from the neurosis of the author and his or her biography. Freud's texts on Leonardo da Vinci, Shakespeare, Goethe and Dostoyevsky, for instance, were largely based on such a deduction. When his pupil Marie Bonaparte wrote a flawed critical text on Poe, Freud passionately eulogized her attempt at psychobiography:

> Marie Bonaparte has directed the light of psychoanalysis upon the life and work of a great writer of a pathological type. Thanks to her interpretative efforts, we can now understand how much of the characteristics of his work

were determined by their author's special nature. (Freud cited in Wright, 1984, 39)

It is, however, worthwhile to note that Lacan in his analysis doesn't deny altogether the consideration of the life and personality of the author. He himself refers to the lives of Gide and Joyce in his literary analysis, '*Jeunesse de Gide ou la Lettre du Désir*' ['The Youth of Gide, or the Letter of Desire,' 1958], and in his seminar on Joyce. Marini believes that the former text remains obscure among Lacanians because Lacan, '[c]ompromised himself with psychobiography' (Marini, 1992, 167). However, Lacan never attempts to deduce analysis from the author's life or what Derrida conceived of as a biographical signified, in his critique of Lacan's seminar on Poe. He ventures from the textual networks of Gide and Joyce into their lives rather than the other way round, for he renounced the deduction of textual knowledge from the life of an author. Moreover, a textual structure for Freud was an index of unconscious codes, and a scene of fantasy through which authors and artists intend to entrap and seduce their audience. Lacan rejects the study of literature by means of the unconscious, and instead sees writing, desire, *jouissance* and the *sinthome* at the heart of narrative, poetics and textual inscription. Lacan's theoretical position posits language as the determinant of the human subject and literature, whereas for Freud, literature and culture were socially acceptable modes for the sublimation of repressed biological and libidinal drives only.

Lacan's theory on the subject and its division between the subject of statement and the subject of enunciation made another major contribution to the better understanding and analysing of literary personae. By positing a subject as an absence and an effect of the signifier, this theory reinforced the poststructuralist fight against the dominance of humanism in Western thought which described the subject or a fictional character as a unified or fixed entity. The entry into language introduces the subject to the signifier and subsequently to desire. As such, the literary subject is Lacan's *parlêtre*, both speaking being (subject of statement) and spoken being (subject of enunciation) in language, a signifier or a constellation of signifiers that functions as a desiring representation for the Other. What the subject speaks comes from the Other. This is how the literary subject is born as a desiring or desired subject.

In his Paris seminar on 12 June 1980, Lacan defines a split subject in terms of a trauma. He argues that the introduction into desire is a fundamental trauma in the life of a subject that splits him into two speakers who do not speak a single common language. As he remarks, '[T]he talking being in question is distributed in general in two speakers. Two speakers who do not speak the same language; two who do not hear each other speak, two who do not understand each other at all. Two who conspire to reproduce a thorough misunderstanding' (Lacan, 1981b, 100). This strand of reasoning reveals a crucial point for literary theory: any interpretation of literature must be grounded on a plurality of voices, because the subject is the subject of the unconscious. In literary discourse, the subject can say something other than what it is apparently saying. This is because literature deals with a particular use of language, a universe filled with galaxies of tropes where each functions as a separate signifying centre. These centres always refer to somewhere outside and beyond their linguistic structures. The subject finds his being in language, a being that is marked by lack. Being in language makes this subject a speaking and desiring being and enables him to find his lack of being in a metonymic illusion by way of his desire. In literature, the position of a subject, the meaning of his speech and his conscious-ego are all determined by his own articulation in the signifying system of language over which he doesn't have control, for a subject enters the symbolic order by adapting to the pre-existing system of language that by definition remains beyond any stable meaning. Literature is a site where the effect of language comes into play in order to become what Lacan calls writing. This notion confirms our claim about Lacan's passion for literature as a writing universe that was the principal inspiration in his own theories, as he said in a Seminar in Caracas (12 July 1980), a year before his death, '[L]anguage is only effective when it becomes writing. That was what inspired my mathemes, if I can talk of inspiration in my work which cost me a vigil where no muse visited me. And it should be believed that I amuse without a muse' (Lacan, 1981c, 106).

It is in this sense that I want to claim that Lacan's approach to literature has a larger provenance than traditional Freudian literary criticism. His psychoanalytic theory, especially his theory of desire, *jouissance* and the *sinthome* provided him with a comprehensive approach to interpret literary semantics, rhetoric, genre, style, intention, discourse, narrative, value, sexuality, performance, structure and so on in literature. He went beyond the focus of psychoanalytic criticism that attempts to appropriate a literary text simply as a simulacrum of the unconscious for diagnostic evaluation. A literary text is a conscious articulation, an artifact, and a fictive product, and it may not represent the unconscious without mediation. In other words, such unconscious residues may well appear in a text only as a 'palimpsest', which by its synchronicity constitutes an inherent textual *jouissance*. It is arguable that a literary text functions as a site where unconscious desire is acted out. Desire lies in the text as a motivating force behind the whole process of literary creation, its aesthetics and even its reading.

In a literary text, desire comes into play in two opposing ways. First, it inscribes a persistent lack in the text; and second, it seeks textual *jouissance* in order to overcome the alienating obstruction of lack. In both cases, discourse will help desire impose its terms on the text. Thus, language allows for erasures in a text as a representation of this lack; it accommodates substitutes for the original object, in order to sustain desire in a metonymic thread, often with recourse to the primary conditions that give rise to desire. This makes everything in language a speech act and a signifying process. Poetry sets scenes more conspicuously than any other literary text in this double play of desire. When a poetic text centres itself on primary loss, it also flirts with the presence and absence of this loss in different ways. By means of a compulsive repetition, poetry endlessly presents an imaginary threshold for the re-enactment of primordial alienation, the traumatic re-experience of archaic loss, and self-identification in the mirror. This loss, with desire as its consequence, is a precondition for entry into language. Poets always remain stuck within the suffering or pleasure of an elusive fulfilment in their verses. Keeping this view in mind, Lacan often argues in relation to poetry that poets are experts of the signifier and the symbol. Poets demonstrate the deep relation between desire and language. Language, for its part, has an enormous effect on poets too in that, in a poetic discourse, it operates beyond the awareness of the poet. As Lacan says, '[t]he verses find their own arrangement without any concern for what the poet does or does not know about it' (Lacan, 1985, 205).

It is important to note that Lacan's approach to literature is not grounded on the assumption that both literature and psychoanalysis have similar linguistic foundations, but on the similarity in their exposure of the truth, which both want to articulate. In this way, both literature and theory are treated like a text. Literature illustrates the truth in its own fictional way, whereas psychoanalysis, in turn, works out an epistemological account of the truth. Lacan's relevance to literature is based on a methodology that places artist and an analyst in a symmetrical relation. However, as Lacan repeatedly admits, literature has always taken the leading and guiding position. With these brief introductory remarks, let us now turn to three crucial proactive components of literature.

L'écriture, Lituraterre and the *Sinthome*

Lacan made a brief foray into the theory of the *sinthome* in *Seminar XVIII: Of a Discourse That Would Not Be On Semblance* (1971), when he draws a link between *jouissance* and the real in relation to *l'écriture* (textual writing). He outlines the function of writing as an operative mechanism in which the reproduction of the real evokes *jouissance*. The very act of writing takes place precisely at the level of *jouissance* too. Lacan develops further his theory of *l'écriture* in *Le Sinthome*, and in a number of different texts written in the final years of his life. A close examination of his texts on writing suggests that they discuss different types of writing and reiterate his previous reasoning rather than presenting a chronological and logical sequence of arguments. Lacan's theory bases itself on the premise that language is a material substance, and a writer uses language in such a way that he or she is capable of playing with the real of the unconscious. Writing as such has primacy and significance over speech and language, for it is not just empty talk but an acting out.

Towards the end of *Encore*, Lacan puts forward a topological model for his theory of writing and the written, in terms of the Borromean chain that functions as a model for the possibility of a topological link between writing and the speaking subject. This Borromean chain in the context of writing marks a new turn in Lacan's thinking, This chain is characterized by a series of interlinked rings where each represents a sentence in a piece of writing. The signifier and its locus, the letter, represent those spatial elements that connect one ring to another. In the meantime, these linking elements or strings that fasten the rings represent the speaking subject in a figurative setting. Lacan's texts on writing suggest that his theory of writing has affinities with poststructuralist theorists associated with the *Tel Quel* school. For instance, Phillipe Sollers promoted an unconventional fresh understanding of writing as material, self-contained and non-representative. He also believed that literature shouldn't be understood as determined historically as a site of representation. As he suggests, '[t]he specific problematic of writing breaks decisively with myth and representation to think itself in its literality and its space. Its practice is to be defined on the level of the "text", a word which henceforth refers to a function writing does not "express", but of which it *disposes*' (Sollers, 1983, 5). Lacan in *Encore* stresses that the letter emerged as writing and the written and as an effect of discourse even before man uses language. As he says, '[t]he letter first emerged from the market, which is typically an effect of discourse, before anyone dreamt of using letters' (Lacan, 1998, 36).

When we are speaking of the letter, we are speaking of Lacan's theory of writing, for it gives us a vantage point from where we can imagine the attachment of the real to writing. What Lacan achieves by this mathematically represented real is a metaphoric way of defining writing as having an effect which remains always beyond speech, as well as a way of representing the sequence of the rings, sentences, words or letters which makes it up. Lacan sees in these letters holes in the real at the heart of which lies an impasse to symbolization and formalization. This is the root cause of Lacan's intensive use of mathematical signs and knots to defy this impasse. Lacan sees these forms of mathematical logic as a means of producing signifierness – the fact of being merely a signifier outside any kind of meaning, or the effect other than the effect of meaning in the normal sense. As Lacan says, '[T]he mathematical formalization of signifierness run counter to meaning – I almost said "a counter-sens". In our times, philosophers of mathematics say "it means nothing" concerning mathematics, even when they are mathematicians themselves, like Russell' (Lacan, 1998a, 93).

Lacan places writing in the same register of the real, '[t]he trace of these writings taking form, in which one can grasp the limits, impasses, and dead ends that show the real acceding to the symbolic' (ibid.). The acceding of the real to the symbolic means that writing makes it possible to bring the real into the symbolic. The letter is one such real object in the symbolic. Furthermore, Lacan seems to have a new insight into the concept of writing as a set of traces that language leaves behind itself, which are in fact the traces of the real.

These elements of the real produce and reproduce the lack which is the lack of being. Lacan's trace here refers to the effect of language and its spell on writing, as he explains:

> Writing is thus a trace in which an effect of language can be read *(se lit)*. This is what happens when you scribble something. I certainly don't deprive myself of doing so, for that is how I prepare what I have to say. It is worth noting that one must ensure things by writing *(de l'ecriture, s'assurer)*. (Lacan, 1998a, 121)

Lacan argues that the '*I*' is a speaking subject that locates itself as a gaping hole in the chain of signifiers that link the rings of the Borromean knot. The gaping holes represent blind spots, opacity and non-meaning in a given literary text. These blind spots are holes and the *littorals* in the structure of discourse, as in the James Joyce and Ashbery texts that we will be discussing in upcoming chapters. Lacan defines the locus of the '*I*', in terms of 'solitude' and a break in being:

> The 'I' is not a being, but rather something attributed to that which speaks. That which speaks deals only with solitude, regarding the aspect of the relationship I can only define by saying, as I have, that it cannot be written par excellence, for it is that which leaves a trace of a break in being. (Lacan, 1998a, 120)

According to Lacan, this being is superimposed on the subject by language, and means nothing in itself. As he writes in *Encore*, '[I]sn't it thus true that language imposes being upon us and obliges us, as such, to admit that we never have anything by way of being *(de l'être)?*' (Lacan, 1998a, 44). Writing should not be read literally in a similar way to mathematical symbols, but in terms of its symbolic function and to what this effect refers. Lacan differentiates writing from language, for its specific feature as writing carries unconscious knowledge within itself, whereas language attempts to resist and displace this knowledge. Unconscious knowledge always dwells in the real, for this knowledge doesn't lend itself to symbolization. In an analogy to clouds and rain Lacan in *Encore* further argues that language functions like a cloud that places its traces on the earth, the traces that designate writing for him. As such, writing is not produced for reading or understanding. Lacan presents his own text as an example of this form of writing: '[t]hat is why you are not obliged to understand my writings. If you don't understand them, so much the better – that will give you the opportunity to explain them' (34).

Writing and the letter don't belong to the same register as the signifier, for the signifier is a semblant and belongs to the symbolic, whereas the letter belongs to the register of the real. That is why it is not available to either understanding or even reading. Writing as an assemblage of mathematical symbols often remains unreadable within its own textual network. In Lacan's sense, writing functions as the trace of the effect of language, sutured with the unconscious. Thus, writing is considered to be an act which brings to life the unthinkable and unspeakable, something that remains beyond imagination. Furthermore, words, signifiers and the letter, could function as the flesh of being that flees language. This being is not being-in-language, but lack of being.

In order to make a textual inquiry into literary discourse, we need to focus on the smallest but determining units in writing (the gram of writing and literature), namely, the letter, the pre-eminence of which in literature is considered by Lacan as analogous to a photon in the theory of light. Lacan wrote a massive amount on the theme of the letter. Our emphasis, however, will be on his later elaborations on the letter especially in relation to writing. The letter, as Lacan argues, has to be taken literally in its relation to writing, but has to be taken metaphorically when dealing with its exact meaning and function. In an exhaustive attempt, Jean-Luc Nancy and Philippe Lacoue-Labarthe in *The Title Of the Letter*, try to interpret the title of Lacan's essay in *Écrits*, 'The Agency of the Letter In the Unconscious or Reason since Freud,' while highlighting the importance of the letter in Lacanian epistemology. They suggest that the 'agency', in the title has to be regarded as both an 'authority' and as 'insistence', with its determining power in the unconscious. As they say, '[T]he agency of the letter could perhaps also be its insistence – something like the suspension of meaning. This does not fail to complicate, as we suspect, the interpretation of the subtitle of the first part' (Nancy and Lacoue-Labarthe, 1992, 22).

The 'insistence', they add, could be negative too, a negativity that insists on the concealment of meaning. As for the second half of the title, '. . . reason since Freud', they suspect that a parody is at work, for after Freud, reason wasn't in the same state as it had been before his discovery of the unconscious. Another nuance of meaning in this part of Lacan's title understands reason in terms of logos. In any case, we are unable to derive a universal definition for the letter. The difficulty arises mainly from the fact that as we have hinted above, the meaning of the letter varies insofar as its function in the unconscious and literature is concerned. When Lacan defines the letter as being indivisible but localizable, he means that the letter functions as the material support of discourse. As such, writing through its primary unit, the letter reveals psychoanalytic truth by its place and functioning position in a literary text.

Thus the letter, according to Lacan, embodies a phonematic structure, and a polysemantic unit of discourse. Strictly speaking, the letter could mean various things such as an alphabetic character, the *sinthome*, a thank-you letter, a love letter in a postman's satchel, and a letter in terms of a man of letters. What interests Lacan is more the function of the letter, as a real entity in the symbolic: opening up a detour to the real, and underpinning the logic of the symbolic itself. As pointed out above, Lacan's interpretation of the letter in terms of mathematics suggests that it often leads us to the real.

Historically speaking, all major scientific revelations have been made in the light of mathematical formulas that cannot be represented simply in language. In *Encore*, Lacan gives the formula of *inertia*, ($mv^2/2$), as an example of how a few small letters explain a scientific truth where verbal expressions fail to do so. Lacan's rationale behind using maths was to formalize psychoanalytic concepts in terms of conventional science. This formalization needs, however, a language for its transmission. This implicit quality of speech is what Lacan calls in *Encore*, an ideal meta-language, which is ex-sistent (and therefore, often sustains itself outside the symbolic order). We know that Lacan often insisted on the non-existence of a meta-language for there was no Other of the Other. His concern, however, is to show that the formalization of the real that subsists in a letter is inassimilable in the symbolic, thus it ex-sists (ex-sistence, is Lacan's neologism that means strange and outside), like a woman who Lacan says ex-sists because a signifier that can represent her in the symbolic is outside this register. When we say the letter is written, it primarily implies that it breaks discourse and always leaves a trace in being. This trace that a letter leaves behind explains the concept of writing. Such a definition and interpretation of the letter arguably gives rise to the question whether it is another name for the signifier. It is true that Lacan gives preference to the signifier in his early teaching when he defines a subject and desire. The letter by its role in the text is never like a signifier, useless and meaningless.

As the content of the letter, a signifier doesn't take part in the signifying process, for it exists only insofar as it is different from other signifiers, while a letter is differentiated from another letter by its meaning. Signifiers arise in the symbolic marked by difference, whereas a letter ties up the real with the symbolic. This is the function that places the letter in a privileged signifying position especially in a literary text. The letter, however, produces an immediate effect of meaning, and allows for meaning to be written. The signifier represents a subject and its desire, whereas the letter, as we have said above, partly harbours *jouissance*, and partly refuses it because of its connection with the *littoral* – the erasure that topologically divides *jouissance* from unconscious knowledge. The letter takes the signifier within its space, and in experience a signifier often returns like a letter, as Colette Soler writes, 'Lacan says that the signifier returns in experience like a letter' (Soler, 1999, 217). Nevertheless, it could be interpreted the other way around, as a letter returns as a signifier in Poe's tale, 'Purloined Letter'. About this, Lacan writes that as soon as Dupin finds the letter and transfers it to the queen, it is by then outside the symbolic chain and this transference equates the letter with, '[t]he signifier, the most destructive of all signification: namely money' (Lacan, 1988b, 49). It is important to note that Lacan territorializes the letter in the field of a literary text in the same way as he did drives and erotogenic zones in the body.

In *Seminar XVIII* (12 May 1971), Lacan takes up the letter and its functions in a literary text in his essay, '*Lituraterre*', probably one of the most difficult texts he has ever written, a translation of which is so far unavailable in English. A reading of this essay is crucial for understanding Lacan's theory of writing. The essay contains a cluster of homophonic puns like *litura, terre, letter, literal, litter, littoral* etc. The *lituraterre* is composed of two parts *litura* and *terre*, the first referring to the letter and the second to land. To identify this letter, Lacan borrows Joyce's slip of the letter into *litter*, and for the meaning of the latter Lacan chooses 'refuse'. The key to the literary criticism is to locate the littering of the letter in the text and find the root and branch cause of the process. This metaphorical statement means that psychoanalysis finds in literature where the letter is littered. In a topological sense, Lacan rethinks and reiterates that a letter makes a *littoral* that functions as a border between unconscious knowledge and *jouissance*. 'As for the pun on *literal* and *littoral* (hence *litura-terre*), the seminar explains it: "[i]sn't the letter the literal, which grounds itself in the littoral"' (Marini, 1992, 229). This *littoral*, in fact, makes a barrier between *jouissance* and unconscious knowledge possible, something of which the subject remains unaware.

The letter has further significance for a number of reasons. It has the capacity to transmit the effect of meaning, and unlike the signifier, is positive in its connection with the real. For Lacan this effect of meaning is like a bar that divides the signifier from the signified, an impossible, a hole, and a nothing. Lacan's subtitle, *La lettre l'etre et l'autre,* (the *letter, being* and *the Other),* in his paper 'The agency of the letter . . .' bears witness to such multiple functions of the letter in writing. The Other in relation to the letter determines the recognition of a subject's desire. What is the meaning of this dense account of Lacan's? In a strictly topological sense, he wants to explain the function of the letter in a literary text. He wants to set up a spatial configuration of the *letter, litter, littoral, literal,* unconscious knowledge and *jouissance*. The *littoral* is like a foreshore that has two borders: one is in touch with the sea and the other is in touch with the land. Lacan metaphorically states that the sea is *jouissance* and the land the *littoral* connected to unconscious knowledge. By this topology, Lacan reveals the map of the letter and its blind spots or non-meanings that traditionally were called lacunae in a literary text. He also has in mind writerly texts like his own, Joyce's, and Beckett's that he insists repeatedly are suitable for '*poubellication*' (Thurston, 2002, xviii). This was Lacan's pun for publication as putting in a dustbin, literally something close to German phrase, *Wegwerflitertur.*

Lacan notes that the *littoral* that separates two homogenous fields namely, *jouissance,* and knowledge, belongs to the unconscious. The *littoral* that separates knowledge from *jouissance* functions as a border between two registers, the symbolic and the real. In other words, the *littoral* is between 'centre' and 'absence', that which escapes the structure. As Lacan remarks, 'The letter be it Roman or Greek or even the loop of an arabesque, circumscribes the edge of the hole that has been left open, by *jouissance*, and then closed by the Symbolic system' (Lacan, cited in Rabaté, 2001, 35). At stake here is the effect a letter produces in a text, an effect that as in Joyce produces the *jouissance* of the author. The letter produces the *littoral* that can be defined as non-signification, equivocation, textual void, ellipses and so on. Elaborating on Lacan's essay '*Lituraterre*', Rabaté writes that 'Lacan is wiser to the fact that letters do not point to a pure void of signification but produce a "hole" in which enjoyment of the most excessive type can lurk' (34). In his seminar on Joyce, Lacan indicates that letters, their fragmentation and littering, produce such pure voids that lead on their part to excessive enjoyment. To put it another way, being located between the two borders, the *littoral* by way of illustration shows the position of the letter that makes holes in unconscious knowledge and thus helps the real to surge forth in a literary text. In this process, the letter excavates a hole in *jouissance* that creates a desire for the reproduction of this lost *jouissance* in an inverted form. Desire is located in the chain of letters, as Lacan says:

> Since the point is to take desire, and since it can only be taken literally [*à la lettre*], since it is the letter's snare that determines, nay overdetermines its place as a heavenly bird, how can we fail to require the bird catcher to first be a man of letters? (Lacan, 2002, 264)

Here Lacan uses the allegory of the heavenly bird to refer to the empowering of the author of a literary text to locate desire in the texture of his writing. The writer as such is like the analyst (armed with a literary knowledge), a bird-catcher or a desire-catcher, so to speak. Lacan then refers to the literary qualities of Freud's theoretical discourse. Lacan insists that poets are very close to their unconscious, and in order to catch those birds, one has to be a poet, as Malcolm Bowie writes:

> Lacan's theory seems to necessitate a certain kind of literary performance. If the unconscious is 'like poetry' in its overdetermined and polyphonic structures, then the writer who chooses to treat the unconscious, and wishes to obey its laws in his writing, must need become more 'like a poet' the closer he gets to the quick of his subject. (Bowie, 1987, 125)

Lacan recasts his theoretical discourse on literature by introducing the idea in *Le Sinthome* that the root cause of art and literature is the symptom. This root cause has to be taken in relation to three factors: first, it implies that the very creation of a literary work is a result of the symptom, and second, it means that the use of literary language that makes writing literature is, like a symptom, an invention. The third factor is the subject's believing in, and identification, with the symptom. As we spelt out earlier, this symptom is not the symptom *qua* signifier that Lacan defines in his earlier teaching in linguistic terms. This symptom is rather a function that ties up the three registers in a fourth ring added to the Borromean knot. It thus invokes *jouissance*, and as an experience of the real, it remains beyond interpretation, analogous to the end of the analysis in the psychoanalytic clinical sense. This loss shows itself in the holes that a literary discourse reveals in the place of the real. The *sinthome* is a kind of compensation for originary loss, or in Joyce's case, what Lacan calls the empowerment of the author to use language in a way that will let him enjoy his unconscious, and transform the symbolic universe into a site of the real and of *jouissance*. To write, for Lacan, therefore, is unlike Barthes who saw it as an intransitive verb, but is related to the ego and the name that an author wants to make for himself. This ego, however, doesn't mean that Lacan validates the ego as an autonomous agency, but as a carrier of the *sinthome*. Joyce's success was his construction of a deeply writerly text as his literary symptom, instead of ending up on the clinical coach. Colette Soler reiterates Lacan's argument that Joyce cured himself by a littering of the letter, something that usually happens only at the end of analysis: '[J]oyce went straight to the best that could be expected at the end of psychoanalysis, says Lacan' (Soler, 1999, 75).

In this way, literature is produced through a symptom that by subverting symbolic articulation produces the real in terms of the *littoral* and an emptiness aimed at defying castration and its lack. The symptom produces pleasures in abundance by allowing the direct satisfaction of the drives. In the light of this view, we can conceive of the *sinthome* as a *suppléance* giving the subject consistency and *jouissance*. This consistency comes from the subject's dwelling in the real of the unconscious. A literary text pockmarked with voids and holes demonstrates that an author is in the real of the unconscious, for as Lacan insists, when there is a hole either in the subject or in the text it means the unconscious is opening itself. These holes in the real are identified with the *sinthome*, and the writing of these holes is part of the author's art. Thus, art, *jouissance*, drives, *the sinthome*, and the possibility of sexual rapport come out of these holes.

Does Lacan devalue literature and art when he postulates literature as the *sinthome?* By no means. Lacan redefines the *sithome* in relation to literature not as a psychopathological concept, but rather as an artistic invention. He emphasizes the representational function of the symptom, which is different from its definition in orthodox Freudian psychoanalysis as abnormality or disease. In this sense, the symptom is a crafted signifier that bears *jouissance* beyond any signification. Lacan's seminar on Joyce defines the symptom as the core of human subjectivity. As he says, no one is without a symptom. It is through the symptom that one finds a way of enjoying one's unconscious. Lacan highly values literature, and he accepts its mastery over psychoanalysis. Literature, by means of repetition, enables the symptom to present itself through and through.

This repetition on its part breaks the signifying chain, supplies *jouissance*, and creates the possibility of experiencing the real of the unconscious beyond the law of desire and the phallic economy and limiting the role of the Name-of-the-Father as a precondition for entry into the symbolic. Although Lacan's postulation of literature as the *sinthome* is a turnaround in the course of his theoretical discourse, reading his previous works bears on the fact that this concept doesn't come into his topos out of the blue. As we have explored thus far, the *sinthome* is deeply rooted in Lacan's earlier teachings, and it seems to be a logical conclusion of his earlier literary theory concerning art and literariness in literature.

Lacan's theory of writing begins with the letter as a signification that emerges by way of the law of metaphor to support meaning as impossible and incompatible with language. This means that the letter is an effect of discourse, it is written, because the written as Lacan says, '[i]s that aspect of language that is conditioned by a discourse' (Lacan, 1998a, 36). The metaphoricity of the letter holds the key for its understanding as a concept. As the effect of metaphor is naturally subjective, and metaphor is creative, we have to notice the function and the process that the network or chain of letters creates in a literary text. As was stated, a letter institutes a hole in *jouissance* and then fills the void or covers the erasure of the object with the veil of language. In his seminar on James Joyce, Lacan winds up his theory of the letter and writing, claiming that the letter in the process of writing functions as the *sinthome*, a position that in his earlier teaching was allocated to the signifier in relation to the symptom. Joyce's writing, as Lacan insists, is in fact a locus for the proliferation of letters as traces of his symptoms. He describes it in terms of '[w]riting as a means of situating the repetition of the symptom' (Lacan, 1982, 166). He identifies the letter as a symptom in a formula $f(x)$, where, f is the function, and x, a letter. The best example will be Joyce's *Finnegans Wake*, where the symbolic has broken down, and language falls into a reservoir of letters inscribed with *jouissance*. In such a text, the unconscious reveals itself in *jouissance*, and meaning is produced not by grammar, syntax or principles of writing, but by an unconscious logic. This shows an inscription of *jouissance* that language brings to the literary text.

> Literature serves, of course, as a vehicle of jouissance, but which jouissance? It is most often the jouissance of meaning, especially in the case where literature is novelistic and makes use of fiction, in other words, of the imaginary. (Soler, 1999, 73)

As said above, the letter as object itself is *jouissance* in the literary text. Apart from being a topological vehicle for analysing literature, *lituraterre* has an additional deconstructing function to which we will return in the next section. Similarly, it is also appropriate at this point to ask: how does the evolution of art and creation end up with the *sinthome*? In order to trace this important theoretical evolution in Lacan we need to explore his literary theory and literary criticism.

Lacanian literary criticism

In order to present succinctly Lacan's literary criticism, we need to bring together his own statements of critical methodology that have arisen from his responses to criticism. Most literary critics in their reading of literary texts ground their judgements in the most cited and imitated psychoanalytic texts. Our emphasis will be on those methods that are unknown or less popular in Anglo-American critical circles. Let us at the outset return to Lacan's *Lituraterre* in order to underline a few of its arguments that are crucial for its adaptation to literary use, the investigation of texts and the question of the essence of literature. While keeping avant-garde literature in mind, Lacan vigorously announces that if literary criticism ever wanted to 'renew' itself, psychoanalysis will be there to help. As he writes, '[i]f literary criticism could effectively renew itself, it would be because psychoanalysis is there for the texts to measure themselves against it, the enigma being on its side' (Lacan, cited in Nobus, 2002, 26). He insists on the power of psychoanalysis to *lituraterre* literature, meaning to carry on an autopsy on writing in order to spot the real, *jouissance,* and symptom in a literary text. He reaffirms his inkling that a psychoanalytic inquiry into literature is consistent with the work of the authors of the literary text. In a psychoanalytic sense, both concern themselves with exploring the single truth that psychoanalysis attempts to conceptualize, and that literature dramatizes and performs. In this context, the concept of the *littoral* within Lacanian literary theory, which resonates with the French *Tel Quel* school of critics in the 1960s, demands attention for its opening of a new critical path that we will explore in relation to poetry in the upcoming chapters. For a literary inquiry into literature, especially contemporary and avant-garde writings, it is important to identify the place and effect of *littorals* – loci of ambiguities that bring writing into play to produce *jouissance* in the real. These *littorals* rupture the textual letters and signifiers in a way that, on the one hand, reveals non-meaning (unconscious knowledge), and on the other, the excesses of *jouissance.* This whole signifying process takes place with an emphasis on the textual and literary speaking subject.

Using an analogy with the flight of bees and swallows Lacan in *Encore* suggests a workable model of reading for a literary text. In the signifying chain, signifiers, like bees and swallows, write the effect of their flight. The signifiers also know how to read the letters in their multidimensional space of absence and erasure. What a critic has to read in the letters is the effect of writing and the play of language that covers and uncovers the textual gaps in relation to the subject. As in the flight of bees, the important thing is the circulation of the 'pollen' among the flowers and in the flight of the swallow, we read the coming 'tempest':

> Consider the flight of a bee. A bee goes from flower to flower gathering nectar. What you discover is that, at the tip of its feet, the bee transports pollen from one flower onto the pistil of another flower. That is what you read in the flight of the bee. In the flight of a bird that flies close to the ground – you call that a flight, but in reality it is a group at a certain level – you read that there is going to be a storm. (Lacan, 1998a, 37)

Lacan insists here that in a signifying operation and in writing too the same thing comes about, the letters are impregnated with *jouissance* and traces of the experience of the real, as for example, in Joyce's *Finnegans Wake.* Lacan prescribes such a reading for analysts, '[w]hat is at stake in analytic discourse is always the following – you give a different reading to the signifiers that are enunciated (*ce qui s'énesce de signifiant*) than what they signify' (Lacan, 1998a, 37).

Lacan's own discussions of a wide range of literary texts draw attention to the fact that any orientation for reading a text has to be grounded in the individual text itself. For example, with Poe, Lacan attempted to detect the circulation of the signifier that like a bee carries the 'pollen', the forbidden *jouissance* in relation to the subject and desire. In Shakespeare, Genet and Gide, desire and its relation to the subject are at the forefront of his inquiry. With Claudel, Lacan saw the breakdown of conventional language and the creation of a new peculiar language that speaks not for itself, but for the unique enjoyment of the author's unconscious. The latter point has become a basis for his groundbreaking seminar on Joyce. In his reading of the Joycean text, Lacan sees behind Joyce's amalgam of encyclopedic knowledge and linguistic subversion the author's symptom and a primal foreclosure of the paternal signifier.

In the field of literary studies, Lacan's difficult critical discourse, however, leads to many misinterpretations of his criticism. To take an example, his statement that the unconscious is structured like a language through its incorporation into literary study has become the source of a common misunderstanding of his intentions. Some critics take for granted that a literary text is a replica of the unconscious message. Even some Lacanians intentionally or otherwise have misapplied his psychoanalytic reading to a number of literary texts. Similarly, Shoshana Felman, whose writing, like Elizabeth Wright's, no doubt reveals some important aspects of Lacanian teaching, mystifies the Lacanian treatment of literature, when in an analogy she compares literature and psychoanalysis to the Hegelian master and slave relation, a dialectical relationship in which both are seeking recognition. In *Jacques Lacan and the Adventure of Insight,* she argues that literature is the unconscious of psychoanalysis and there is an exchange of knowledge between them. Similarly, Ben Stoltzfus, somewhat naively, applies

Lacan's theory of the unconscious to a selection of literary texts in *Lacan & Literature: Purloined Pretexts.* He sees literature as a mirror reflection of the unconscious. He argues that the Lacanian statement, the unconscious is structured as language '[o]pened a royal road between literature and the unconscious' (Stolzfus, 1996, 51). He goes further in his misinterpretation of Lacan when he states that '[L]iterature and the unconscious enjoy a special affinity because language is the magnetic field that joins the two, but it is a union that can function only when a reader activates the circuit between them' (11). As we have stated earlier, Lacan vehemently rejects the reading of literature as unconscious discourse.

Lacan's interpretation of literature, instead, is a guideline, a street directory that shows us the causes of events and behaviour of characters in a text and of the content, messages, structure, plot, rhythm and other fundamental constituents of literature. Because everything in literature and poetry is crafted and fictionalized, it should be interpreted the way the author himself wanted it to be, as we argued above in terms of engagement with the text. As the seminar on Joyce indicated, the life and person of the author may also be accounted for by a psychoanalytic interpretation, but not as a determining factor in criticism.

As it was hinted above, in Lacan's thinking, literature and psychoanalysis have symmetrical functions and objects. Since time immemorial, literature has been defined by its distinctive use of, and play with language. The play of language in literature reveals itself in terms of textual deviation, lapses, slips and grammatical subversion. The psychoanalytical reading of the text dwells in these pregnant textual moments. If a feeling finds expression or representation in literature, psychoanalysis attempts to problematize and translate it into the truth of unconscious desire. The frontier between the two fields of literature and psychoanalysis often remains unchecked and unguarded. It happens with some writers that their literary discourse is often punctuated with their own interpretative discourses. Authors by taking the position of an analyst, produce unmediated psychoanalytic truths. In Dostoyevsky, Shakespeare, Joyce, Proust as well as in classical writers like Sophocles and Plato, we frequently come across some sporadic comments similar to psychoanalytic discourse. For example, Plato gives us a prototype of Lacan's definition of desire and love: '[A]nd love is simply the name for desire and pursuit of the whole' (Plato, 1956, 64). Isn't this 'whole', what Lacan calls the Thing or its symbolic representation, the Other? Plato knew this before Lacan when he stressed in the *Symposium* that Zeus was responsible for breaking that wholeness. Dostoyevsky punctuates his discourse with almost psychoanalytic speech about the unconscious, fantasy and phobias: '[E]ven in my underground dream I did not imagine love except as a struggle. I began it always with hatred and ended it with moral subjugation, and afterwards I never knew what to do with the subjugated object' (Dostoyevsky, 1992, 88). Dostoyevsky is talking about Oedipal trauma and its associated guilt that has become a subjugated object in the symbolic order.

The concluding lines in the *Notes from the Underground* express this in the guise of suffering as self- punishment, and the need for expiation: '[I] believe I made a mistake in beginning to write then, anyway I have felt ashamed all the time I've been writing this story; so it's hardly literature so much as corrective punishment' (90).

Likewise, Lacan discovers instances in Shakespeare and others of a version of his theoretical formulation. For instance, in *Hamlet,* fascination with the etymology of the name Ophelia incites Lacan to write it as O(phallus). Lacan doesn't hesitate to interpret the following Shakespearian lines in which he translates the 'thing', of the 'nothing' as nothing but the phallus, the lack in the Other:

> Hamlet: The body is with the King, but the King is not with the body. The King is a thing –
> Guildestern: A 'thing', my lord?
> Hamlet: Of nothing . . .
>
> (*H,* IV-ii, 27–30)

Every theoretical adventure in Lacan moves from literature towards psychoanalysis so that literature reveals its own inherent psychogenesis. On many occasions, Lacan makes his theory fit with literature. With Duras, for example, he affirms the theory of sublimation in relation to the creation of art and literature. He concludes that in the case of Leonardo da Vinci it is originary fantasy at work in his art. The existence of desire makes a classic drama a tragedy. As Lacan notes in his seminar on *Hamlet,* Hamlet's desire has been blocked, but his melancholy unblocks it. We will return to this in the coming chapters. For Lacan, tragedy as a genre was a re-enactment and re-experience of the primordial trauma that gives birth to desire. He finds a psychoanalytic narrative in tragedy, and sees desire as the basis of the suffering of the hero in classic drama. Tragedy in Lacan's thought shows us how a human subject is doomed to a desire that remains unknown to him or her as Lacan '[e]mphasises that the genre of tragedy shows that the root of human experience is tragic' (Ragland, 1999, 102).

After Lacan, psychoanalysis is no more a foreign discipline to literary studies. Lacan's contribution to criticism and the literary use of his theories are important in the fact that he integrated psychoanalytic literary criticism in the overall project of poststructuralist literary and cultural studies. Lacan's concepts such as desire, the *mirror phase,* the gaze, the phallus, the object *a,* the *sinthome* and *jouissance* are familiar terms across a range of literary and cultural studies such as feminist literary criticism, film studies, music, opera, painting and so on. It is not accidental that in North America, Lacan was discovered first by professors of literature, not psychoanalysts. Schneiderman, the author of *The Death of an Intellectual Hero,* is an interesting case in point, who under the spell of Lacan's teaching, left his career as a professor of English to join his guru in Paris and become a psychoanalyst. Malcolm Bowie explains Lacan's importance for literary critics when he says, '[i]t would be convenient to see the relationship between Lacanian theory and literary studies as one of reciprocal support and enhancement. Many critics' writings in the penumbra of that theory have derived special advantages from it' (Bowie, 1987). Lacan's tremendous influence on contemporary literary theoreticians and critics attest to the significance of his reading and criticism of literature. A close reading of *Mythologies* (1957), *S/Z* (1970), *The Pleasure of the Text* (1973), *A Lover's Discourse* (1977) and *Camera Lucida: Reflections on Photography* (1980) shows that Barthes' fundamental theories were centred on Lacan's *oeuvre.* In *Mythologies,* Barthes takes up Lacan's theory of signs as a point of departure. In *S/Z,* as Jane Gallop hints in *Reading Lacan,* Barthes is influenced by Lacan's formulation, '[t]he written as not-to-be-read' (Lacan, 1985, 47). Similarly, *The Pleasure of the Text* follows the lead of Lacanian *jouissance* by positing pleasure and desire at the heart of the literary text. Here, like the subject, the text itself calls for desire, through which pleasures are in store for both the writer and the reader.

> Barthes had systematized the application of the Lacanian term of jouissance to these avant-garde texts he found so tantalizingly opaque and experimental in their attempt to disclose the pure functioning of textuality which made them boring therefore 'interesting'. (Rabaté, 2002, 92)

Barthes' last two books take up Lacan's theory of the gaze and of imaginary identification in the mirror phase. However, since for Barthes, pleasure was the ultimate end in a text, he criticizes psychoanalysis in *The Pleasure of the Text* for policing pleasure and replacing it with desire. Barthes brings his literary theory to the limit by dwelling in pleasure alone:

> No sooner has a word been said, somewhere, about the pleasure of the text, than two policemen are ready to jump on you: the political policeman and the psychoanalytical policeman: futility/or guilt, pleasure is either idle or vain, a class notion or an illness. (Barthes, 1993a, 411)

For Kristeva, nevertheless, it wouldn't have been possible to formulate her theory of poetry on the basis of semiotics without Lacan's theory of the imaginary, the letter and its agency in the unconscious, and *lalangue.* Before her theory of poetic language, Lacan postulated in *Écrits* that poetry inaugurates metaphor, polyphony and music, '[a] polyphony to be heard and for it to become clear that all discourse is aligned along the several staves of a musical score' (Lacan, 2002, 146). When Derrida is reading a literary text, he follows Lacan in his analysis of the textual system while ignoring anything that Lacan says about such things as the momentary halting of the play of signifiers (in which the signifiers play the role of the signified or the subject). His project of deconstruction in relation to the interpretation of literature produces the effect of *jouissance* borrowed from Lacan and Barthes. As he says, '[e]verytime there is "*jouissance*" (but the "there is" of this event is in itself extremely enigmatic), there is deconstruction. Effective deconstruction. Deconstruction perhaps has the effect, if not the mission, of liberating forbidden *jouissance*' (Derrida, 1992, 65). We can trace a similar Lacanian influence on the important works of literary critics such as Philippe Sollers, Maurice Blanchot, Harold Bloom and so on. We are equipped now to interpret and criticize literature in the next chapter.

Chapter 5

Shakespeare's Theatre of Desire

From our theoretical inquiry into desire as well as our exploration of Lacan's modes of reading literature and critical methodologies in the previous chapters, we are now able to examine desire in Shakespeare. This chapter is divided into two parts in order to investigate the structure and textual modes of both masculine and feminine desires in a selection of key Shakespearean texts. In light of Lacan's seminar on *Hamlet,* the first part will scrutinize the literary articulation of masculine desire in that play, with special focus on some of Lacan's important theoretical points that have been mostly omitted in post-Lacanian literary debates. I wish to consider those important points that make this play the epitome of a masculine desire in deep crisis. This crisis will be followed by a reading of Hamlet's soliloquies – a metonymical vehicle for sustaining the mourning that is constitutive of his desire. Then we will explain Hamlet's interpersonal swing between the object *in* and *of* desire, the theme of the hour of the Other, and Hamlet's conversation with Gertrude, as the dénouement of a chaotic desire. This section ends with a study of the play-within-the-play, Hamlet's 'mouse trap', not as a traditionally Oedipal allegory, but as textual evidence for the return of Hamlet's desire. In the second part of the chapter, the focus will be on paradigms of feminine desire in *Coriolanus, Macbeth* and *The Merchant of Venice.* The latter texts will allow us to demonstrate the multiplicity of feminine desire, and the interdependence of masculine and feminine desires not as two opposite categories but as two types of unconscious preference. We will examine two kinds of the phallic mother in *Coriolanus* and *Macbeth.* We will conclude with a survey of the fluidity of feminine desire in *The Merchant of Venice.*

These plays are selected because: first, they offer a fertile ground for Lacan's theory of desire in which literary experience converges on psychoanalytic experiment; and second, some of the texts display prototypes and models of theoretical material that Lacan was to develop later. This also reveals that Lacan seems always keen to see *Hamlet* like any other literary text, representing a pre-existing truth about desire. From this vantage point, Lacan and Shakespeare make an ideal match, as the former postulates a psychoanalytic theoretical position for which the second has already produced textual illustrations.

Hamlet and the crisis of desire

The tragedy of *Hamlet* interested Lacan chiefly because of its spectacular structure, Oedipal backdrop, and Shakespeare's unique poetic skills in dramatizing desire in crisis. Lacan admits this at the outset of his remarks on *Hamlet* in his *Seminar VI: Le Désir et son Interprétation* when he says that the play has '[a]n exceptional power of captivation' (Lacan, 1977, 11). Lacan's theory of desire comes into full swing in his criticism of *Hamlet* and is of special significance for literary studies because, for Lacan, Hamlet was a modern hero caught up in the Other's desire. This point is cardinal because it answers the question raised by traditional Shakespearean studies about the play: why did Shakespeare subvert the traditional Aristotelian definition of tragedy? From Dr Johnson to Eliot, for many critics the character of Hamlet was a mistake on Shakespeare's part because he fails to provide a clear-cut reason for Hamlet's indecision. T. S. Eliot continued such an arguably humanist literary exegetics in expressing difficulty with both *Hamlet* as a drama and Hamlet as the character in his brief essay on the Shakespearean text. In order to show the significance of Lacan's sustained criticism of *Hamlet* for contemporary poststructuralist Shakespearean studies, we will first clarify Eliot's trouble with *Hamlet*. T. S. Eliot writes, '[s]o far from being Shakespeare's masterpiece, the play [*Hamlet*] is most certainly an artistic failure. In several ways the play is puzzling, and disquieting as is none of the others . . . It is the "Mona Lisa" of literature' (Eliot, 1975, 47). Eliot seems to have trouble with Shakespeare's subversion of the traditional norms of tragedy and the tragic hero. He highlights the following enigmas in his reading of *Hamlet*: the neither effect of Hamlet's mother's guilt on her son that neither can be expressed, nor does Shakespeare succeed in treating it properly, or articulating the two of them in art; and Hamlet's emotions and feelings are so intense and excessive that they remain beyond objectification. Such a mental state makes Hamlet '[d]oubtless a subject of study for a pathologist' (49). We can see these statements as the final words of traditional humanist literary criticism of the play. On the other hand, Lacan's reading of Shakespeare's text as a drama of desire helps unravel many of the mysteries of *Hamlet*.

Let us begin with answering the important question: why is *Hamlet* a tragedy of desire?

Lacan points to a major breakdown in the path of Hamlet's desire, a breakdown through which he ends up lost in a chaotic desire. He doesn't know how to desire, mainly because his desire is not his own. Instead, he carries Gertrude's desire as his Other. Hamlet's total reliance on the Other's desire brings out an effect of incongruity within the structure of registers, mainly because of an incoherent incorporation of the imaginary and symbolic in his subjectivity. This makes it impossible for him to be integrated successfully into the symbolic register. In other words, Hamlet's inability to assimilate his desire beyond the Oedipal triangle into the symbolic is the primary reason for this chaotic desire that Lacan terms the tragedy of desire in *Hamlet.* Lacan translates Freud's term for *Hamlet,* a 'tragedy of destiny', into the tragedy of desire. As Freud says in 'On Hamlet and Oedipus', *Hamlet* is a Renaissance immitation of *Oedipus Rex.* Freud saw the play as an effect of the incompatibility of the will and destiny, as was Sophocles's play: '[i]ts tragic effect is said to lie in the contrast between the supreme will of the gods and the vain attempts of mankind to escape the evil that threatens them' (Freud, 1970a, 81). In the Lacanian approach, this tragic effect is seen to develop because of the conflict between human desire and the law of the super-ego. This conflict in desire shows itself in Hamlet's hesitation, procrastination, mourning, indecision, feigned madness and so on that make his self divided between his weak ego, the object of his desire and the Other, the place from where he gets the assurance of his own existence and discourse.

Contrary to Eliot's assertion, Shakespeare has successfully illustrated the ambiguous state in which Hamlet continuously procrastinates and remains indecisive through unpredictable changes of behaviour. He breaks with Ophelia for no reason, an event which shows the rise of an imbalance in his unconscious fantasy. Because of this imbalance, Hamlet loses any guarantee of the stability of his desire. This is the moment identified by Lacan as the moment of Hamlet's depersonalization, when he rejects Ophelia, because from then on she is no longer an object *a* in relation to Hamlet's desire. She represents the primal object of desire of which he is deprived in the symbolic. When Hamlet was still in love with Ophelia, her position as an object *a* in fantasy had offered him a stage on which to play out his desire. Ophelia, from this point on, leaves the stage of fantasy in Hamlet's desire. We learn of this when Ophelia brings the news of the sudden change in Hamlet's behaviour to Polonius. This sudden change means for Lacan a subjective rupture that is caused by a disparity between the components of fantasy, the barred subject and the object *a.* This shift also triggers an outcome that reveals a pathological crossover from unconscious thought into a conscious message. Lacan further observes that because of such a disparity, Freud conceptualized the *Unheimlich* (uncanny), a moment in which the imaginary limit between the subject and the object changes. This sudden change freezes the subject and something that was hidden from him becomes visible. Ophelia discloses this irruption in Hamlet that changes him from what she has earlier described as 'the glass of fashion', and 'mould of form', into someone who has just emerged from 'hell':

My lord, as I was sewing in my chamber,
Lord Hamlet, with his doublet all unbraced,
No hat upon his head, his stockings fouled,
Ungartered, and down-gyvèd to his ankle,
Pale as his shirt, his knees knocking each other,
And with a look so piteous in purport

As if he had been loosed out of hell
To speak of horrors, he comes before me.

(*H*, II, i, 87–94)

This uncanny irruption in Hamlet once again reveals itself in the graveyard scene, where the dead Ophelia, the abandoned object, becomes a fetishized object of his desire. Hamlet shows his passionate love for the dead Ophelia, an object that he cannot have any more. This produces '[a] reintegration of the object *a*, won back here at the price of mourning and death' (Lacan, 1977, 24). This restoration of the object brings Hamlet's desire to boiling point and causes him to jump into her tomb in order to prevent his rival, Laertes, from grabbing the symbolic phallus. When she is loved, she is an object *a*, and when dead in a tomb she represents the empty space, the dead body, and the lack of the phallus. Such moments, in which rivalry, aggression and ambivalence towards the idealized object take place, are repeated several times in the play. The fencing scene, for example, upsets the balance in desire when the resurgence of the imaginary into the symbolic register takes place, changing Hamlet from an indecisive posture into an aggressive stance of action. In such instances, as Lacan puts it, '[t]he playwright situates the basis of aggressivity in this paroxysm of absorption in the imaginary register, formally expressed as a mirror relationship, a mirrored reaction' (31). In the graveyard scene, an imaginary inscription of desire emerges in the symbolic, and the ghost in the play represents the emergence of the real in the symbolic. Lacan sees the symptomatic aspect of Hamlet's desire in this imbalance that is inscribed in the play in a series of bizarre actions. The real cuts through the symbolic in terms of uncanny and bizarre in this play, for it as we often insist are inassimilable in the symbolic. Lacan observes Hamlet's dragging of Polonius' body, the hiding of the corpse and the graveyard on the stage as among the gaps in the real that emerge uncensored in Shakespeare's play. The gap in the real and consequently in the existence of the subject, as Lacan emphasizes, cannot be articulated in the signifying chain because of the limit of language in homogenizing the real. These gaps locate Hamlet and his desire in what Lacan calls 'the blackout of signifiers' (49). This blackout or syncope means that when an act or gesture doesn't lend itself to signification, it emerges in the real. This is a situation of a total loss where the function of speech – the symbolic exchange and the function of love – transference – all fail. This means that the configuration of the Oedipal love-bond fails to cross over to the symbolic bond of love. Desire of man is indeed hell as Lacan said in response to a question by Marcel Ritter (Marini, 1992, 243). This hell is where Hamlet turns into a 'coward', a natural result of a chaotic desire, as Lacan writes, '[d]esire, what is called desire, suffices to make life meaningless if it turns someone into a coward' (Lacan, 2006, 661).

This crisis shows itself in Hamlet's monologues on mourning, for they function as a backlash against Hamlet's desire that remains still stuck in Oedipal conflict. Hamlet's seven soliloquies about mourning serve him as a metonymic chain, carrying his deepening agony from one stage to another.

Seven meditations on mourning

From a psychoanalytic perspective, Hamlet's soliloquies each have significance beyond being merely dramatic devices. Apart from expressing the protagonist's philosophical thoughts, they are, in fact, sermons that address Hamlet himself more than the audience. Far from being a device for the development of plot, a soliloquy reveals a whirlpool where Hamlet finds himself increasingly sucked into his interiority. The goal towards which Hamlet's desire moves is impossible and yet, the seeking of this impossibility lies at the heart of his desire. We find Hamlet always at a loss, because he is unable to articulate the impossibility of his desire in the symbolic order. This impossibility designates a gap in his existence that is reinforced and widened with the progress of the tragedy. The seven soliloquies metonymically repeat, confirm and brood on what has been inscribed in the first soliloquy. They are different in tone, content and message from Claudius's soliloquy that sheds light on his secret intentions and his guilt for murdering his brother. Each soliloquy consciously emboldens Hamlet, but action still mysteriously remains deferred. Even when occasionally they reveal Hamlet's nihilistic world outlook, the principal goal of his thoughts is to reinforce his pathological mind-set on mourning and procrastination, as well as his self-reproach.

The first soliloquy presents Hamlet utterly engrossed in his mother's hasty marriage rather than the murder of his father, or even mourning for his father's death. He seems to project his chaotic inner world onto the whole order of nature and the whole universe.

> She married. O, most wicked speed, to post
> With such dexterity to incestuous sheets!
> It is not, nor it cannot come to good.
> But break my heart, for I must hold my tongue.
>
> (*H*, I-ii, 161–164)

After he sees and talks to the ghost of his father, Hamlet, in the second soliloquy, vows to do everything to fulfil the demand of the dead father. The ghost's injunction contains three commandments: avenging the murder of the father, bringing a split between Gertrude and Claudius, and most importantly, commitment to his father's memory. Amidst his horror, we find Hamlet swearing to cleanse his mind of anything but the ghost's commandments. The soliloquy parallels the utterance of the ghost except for the two lines, 'O most pernicious woman!' and 'O villain, villain, smiling, damned villain!' (*H.* I-v, 114–115) is punctuating the soliloquy's semantic texture.

The third and the longest soliloquy brings the second part of the play's action to a close, where Hamlet's behaviour confirms our view of his procrastination, which is a source of his unconscious pleasure, which he continues to avoid at the ego level. In Lacanian psychoanalysis, the subject's ego with its comic existence, tries to master duplicity and misunderstanding. In Hamlet's case, it doesn't seem to cope with his increasing inner crisis nor does it submit to the mastery of the unconscious. Throwing labels such as 'rogue', 'coward',, 'ass' and 'rascal' at himself, his speech bears witness to the duplicity and submission of his ego. His masochistic self-destruction goes hand in hand with his incrimination of his indecision and procrastination. Hamlet's craftiness in making up excuses and pretences can be seen from the beginning to the end of the tragedy. Long before Freud and Lacan, William Hazlitt revealed in 1818 his own psychoanalytical insight when he said that as soon as Hamlet was bound to act he was also bound to inaction. He would leave things cool off until the event was forgotten, then he would find another pretence to delay his mission. The third soliloquy is a vivid example of such thoughtfulness and cunning. Towards the end of the soliloquy, he seems happy because he has discovered another excuse for putting off real action. This game of action in inaction is at the heart of the metonymy that sustains Hamlet's desire.

In light of the preceding argument, what is at stake for Hamlet is support for his desire in the visual field, as this field opens up a game of seeing and being seen, capturing and being captured reminiscent of a subject in the mirror stage. This game thus sets the stage for his desire in a visual field, which is connected with the bodily drives that function in the domain of desire, through which Hamlet identifies with the outside image, and sees, in the imago of his father, his own idealized identity:

> HAMLET: My father – methink I see my father.
> HORATIO: Where, my lord?
> HAMLET: In my mind's eye, Horatio.
>
> (*H*, I-ii, 191–193)

His father too reciprocates this Oedipal interest through the ghost, and it is clearly comprehended by Horatio who desperately tries to talk to the ghost, but in vain. This is what Horatio says to Hamlet in Act I, Scene IV:

> It beckons you to go away with it
> As if it some impartment did desire
> To you alone.
>
> (*H*. I-iv, 63–65)

In Act III Scene I, we are in the midst of yet another visual field in which Hamlet is put to the test. This time, however, the craft of the scene belongs to Polonius whose psychoanalytic wisdom is praised by Lacan for revealing the diagnosis of Hamlet's madness that he attributes to frustration with Ophelia's love. This visual field places Hamlet at centre stage where Claudius wants to see Hamlet's encounter with Ophelia, in order to figure out what has caused his madness. But before the inception of this visual game, Hamlet's meditation on death and suicide in the *to be or not to be* soliloquy occurs. Now, we see the depth of Hamlet's inconsolable inner crisis and the paranoia that leads him to choose between life and death. His very existence is a burden to his own self, for the impossibility of his desire has plunged him in a sea of existential anxiety. At the outset of the soliloquy, he puts in front of himself the hard question of fight or flight that now turns out to be a moral question in relation to his destiny. Hamlet's solution involves the power of the conscience turning against one's own self. Isn't this an antecedent to the tyrannical Freudian super-ego, which brings the ego under the thrall of its moral power: '[t]hus conscience does make cowards of us all' (*H*, III-i, 85).

The graveyard scene shows that Hamlet's desire is fixed at 'not to be', rather than 'to be'. At the ego level, he tries to convince us that he prefers thoughts to action, yet his thinking gets him nowhere. He is plunged into the imaginary when he plays with Yorick's skull in the same scene in which he compares the skull with his own self.

The fifth short soliloquy ends the turbulent Act III, Scene II, where in his mind Hamlet projects his anger onto his mother. This is ironic considering we would expect his anger to be directed against Claudius, whose guilt had been confirmed after the 'mouse trap'. Polonius's words informing Hamlet that his mother wanted to see him, might have triggered his indignation towards Gertrude. He goes too far when he compares himself to Nero, who murdered his mother Agrippina.

> O heart, lose not thy nature; let not ever
> The soul of Nero enter this firm bosom.
> Let me be cruel, not unnatural.
>
> (*H*, III-ii, 426–428)

As the soliloquy ends, he is split between feelings of wrath and passion but pledges to be gentle and kind to his mother when he enters her closet:

> I will speak daggers to her, but use none.
> My tongue and soul in this be hypocrites.
>
> (*H*, III-ii, 429–430)

Hamlet, minutely and with great passion, describes the intimate love acts between Gertrude and Claudius. This is not without importance when we bring it into the light of the Lacanian theory of desire. Such a narrative of sexual episodes portrays the subject's encounters with his own unconscious fantasies. The encounter is not necessarily a return of the same thing, a thing that is already there, but the process of return, according to Lacan, is a return that allows us to see Hamlet's desire in crisis, for it is difficult for him to locate his own fantasy outside of the Oedipal space.

The sixth soliloquy places Hamlet very close to Claudius, but it ends in his moral decision not to strike, for Claudius is in the middle of saying a prayer. For Hamlet, any attack at this moment would be 'hiring' and 'salary', not revenge. Thus, the prayer serves both Hamlet and Claudius. The former finds a reason for delay, and the latter is saved:

> . . . My mother stays
> This physic but prolongs thy sickly days.
>
> (*H.* III-iv, 100–101)

Hamlet's obsession with the visual field again resurfaces when he reveals his intention to strike at Claudius when he 'is drunk asleep, or in his rage/Or in th' incestuous pleasure of his bed' (*H.* III-iv, 94–95). There are two visual fields juxtaposed in this soliloquy. The first reveals Claudius at prayer when Hamlet unsheathes and sheathes his sword, and the second is the one which Hamlet nurtures in his imagination, the bed where Claudius makes love to Gertrude.

Finally, Hamlet delivers his seventh soliloquy, which poses questions about the power of thinking and its implication for him. He is once again at the mercy of his compulsive depressive thoughts, thoughts of death, nihilism and the absurdity of life. Even the life of the kings with their invading armies looks meaningless to him. He deludes himself that a series of unforeseen events and circumstances have stopped him from taking revenge so far. After talking to Fortinbras, the prince of Norway, he shows his dualistic outlook on life and death. In the final soliloquy, he again projects his own crisis onto the world. Surprisingly, at the end of his monologue, he vows revenge, when the semantic texture of the soliloquy is broken. The last lines of the soliloquy represent another ploy of which we now know that Hamlet is an unquestionable master:

> O, from this time forth
> My thoughts be bloody or be nothing worth!
>
> (*H.* IV-iv, 68–69)

The metonymic insistence on mourning in the soliloquies works as a device for a subject to compensate for the lost object of desire. This is a crucial point in the whole logic of Hamlet's chaotic desire, as Lacan remarks:

> The work of mourning is first of all performed to satisfy the disorder that is produced by the inadequacy of signifying elements to cope with the hole that

has been created in existence, for it is the system of signifiers in their totality, which is impeached by the least instance of mourning. (Lacan, 1977, 38)

Hamlet, in fact, detaches himself from the primal object by fixing his libido to a new imaginary object. This imaginary object for Hamlet is his dead father whom he idealizes in a way that expresses his desire for the primal object. His final words, in fact, show the ultimate goal of his desire to be silence and death, the result of his act of selecting 'not to be'. This death is what Hamlet desires like the hero of every classical tragedy, as death brings about freedom from the symbolic and its laws. This is how desire brings a split and barred subject to silence, because as Hamlet says, '[t]he rest is silence, (O,O,O,O!)' (*H.* V-ii, 395).

The metonymic structure of the soliloquies on both textual and thematic levels in *Hamlet* insists on mourning as a primary condition of desire, for mourning, as Freud and Lacan suggest is not for a person, mother or someone else, but for an object. Therefore, mourning develops as the objectification of desire and its related feelings and emotions. Eliot's inability to see this objectification in *Hamlet* is apparent in his conclusion that the protagonist cannot objectify his feelings: 'Hamlet's bafflement at the absence of objective equivalent to his feeling is a prolongation of the bafflement of his creator in the face of his artistic problem' (Eliot, 1975, 48). This is the central point of Eliot's argument in his essay on *Hamlet.* The solution of this problematic necessitates the intrusion of a pathologist. The object lost is the cause of desire insofar as it is an object *a*, the phallus which when it is hidden, designates the relationship of the subject with the imaginary. At the bottom of Hamlet's mourning lies a choice in relation to the objects of desire, the choice that consolidates and sustains desire. For this purpose, the objects, the phallus and the object *a*, have been located in relation to Hamlet's desire. At this stage of our discussion, we need now to clarify and scrutinize the place and effect of object *a* and the phallus in relation to Hamlet's chaotic desire.

Object *in/of* desire

Lacan postulated the object *in* desire and distinguished it from the object *of* desire, by way of his formula of fantasy (*$<>a*), where the barred subject (*$*) is irreducibly affected by the signifier; the *poiçon* (<>) shows the subject's relationship to the imaginary juncture '[w]hich is not the object of desire but the object in desire' (Lacan, 1977, 28). Lacan revealed the existence of this object in two literary texts, 'The Purloined Letter', and *Hamlet.* In *Hamlet,* Lacan articulates the absence of the signifier of desire or the phallus and sees Hamlet himself as a subject lacking the phallus. This signifier alienates him from the signification in which he has lost part of his life. Lacan calls this lack a deprivation of the phallus. Deprivation of the signifier urges the subject to fixate on a particular object to be his object of desire. This object *in* desire, according to Lacan remains concealed, and can be defined as the imaginary complex number (*i*) or the square root of minus one in mathematics. This object returns in the symbolic as an object *a*.

Lacan's exhaustive search for the phallus, its place, and its inter-changeability with the object *a* illustrates a game of objectification that has a link with Hamlet's desire throughout the play. Hamlet's relation to each of these objects links him with the Other in an imaginary dimension that works essentially towards the establishment of a substitute for the primal subject/object relationship as well as something to fill the void created by castration. Hamlet as a literary subject is also caught up in the double game of the object as signifier and the object as the cause of his desire. In addition, on occasions Hamlet takes the place of these objects, as we will see shortly. In this event, however, the transposition goes back to the paradoxical imaginary relation between the ego and the ego-ideal, where the ego-ideal becomes the ideal signifier that brings a subject's position under its control in the symbolic register. Lacan has clarified this at the outset of his seminar, as he identifies Hamlet's desire as caught between the ideal, but dead father, and Claudius. Here Hamlet introverts the ego-ideal into his own self. The objectification game and the occurrence of transposition between the subject and its object again go back to the imaginary in which there is no identification proper, but only an identification which is elusive, paranoiac and often exposed to misunderstanding. The whole process aims to disrupt the congruity of the symbolic structure, the motivation for which is inherent in a desire that, in Hamlet's case, is not understood and not integrated successfully in the Oedipal triangle.

The object *a*, which causes and sets desire in motion, is connected to the real but always carries with itself its imaginary status. It functions in the symbolic as a leftover of the real and primal object from which it gets all its privileges of transcending the entry of the real into the symbolic. That is the reason that Lacan writes this object as the algebraic letter *a*, for it is unsymbolizable. This is also the reason why at the outset of his seminar, Lacan calls Ophelia 'bait' in relation to Hamlet's desire. As Lacan insists in *Encore*, the object *a* is the semblance of being in the symbolic. In other words, it is a semblance of the Other or the primary subject of the demand. Lacan saw the transposition of Ophelia take place in three crucial stages in the play. She appears first as an object *a*; then her position is shifted into a rejected phallus, and finally, she comes back to the position of forbidden *jouissance* or object *a* again. It is Ophelia's position as the phallus and its importance for the structure of desire that made Lacan call her '(O) phallus', and the whole play a 'phallophony'. She provides evidence of her key position in the structure of desire first, when she apparently drowns herself, and later in her funeral. She drowns herself in water full of *Orchis mascula*, plants representing phallic objects, as Lacan says: '[t]he plant in question is Orchis mascula, which is related to the mandrake and hence to the phallic element' (Lacan, 1977, 23). The oscillation of Hamlet between these objects splits his desire itself into three stages: the first stage is indicative of a time, during which Hamlet has been entrapped in a love-relationship by Ophelia. This relationship makes it possible for him to sustain his desire of/for the Other. The second stage begins when the object *a* is going to shift into a phallus that empowers Hamlet to fill the void of castration in his unconscious. In this stage, Ophelia is repudiated as an object *a*. The final stage refers to a time in which the object *a* is restored to its previous status. The graveyard scene enhances Ophelia's position as object *a*, when Hamlet boasts about his love for her.

Simply put, like an object *a*, the phallus functions as the signifier of desire, and as a signified of lost *jouissance*. When Ophelia is assigned to act as the phallus, she stands to ensure Hamlet's desire for the Other. By contrast, when we find Hamlet fixated on Ophelia as an object *a*, she is a substitute for the primal object, as can be seen in a letter Hamlet writes to her:

> Thine evermore, most dear lady, whilst
> This machine is to him, Hamlet.
>
> (*H*, II-ii, 131–132)

However, this machine is soon defiled when he denounces his love for her:

> Get thee (to) a nunnery. Why wouldst thou be
> a breeder of sinners?
>
> (*H*, III-I, 131–132)

A continuum of change in the modulation of objects explains another law of desire, namely, desire is always for something else. You cannot desire something which you already have. In the graveyard scene, Ophelia reclaims her position as an object *a* for Hamlet's desire, because she is now dead and Hamlet is no longer able to have her. She is an impossible object that fits an impossible desire. In the meantime, the dead Ophelia functions once again as a phallus, because she has become the object of Hamlet's desire based on her absence of lack. This is a crucial moment for the representation of Ophelia, as she acts out a double function for Hamlet's desire. In Act V, Scene I, there is an intense event in the imaginary when Laertes mourns his sister, and Hamlet cannot bear it. That is why he jumps into the open grave and begins a brawl with his rival. Why should there be such a leap inside the tomb? This quantum leap is, in fact, into his own imaginary, which sees Laertes as his specular image in the mirror. The Lacanian imaginary confirms this because rivalry, aggression as well as love are among the important ingredients of this register. Here Ophelia, as the phallus, can fill the void in Hamlet and thus consolidate his desire. Hamlet cannot bear Laertes' ostentatious sorrow at Ophelia's burial. The imaginary has a magic and captivating power over the subject. Therefore, Hamlet can neither lose the phallus nor allow the phallus to be taken by his rival:

> I loved Ophelia. Forty thousands brothers
> Could not with all their quantity of love
> Make up my sum. What wilt thou do for her?
>
> (*H*, V-i, 285–287)

It is important to note that desire doesn't have a real object. Otherwise, it would have been easily satisfied like a drive, but it needs an object *a* as its cause and the phallus or an object to substitute the lack on which desire stands. Thus, the objects we are talking about here are either substitutes or residues of the original object. They irreducibly stabilize the desiring subject and its relationship with the Other in the symbolic. This explains the ever-changing status of the object *a* and the phallus. An object is an object *in* desire, insofar as it functions as the phallus and stands as a symbol of lack.

> Something becomes an object *in* desire when it takes the place of what by its very nature remains concealed from the subject: the self-sacrifice, that pound of flesh which is mortgaged [engagé] in his relationship to the signifier. (Lacan, 1977, 28)

The phallus appears in many guises in the play, the ghost, Claudius, Ophelia, the skull and Hamlet and each occupy the place of the phallus alternatively in relation to the desire of the Other that reveals the intersubjective nature of human desire. The phallus is always veiled and hidden and emerges always suddenly, as the dead Ophelia emerges to be the phallus for Hamlet. Hamlet too becomes the phallus for Laertes, as Claudius has become a phallus for Gertrude. By the same token, then, Hamlet functions as the phallus for Claudius, because Claudius is Gertrude's phallus, whereas Hamlet is deprived of having one here. As Lacan says, Shakespeare opens up a gallery of objects with an outstanding visual effect in the last scene of the play. The phallus and the object *a* appear all over the place, some veiled and some unveiled: Claudius and Laertes wager on Barbary horses, French rapiers and poniards, and there is Claudius's pearl dropped in the chalice. As soon as the duel breaks out, Hamlet identifies with the phallus for Laertes:

> I'll be your foil, Laertes. In mine ignorance
> Your skill shall, like a star i' th' darkest night
> Stick fiery off indeed.
>
> (*H.* V-ii, 272–273)

The above gallery of objects becomes richer when, as Lacan argues, Shakespeare uses the word 'foil' as a 'pun' for the phallus. The word 'foil', etymologically means both a fencing sword as well as a case for jewellery. Lacan argues that its French equivalent is *feuille* (from Latin *folia*, the plural of *folium*) representing here the signifier, the phallus, for in punning, figurative language functions to express the hidden and inexpressible. Besides, for Lacan, a pun gives preference to a signifier over a signified. In addition, *The Oxford English Dictionary* explains the word 'foil' as the setting of a precious stone, and according to *The Concise Oxford Dictionary of English Etymology* the word 'foil' and its French *feuille*, denote a thin metallic leaf that the goldsmiths put under a gemstone in order to increase its shine. So the foil and its shine is what Lacan calls here the object in desire or the phallus.

These changes in position are not limited to Hamlet. Every subject is predisposed to alter his position in order to remain in his desire. Lacan reveals such alterations of position in relation to desire. There are two points of interest in Lacan's comments on the final scene of the play. The place of the Other for Hamlet changes from Gertrude to Claudius. For the mother who was up until now his Other, she gives her place to Claudius, who is now Hamlet's Other in the symbolic register, with whom Hamlet tries to identify. This is the hour that determines Hamlet's destiny in psychoanalytic terms when he succumbs to the symbolic Other and its trap:

> Thus, he [Hamlet] rushes into the trap laid by the Other. All that's changed is the energy and fire with which he rushes into it. Until the last term, until the final hour, Hamlet's hour, in which he is mortally wounded before he wounds his enemy, the tragedy follows its course and attains completion at the hour of the Other. (Lacan, 1977, 19)

What makes all these shifts in objects possible? Fantasy holds the answer, for, according to Lacan, unconscious fantasy provides a transition period for an object to be replaced by another. In this sense, an object only becomes the phallus when it posits itself as the end term of fantasy and thus as the end term of desire as well. Fantasy is knotted to the unconscious and enjoys some connection with conscious demand. In a normal situation, a crossover from the realm of the unconscious into the realm of the conscious doesn't occur, because fantasy in this case tends to stick to the unconscious. It is, nevertheless, only in pathological events that fantasy makes this crossover. The object gets its function in fantasy from the phallus, and through the phallus, '[d]esire is constituted with the fantasy as its reference' (Lacan, 1977, 15). The essential thing is the role of the fundamental lack that determines the identity of the phallus in relation to desire. Within this lack, which signifies the lack of the phallus, Hamlet experiences himself as nothing but a desiring self who doesn't know how to desire. Because as we have remarked at the outset, his submission to the Other puts him in a pathological melancholia and probably a feigned madness. This dependence on the Other can be derived in the text from the signifier that produces its signification only by a deferred action.

The objects, in sum, merge and change their status in relation to the fantasy that sets the stage for desire. In the process of desire, an object *a*, and the phallus that mark a subject's desire are closely interconnected. Lacan says in *Television*, '[t]he a, the object, falls. The fall is primal' (Lacan, 1990, 85). That fall creates a gap and a void in the subject, which has to be filled by another object, the phallus. The object takes the status of an object *in* desire, insofar as it is the phallus, a signifier for desire; and it takes the status of an object *of* desire, insofar as it is a substitute and a residue of the primal object of demand. The phallus, however, has a privileged position when it operates in the whole configuration of desire. As Lacan says, '[a]nd it is from the phallus that the object gets its function in the fantasy, and from the phallus that desire is constituted with the fantasy as its reference' (16).

The final scene of the play as Claudius becomes Hamlet's Other and when Laertes wounds the prince, is crucially important in Lacan's criticism. Because, from this moment on, Hamlet is no more in the time and place of the Other. Encounter with Laertes, his Other, emboldens him to act and kill Claudius.

Hamlet's hour of the Other

The idea of the hour essentially comes into Lacan's discourse in his writing on Oedipus Rex. '[A]m I made man in the hour when I cease to be?' (Lacan, 1991a, 229) is the question that Oedipus asks when he is going to mutilate himself. For Lacan this hour is crucial in Shakespeare's play too, for Hamlet lives in this hour, that like his desire, is not his own. He enters into his own hour the moment he anticipates his death, at the end of the play, after he is wounded fatally. What becomes problematic, according to Lacan, is that since the Other itself is elusive, lacking and non-existent, there is no hour of the Other, and Hamlet is not in anyone else's hour but his own. The hour of the Other is as elusive as a mirage.

Lacan writes in *Seminar II: The Ego in Freud's theory and in the Technique of Psychoanalysis* that unlike the pervert, the neurotic lives all his time in the time of the Other. For the neurotic is faced with a crucial question of 'to be or not to be', the determinant of which is desire. This means that desire gives the neurotic his structure, which is prior to any conceptualization to the extent that '[e]very conceptualisation stems from it' (Lacan, 1991a, 225). In fantasy, the neurotic subject has a relation to the object which is often '[o]n the basis of the relationship of the subject to time' (Lacan, 1977, 17).

Furthermore, Lacan's theory of time is puzzling because it is distinguished from the conventional sense of time as linearity and chronological order. Lacan introduces the concept of time or the hour in relation to the subject, desire and language. In this hour of truth, the Other is often in another hour. It is part of Hamlet's desire from the beginning to the end of the play that makes him chase the hour of the Other. Hamlet falls in his own hour when he receives a wound.

This explains why we often find Hamlet in a narcissistic bond with the object *a*. In order to figure out what this 'hour' means, we need to draw on the subject's entry to language and the effect this entry places on the subject in the symbolic. The very moment of this entry into language is what Lacan calls the hour of the Other, or the hour of the truth, to which Hamlet is linked. From Lacan, we know that this entry into language places a subject, in the meantime, in a place between two deaths. The first death occurs when the subject becomes discontinuous in the real with entry into discourse, and the second, when he dies in the real world. In neurosis, the relation a subject builds vis-à-vis the object designates a relation that exists between the subject and time. As Lacan says, '[t]he object is charged with the significance sought in what I call the hour of truth, in which the object is always at another hour, fast or slow, early, or late' (17). As for the second problem, it has to be pointed out that Lacan's concept of truth is extremely complex, and this results from the different contexts in which truth defines itself. In the case of Hamlet, however, Lacan's aim is clearly the truth of the real. This is the truth that emerges from a subject's alienation in language, a truth that is also the truth of desire, which a subject always wants to repress. Thus, the hour and truth refer to the occasion when a subject enters language.

The death of Hamlet, according to Lacan, like that of Oedipus, happens in the hour of truth, because this hour unites the subject with the Other. In this context, Lacan claims that Hamlet's hour arrives when he dies. For Lacan, everyone in the play has an hour: Ophelia's hour is when she commits suicide, Gertrude's hour is when she is poisoned and Claudius' hour comes when he dies:

> When he [Hamlet] stays on [Lacan refers here to staying in Denmark instead of going to Wittenberg], it is the hour of his parents. When he suspends his crime, it is the hour of the others. When he leaves for England, it is the hour of his stepfather. It's the hour of Rosencrantz and Guildenstern when he sends them on ahead to death – with a casualness that amazed Freud – by means of a bit of hocus-pocus that he brings off not half badly. And it is the hour of Ophelia, the hour of her suicide, when the tragedy will run its course, in a moment when Hamlet has just realised that it's not hard to kill man, the time to say 'one' . . . he won't know what hit him. (Lacan, 1977, 18)

When the hour of truth arrives, there is death, and no further time for the subject. We can take the following lines, which shortly before his death, Hamlet utters, to Horatio, as textual evidence of this claim:

> Had I but time (as this fell sergeant, Death,
> Is strict in his arrest), I could tell you –
> But let it be – Horatio, I am dead.
>
> (*H.* V-ii, 368–370)

And this is the hour that the ghost of Hamlet's father has told us about:

> My hour is almost come
> When I to sulph'rous and tormenting flames
> Must render up myself.
>
> (*H.* I-v, 5–7)

When this paradoxical ' hour' arrives, a subject 'leaps' to his own death. This is what Hamlet does in the play. Hamlet's duel takes place at this hour. Lacan stresses that Hamlet '[i]s suspended in the time of the Other, throughout the entire story until the very end' (Lacan, 1977, 17). Lacan connects Hamlet with neurosis that, unlike perversion, links the subject with the time of the object. Hamlet's own hour is destined to coincide with the hour of the Other, as Lacan remarks: '[u]ntil the last term, until the final hour, Hamlet's hour, in which he is mortally wounded before he wounds his enemy, the tragedy follows its course and attains completion at the hour of the Other' (19). We also know that, according to Lacan, Hamlet is always in the hour of the Other and his desire too is the desire of the Other, but these Others subsequently refer to Claudius and Gertrude. However, Claudius is the Other of Gertrude's demand, for the father for Lacan represents the desire of the mother. Lacan clarifies his position that this Other is only a mirage, for there is no Other of the Other, '[f]or Hamlet there is no hour but his own. Moreover, there is only one hour, the hour of his destruction' (25). As we have pointed out earlier, the hour of the Other is identical with the subject. Bruce Fink takes on Lacan in his essay, 'Reading Hamlet with Lacan', asserting that Hamlet never arrives at his own time: 'I do not entirely agree with Lacan's conclusion that "Hamlet does take the leap in the end", It is not clear to me that Hamlet is ever able to act in any full sense of the term' (Fink, 1996,196). On the contrary, Hamlet is able to act, he self-consciously kills his uncle when in the last scene of the play, he calls the courtiers to lock up all the doors and catch the king. Fink relies on a quote from Hamlet's last words for evidence:

> I am dead, Horatio. – Wretched queen, adieu!
> You that look pale and tremble at this chance,
> That are but mutes or audience to this act,
> Had I but time,– as this fell sergeant, death,
> Is strict in his arrest, – O, I could tell you, –
> But let it be.– Horatio, I am dead;
> Thou liv'st; report me and my cause aright
> To the unsatisfied.
>
> (*H.*V-ii, 285–292)

Hamlet's words, 'Had I but time;, are taken here by Fink to mean that 'Hamlet's time never comes – now he is *à l'heure de la mort.* He remains as neurotic as ever, his time is never now, he cannot speak his piece, someone else must speak for him and plead his cause before the world' (Fink, 1996, 196). A close reading of the play suggests that Hamlet wants Horatio to be alive in order to tell the public about Claudius's heinous crime after his death, something that remains outside the realm of his unconscious desire. He forcefully takes the poisoned cup away from Horatio who was about to drink at the last moments of the play, for he doesn't want the blame of the kill to fall on him in the eyes of the public. As Horatio promises, he will tell the full account of the story before the council summoned by Fortinbras upon his coronation.

In Gertrude's closet

The closet scene highlights two major points beyond its dramatic significance: first, a frustrating quarrel between the son and the mother that shows Hamlet in his rage and distemper; second, Hamlet's demand that his mother not go to Claudius's bed and give up on her *jouissance.* Persuaded by Polonius, Gertrude calls Hamlet into her closet, apparently to find out about the secret of his madness, though she has stated early in the play that Hamlet's madness was caused by her hasty marriage and King Hamlet's death. Almost the whole scene is occupied by a question/answer conversation that is symmetrical and reciprocal in rhythm and tone.

QUEEN
Hamlet, thou hast thy father much offended.
HAMLET
Mother, you have my father much offended.
QUEEN Come
Come, come, you answer with an idle tongue.
HAMLET
Go, go, you question with a wicked tongue.
. . .
HAMLET
Come, come, and sit you down; you shall not budge,
You go not till I set you up a glass
Where you may see the innermost part of you.

(*H.* III-iv, 12–25)

Hamlet's sharp and passionate words overcome his interlocutor until she is wordless, for as his Other, she doesn't know how to answer the subject's *Chè Vuoi? (what do you want?)*

Be thou assured, if words be made of breath
And breath of life, I have no life to breathe
What thou hast said to me.

(*H.* III-iv, 219–221)

Gertrude's behaviour at this moment is of great importance, as it gives us an idea of how Hamlet desires, and why his desire remains dependent on her. As Lacan remarks:

> This fall, this abandon, gives us a model that enables us to conceive how it is that Hamlet's desire – his zeal with respect to an act that he so longs to carry out that the whole world becomes for him a living reproach for his perpetual inadequacy to his own will – how this zeal always flags. The dependence of his desire on the Other subject forms the permanent dimension of Hamlet's drama. (Lacan, 1977, 13)

Hamlet's desire is best defined by Gertrude's refusal of his demand. The desire of the subject always, at the last minute, wants the Other to refuse his demand, for desire is always for something else. Therefore, Hamlet's unconscious desire insists Gertrude go to his uncle. Lacan metaphorically says in *Ou Pire* (Seminar of 9 February 1972) that a subject's demand may say *no* but his desire *yes* to the same question:

I ASK OF YOU
TO REFUSE OF ME
WHAT I OFFER YOU
BECAUSE: THAT ISN'T IT

(Lacan, 1973, n. p.)

Why does Hamlet have to make a demand while his desire is essentially a demand for rejection? From Lacan, we know that a subject's desire is always an impossible desire for an impossible object. We also know that a demand has always a double function, for it contains need and love for the Other. There is thus an impossibility that Hamlet wants to cultivate beneath his demand, because his desire is always circling around impossibility. As Lacan says, Hamlet '[s]ets everything up so that the object of his desire becomes the signifier of this impossibility' (Lacan, 1977, 36).

As Lacan insists, the ghost in Shakespeare's play appears and reappears often as the 'veiled phallus' in order to take the place of the signifier of the Mother's desire and the Law-of-the-Father. The father, whom this ghost stands for, reappears in the real in order to replace Hamlet's desire with the fundamental lack that it signifies. Lacan argues that the ghost emerges from the primal and irreparable crime of the Oedipal drama. The ghost clearly in its earlier appearance states this when he refers to '[t]he blossoms of my sin' (*H*, I-v, 83), as well as to Claudius's horrible crime. Why is Gertrude unable to see the ghost? Was this because this time the apparition wasn't real or was only Hamlet's hallucination? From what is revealed in the scene, one might suggest that it is a false apparition, because Hamlet and his mother are talking at length about this issue and Gertrude is becoming convinced that Hamlet is now really mad. Besides, in its first appearance, Barnardo, Francisco, Horatio and others saw the ghost.

In addition, in this scene, we can argue that Hamlet and the ghost have to be reckoned as a couple as they complement one another. This helps us find another dimension in Hamlet's desire: a desire on the side of the law that is represented by the super-ego. Quoting Ludwig Jakels in his essay 'Those Wrecked by Success', Freud suggests that Shakespeare's unique skill in characterization was to create a double for each character. The ghost is the messenger of Hamlet's super-ego. The ghost's horrible sins echo, in fact, Hamlet's own Oedipal guilt. In a footnote in *Écrits,* Lacan also refers to this motive behind Shakespearean characterization that was also admired by Goethe:

> Indeed, one can recognize in such oblique forms of allegiance the style of that immortal couple, Rosencrantz and Guildenstern, who are a set that cannot be broken up, not even by the imperfection of their destiny . . . and for the very reason for which Goethe praised Shakespeare for presenting the characters in double. (Lacan 2002, 167–168)

With the conflation of Hamlet's and the ghost's speeches, we have a full account of the conflicts of desire in Shakespeare's tragedy. We can see this easily, for instance, when the ghost confesses. This is in fact a projection of Hamlet's own unconscious guilt, as Lacan takes the 'cut off' and 'the blossoms of my sin', as Hamlet's own Oedipal sin revealed by his double, the ghost. The 'cut' here refers to the primal cut between the subject and the Other that happens in the Oedipus Complex. The ghost reveals King Hamlet's sins when he mentions the horrible fire in which he is burning. In Act I, Scene-V, a father is saying to his son, 'O son, can't you see I am burning":

> I am thy father's spirit,
> Doomed for a certain term to walk the night
> And for the day confined to fast in fires
> Till the foul crimes done in my days of nature
> Are burnt and purged away. But that I am forbid
> To tell the secrets of my prison house,
> I could a tale unfold whose lightest word
> Would harrow up thy soul, freeze thy young blood,
> Make thy two eyes, like stars, start from their spheres,

Thy knotted and combinéd locks to part,
And each particular hair to stand on end,
Like quills upon the fearful porpentine.
But this eternal blazon must not be.

(*H.* I-v, 14–26)

King Hamlet discloses this crime and sin even before he reaches the real and accomplished crime of Claudius. This 'eternal blazon' of the divine punishment for sin is what Hamlet compensates for by his eternal mourning and melancholia. What Hamlet shows by his desire and its tragic outcome is told by the ghost. The reverse of this story is told in the last dream analysed by Freud in *The Interpretation of Dreams* that Lacan touches upon in his *Four Fundamental Concepts of Psychoanalysis.* A father sees in his dream his son's crying: '[f]ather, can't you see I am burning' (Lacan, 1977, 34). Both stories tell the same tale of Oedipal sin. Hamlet goes even further when he dramatizes this sin, as though the ghost's confession and Hamlet's mourning were not enough. His dramatization of the event occurs in the play-within-the play.

The play-within-the-play

Hamlet's intention is to capture Claudius's gaze, by looking at the gaze that turns out to be the object of his scopic drive, which is already in the field of desire. Hamlet's look and Claudius's gaze come from two different fields, the field of the subject and the other (in the Imaginary) that according to the Lacanian theory of the gaze are essentially cut off from one another. This separation shows us why Hamlet wants to capture Claudius's guilt in his gaze. This capture of the gaze only takes place in the imaginary that Hamlet has gained access to. Hamlet initiates and directs the staging of this play, in much the same way as did Dupin in Poe's 'Purloined Letter', in order to create a fiction that will order to reveal the truth. The imaginary capture in which we find Claudius in the play-within-the-play (Act III, Scene iii) is enacted by dumb show. Claudius doesn't succumb to Hamlet's so-called 'mousetrap'. However, he is affected by the play when the characters re-enact his crime. Claudius reacts when he moves from the imaginary into the symbolic. The dumb show is punctuated at the end by Hamlet's comments about the murderer of Gonzago, the murderer who, in fact, is re-enacting Claudius's crime. After killing Gonzago, the murderer marries his wife. The dumb show contains the imaginary capture that holds Claudius dumb-founded but not distracted. Later when he hears Hamlet's loud and angry comments, Claudius reacts violently to the show and rises up, crying out: '[g]ive me some light. Away' (*H*, III-ii, 295). He is no more in the imaginary capture, but in the symbolic. Claudius wants more light because as we stated a moment ago, in the gaze, the subject and the Other don't see each other from the same place. As Lacan says: '[y]ou never look at me from the place from which I see you' (Lacan, 1979a, 103). In this capture, Hamlet expresses his desire, for he gets recognition of his own desire in capturing Claudius's guilt, as in his fantasy he has already accomplished what Claudius did.

Freud applies an Oedipal explanation to the play-within-the-play in *The Interpretation of Dreams.* Claudius is showing Hamlet his own infantile guilt: '[t]he man [Claudius] who shows him the repressed wishes of his childhood realised' (Freud, 1991, 367). This, for Freud, was the Oedipal fantasy. As stated above, Hamlet by setting the *mis-en-scène* and direction of this play successfully reveals Claudius's guilt. He is, indeed, like an analyst here, because he is the one who creates tense emotions in a fictional space: '[h]e begins by reflecting in a syntactically complex question on the paradox of an actor's ability to display real emotion in a fictional situation' (Cantor, 1998, 80). To this end, as Ophelia notes, '[y]ou are as good as a chorus, my lord' (*H.* III-ii, 269), Hamlet undertakes the role of the chorus, suggesting that the clowns have to be silent so that they do not incite laughter. Any strong response within the audience would have spoiled his principal goal.

To conclude our discussion of *Hamlet,* the tragedy offers us a quintessential topological structure of desire, which attracted Lacan to the study of Shakespeare. Lacan's criticism highlights Hamlet's importance as a modern hero, for on textual and aesthetic levels, the play reveals the subversion of the classic genre of tragedy. The endless inaction and procrastination have violated the fundamental dramatic and textual tenets of traditional drama. This was at the heart of the trouble in traditional literary criticism with regard to both *Hamlet* as a play and Hamlet as a protagonist. Lacan goes even further in this respect when calling Hamlet one of Shakespeare's clowns and fools who reveal the most intriguing and important motives. In this sphere, Lacan claims that Hamlet put an end to the emergence of fools in tragedies. Lacan's criticism clarifies the mythopoeia in relation to the emergence of the ghost in *Hamlet,* who signifies the lack and absence of the phallus as the signifier of desire.

Hamlet illustrates a desire in crisis. The crisis begins early in the play when Ophelia falls out of the orbit of his desire as an object *a,* and ends with the death of Hamlet. This shows a dramatic itinerary in which the prince of Denmark loses his sense of how to desire. His desire remains locked up in the Oedipal triangle that can never be integrated into the symbolic order. That is why his desire is the Other's desire, and he remains to the end, in the time of the Other. The disintegration of Hamlet's desire reveals itself in Hamlet's bizarre behaviour when his unconscious fantasy ceases to hold together and there is a crossover to the level of consciousness. In the dumb show, Hamlet falls once again into the imaginary with Claudius. Here Claudius occupies the place of the specular image. At the textual level, Hamlet repeatedly unfolds the rocky path of his desire by his feigned madness, puns, conceits, wordplay and use of ambiguities. In Hamlet's discourse, we frequently notice inconsistencies and disruptions, revealing his unconscious lack and voids. At the heart of Hamlet's desire is the persistence of the lack of the signifier. This problem always emerges on the borderline between the imaginary and the symbolic, showing a failure on Hamlet's part insofar as his Oedipus Complex is concerned. This failure emerges through Hamlet's endless mourning and despair that metonymically in a chain of seven soliloquies. Shakespeare illustrates Gertrude's desire and Hamlet's dependence on it; in this encounter, Hamlet's demand carries its own rejection in the play-within-the-play. Hamlet's desire lingers on a repeated swing in relation to its objects. When he is deprived of the phallus, he is alienated in signification, and compensates for it by his love relation with Ophelia as his object *a*. At the unconscious level, Hamlet's desire thus swings between the object *in* and *of* desire.

What we have explored in *Hamlet*, however, accounts for a paradigm of masculine desire. In order that we have a full account of desire, we need to unravel other Shakespearean texts that specifically deal with the deployment of feminine desire.

Shakespeare's ladies in *Coriolanus*, *Macbeth* and *The Merchant of Venice*

Lacan's theory of femininity defines woman's desire as delicate, paradoxical and plural. The core of the issue is the phallic function (symbolic castration that has the phallus as its symbol) as an absolute condition for masculine desire, and the impossibility of woman's assimilation within this function, which makes her what Lacan calls not-all, and not-whole. A woman has to solicit her own desire by submitting to masculine desire while sacrificing her own essential femininity. In view of such a paradox, I wish to outline three fundamental structures of feminine desire, structures that should not be understood as a nosographic model of feminine desire. On the contrary, they constitute fluid and alternative unconscious positions. A woman would subscribe to one or more of these modes of desire beyond biological or gender determinants. The first paradigm of feminine desire is the desire of the phallic mother, the *femme à pastiche*, or Kristeva's *archaic mother* as a source of plenitude and power. The desire of the phallic woman itself appears in two types. One is the all powerful and devouring mother of the infantile fantasy in the imaginary. This mother is like the real father of the symbolic with a castrating power. The second is a woman who responds to her lack of *having* the phallus by adopting a masculine paradigm, which is identified with the possession of the phallus. This paradigm constitutes an unconscious masculine desire by virtue of which a woman recovers her lack of being in the symbolic by positing her desire as related to the whole and the universal, which as we have just pointed out, is essentially pertinent to masculine desire. This is because man's desire has the support of the signifier in the symbolic register.

The second structure is referred to by Lacan as the 'real woman', or the 'true woman', of the symbolic, who accepts and affirms her lacking status by locating herself in a position where her whole being will operate as an object for masculine desire. This feminine position drives a woman herself to be the veiled phallus. Finally, the third structure of feminine desire, which Lacan conceptualizes in *Encore,* is related to the feminine *jouissance* that operates outside the phallic economy. This may well be called the polymorphous, unbound and pure essence of femininity that is free from being the absolute condition of the phallic function. Let us term this condition and a transcendental space for feminine *jouissance* the 'suspension of desire'. This suspension enables a woman to experience the real beyond the boundaries of phallic desire. This gives woman all the privileges and, according to Lacan's theory of sexuation, as S (A) [the signifier of the lack in the barred Other], a woman has a direct access to the real. A man can only open a detour to the real by means of the object *a,* or by taking up a virtual feminine position in his relation to his desire. The important thing for a woman is the loss of an essential part of her femininity as a payoff for the configuration of her desire. This loss, in fact, implies a gap between a woman's own desire and a foreign desire she is ordained to escort. This gap has to be understood as the cause and meaning of feminine masquerade. Shakespeare's theatre exhibits a great number of female personae who fall into one or more of the above modes of feminine desire. However, three of his plays, *Coriolanus, Macbeth* and *The Merchant of Venice,* require special attention as they set the stage for the shifting paradigms of feminine desire.

The phallic mother Volumnia

Coriolanus both begins and ends with two more or less identical scenes in which a formidable Roman matriarch, Volumnia, stands in the midst of a sociopolitical crisis, playing a decisive role in the death of her son and the destruction of her country. We come upon a Roman state torn apart by confrontation between the Patricians and Plebeians. This crisis has pushed the nation to the brink of defeat by the Volscians. Coriolanus's mother, Volumnia, is the one who from behind the scenes rules both her son Coriolanus and Rome. Although Shakespearean dramatic irony makes her absent in the first and final scene of the play, her absence is present everywhere with her haunting influence and power, overshadowing Coriolanus's absent father.

Volumnia disavows femininity by locating herself in a position from which she has obtained all the masculine attributes of the symbolic order. She appears as the image-object of infantile fantasy that is related to a moment in the *mirror phase* where a child imagines that the mother has the phallus. By showing a pathological hubris, virility and savagery, she places herself in a castrating position, seeing men as weak, worthless and contemptible creatures. Lacan says of the phallic mother that she enjoys herself and her life as a man, for '[t]o enjoy in this way is to enjoy *like* a man' (Lacan, 2002, 37). The first sign of Volumnia's lack of the mothering instinct arises in Act-I, Scene-iii, when she condemns Virgilia for her worries about her husband's absence in Rome's wars. Instead of sharing Virgilia's anxiety, she wants to see her son stained with blood and even dead. Volumnia's words foreshadow the disparity between herself and Virgilia in their response to Coriolanus's absence. When Virgilia shows surprise and bewilderment at Volumnia's tone: '[h]is bloody brow? O Jupiter, no blood!' (*C*, I-iii, 39). Volumnia's unusual savagery for a mother reveals her repositioning as a male who *has* the phallus. She compares the warrior's wounds to the mother's breast, a gesture of contempt for her own role as a mother:

> Away you fool! It more becomes a man
> Than gilt his trophy. The breast of Hecuba
> When she did suckle Hector look'd not lovelier
> Than Hector's forehead when it spit forth blood
> At Grecian sword, contemning.
>
> (*C*, I-iii, 40–44)

She reiterates this gesture as she thanks God when she hears about her son's wounds in the war, and then surprisingly shows much less delight in the scene when her son is honoured with the title Coriolanus for his patriotism and bravery. She lashes out at Virgilia for showing concern and emotion about her husband's mishap in the war. The scene when her son, not yet awarded with the title returns home triumphantly with bloody scars on his face, is a great moment of joy. However, the only source of her embarrassment is Virgilia.

> My gentle Martius, worthy Caius, and
> By deed-achieving honor newly nam'd –
> What is it? – Coriolanus, must I call thee?
> But oh, thy wife –
>
> (*C*, II-i, 173–176)

Furthermore, Volumnia's hostility towards Virgilia not only portrays her as Virgilia's rival, but also as an oppressor who attempts to intrude into the latter's love relationship with her husband. By disapproving of the love relationship in this way, she reinforces her status as the possessor of the phallus. She over-rides Virgilia's love for Coriolanus with her own cultural position as a devouring mother who rules all. As she says:

> If my son were my husband I should freelier rejoice in the absence wherein he won honor, than in the embracement of his bed, where he would show most love. (*C*, I-iii, 2–5)

Volumnia's own desire is to desire what she lacks by placing this lack in Virgilia and Coriolanus's love relationship, for, as the phallic mother, she needs to get an assurance about her masculine demeanour. As Kroker says:

> The phallic mother as the original real Other, must abdicate her position because she lacks the signifier of desire, the phallus, lacking it, she therefore desires it, since desire, in the Platonic terms which Lacan has appropriated, is the desire, amongst other things, to have what one lacks. (Kroker, 1991, 22)

Volumnia's comparison of herself to Hecuba and Coriolanus to Hector culminates when she associates her masculine attribute with the canniness of the phallic mother, that Lacan often refers to. She admits that each drop of valour had come to her son from her milk that he sucked in his childhood, but not his pride, thoughtlessness, senseless hostility and hatred for the common people. She exhibits her canniness by advising her son that his words and language to the Plebeians have to be learnt by heart but not felt by heart:

> VOLUMNIA: Thy valiantness was mine, thou suck'st it from me,
> But owe thy pride thyself.
> (*C*, III-ii, 129–130)
> CORIOLANUS: . . . I'll mountebank their loves,
> Cog their hearts from them, and come home belov'd.
>
> (*C*, III-ii, 132–133)

The phallic mother disclaims everything feminine and often identifies feminine attributes with masculinity, for following Freud, Lacan says that bearing a child and particularly a son functions in a feminine fantasy as a guarantor of *having* the phallus. Since a feminine subject lacks the signifier of her desire, she has to replace it with a pure femininity. For her 'milk' (the signifier of femininity) is replaced by the masculinity she claims she passed on to Coriolanus.

In order to remain a desiring phallic mother, Volumnia cannot stay outside of the world of savagery, ruthlessness, death and horror. As she says '[a]nger's my mean: I sup upon myself' (*C*, IV-ii, 50). She abuses Brutus and Sicinius, two tribunes, for their conspiracy to drive Coriolanus to his fall in Act-IV, Scene-ii. Her action shows her son's dependence on her. Likewise, the banishing of Coriolanus from Rome would mean for Volumnia the separation of mother from son:

> Ay, fool; is that a shame? Not but this fool.
> Was not a man my father? Hadst thou foxship
> To banish him that struck more blow for Rome
> Than thou hast spoken words.
>
> (*C*, IV-ii, 8–12)

In the symbolic register, a feminine desire must be veiled, rejected and metamorphosed. Antigone doesn't accept the veil; that is why she lives outside the symbolic. She doesn't want to succumb to the status of either *having* or *being* the phallus. Volumnia, on the contrary, wears the veil of the symbolic, a veil that masquerades her womanliness and thus conceals her own genuine desire.

One of the persistent dramatic techniques in *Coriolanus* is the repetition of scenes in which a character's behaviour is both revealed and confirmed. The mother-son nexus is displayed by a triumphant mother who always makes her son succumb to her will. As she says of her son, '[t]here is no man in the world more bound to's mother' (*C*, V-iii, 160–161). Volumnia often shows her power as part of her phallic rivalry for control of her son's will and power. And she is the one who makes her son's 'stout heart', into 'the ripest mulberry' (*C*, II-ii, 78–79). In Act-III, Scene-ii, we come upon Coriolanus's uncompromising determination to pursue his hatred of the Plebeians in public. Ultimately, his pride is eroded as he accepts his mother's order by going to the marketplace and apologising for his behaviour, though in the end he fails to do so. The mother-son nexus comes again into full view in Act-V, Scene-iii, when the angry mother succeeds in persuading her son to make peace between the Romans and the Volscians. Shakespeare ironically foreshadows the true nature of his character when Coriolanus says to his mother, 'My hazards still have been your solace' (*C*, IV-i, 28). Once he is with the Volscians, she wants him back in Rome:

> O my mother, mother! O!
> You have won a happy victory for Rome;
> But for your son, believe it, O, believe it,
> Most dangerously you have with him prevail'd,
> If not most mortal to him. But let it come.
>
> (*C*, V-iii, 188–192)

There is an inverted imaginary drama within the drama at work in *Coriolanus*. The father is dead and absent, but the mother, instead, is omnipresent, all powerful and menacing. The effect of the phallic mother on her son is revealed when Coriolanus announces that he is ready to replace his relationship with Virgilia with a homoerotic bond with Aufidius, the Volscian general. This is revealed in Act-IV, Scene-iv, when Coriolanus knocks at the gate of the enemy city:

> My birthplace hate I, and my love's upon
> This enemy town. I'll enter. If he slay me,
> He does fair justice; if he give me way
> I'll do his country service.
>
> (*C*, IV-iv, 23–26)

He takes the position of the phallus, the marker of Aufidius's desire in this scene when Aufidius welcomes him. This is a manifestation of a son in the grip of a phallic mother for, as Dor says, '[t]he imago of this phallic mother will determine the pervert's later relations with other women. He will not renounce women even though, as in the case of homosexuality, he may look for them in other men' (Dor, 1999b, 57):

But come in.
Let me commend thee first to those that shall
Say yea to thy desires. A thousand welcomes!

(*C*, IV, v, 144–146)

There is another important thread of feminine desire in Virgilia, described by her husband in Act- II, Scene-i, as 'gracious silence'. We can take this silence as an irony in relation to her desire, which is only a desire dependant on Coriolanus's desires. For a woman, desire is always dependent on masculine desire. Coriolanus compares her eyes with the eyes of those mothers who don't have sons (the phallus). The son always functions to fulfil a woman's desire to have the phallus. This is evident when Coriolanus says to Virgilia:

My gracious silence, hail!
Wouldst thou have laugh'd had I come coffin'd home,
That weep'st to see me triumph? Ah, my dear,
Such eyes the widows in Corioles wear,
And mothers that lack sons.

(*C*, II-i, 174–178)

Her silence in the drama shows her feminine desire that is a masquerade and is contingent on her husband's, thus ensuring her status as *being* the phallus, not the masculine position of *having* the phallus. This contingency is displayed when she stops venturing out of home while Coriolanus is away.

The Coriolanus-Aufidius relationship in the play makes it clear that desire is infinitely fluid. Coriolanus practically falls into the position of *being* the phallus for Aufidius, his enemy-cum-ideal ego when he returns to him as a prodigal son. When in Act-IV, Scene-iv, as Coriolanus reaches the gate of his enemy's city, his status reverts from being the hero warrior to that of a humiliated beggar. However, he also reveals here his unconscious love for Cominius:

My birthplace hate I, and my love's upon
This enemy town. I'll enter; if he slay me.

(*C*, IV-iv, 24–25)

As though seeing each other in a mirror, Aufidius reciprocates this love by identifying 'Worthy Martius', as a site of the phallus. Coriolanus takes the feminine position in his desire, becoming the phallus for Aufidius:

> Thou noble thing, more dances my rapt heart
> Then when I first my wedded mistress saw.
> (*C*, IV-v, 117–118)

> Twelve several times, and I have nightly since
> Dreamt of encounters 'twixt thyself and me –
> We have been down together in my sleep
> Unbuckling helms, fisting each other's throat –
> And waked half dead with nothing. Worthy Martius. (*C*, IV-v, 123–127)

This is a very dramatic development in the whole play, and comes to a climax in Act-V, Scene-i, when Coriolanus is ready to sacrifice everything for this love. When Menenius and Cominius arrive at the Volscian camp to unsuccessfully try to persuade Coriolanus to return home, he says:

> Wife, mother, child, I know not. My affairs
> Are servanted to others. Though I owe
> My revenge properly, my remission lies
> In Volscian breasts.
> (*C*, V-I, 82–85)

When a male subject shifts the status of his desire from *having* to *being* the phallus, this gives rise to a deep-seated rivalry between the partners, because such a shift is censured by the phallocentric culture. When Coriolanus decides to return home, Aufidius becomes his enemy and murderer. In the earlier scenes of the play, Coriolanus had similar feelings for Aufidius. Another example of such love/hate relationship can be found in Shakespeare's narrative poem, *Rape of Lucrece*, where Tarquin arrives in Collatium, and in the depth of the night visits Lucrece's chamber only to rape her. This rape displays significant rivalry between Tarquin and Lucrece's husband Brutus.

Virgilia represents the extreme opposite of the phallic mother in *Coriolanus*. She is the epitome of the *true* woman to which I will return in a moment. I wish now to present another version of the desire of the phallic woman, identified as the phallic mother in the pre-Oedipal fantasy, often associated with horror and fear. Such phallic mothers with supernatural powers are abundant in literature. Beside the Gorgons in Greek mythology of which Medusa was one, in Euripides' play *Medea*, the female protagonist kills her children and her husband. Dostoyevsky's *Crime and Punishment* revolves around an evil old ruthless female moneylender whose murder is the recurrent obsession of the novel.

In *Ulysses*, Stephen Dedalus refuses to pray for his mother at her deathbed. No other literary text can reveal this version of the phallic mother and its surrounding horror and mayhem better than Shakespeare's *Macbeth.*

The phallic lady Macbeth

Shakespeare offers another model of the phallic mother, Lady Macbeth, a wo(Man) of action in *Macbeth.* She does what Volumnia would have been happy only to fantasize about. The criminality of Lady Macbeth's actions remains the only difference between these two characters. Lady Macbeth plans and assists in the murder but refrains from killing the king herself only because as she says he looked like her father in sleep. More ironically, she wants to kill him but by way of someone else. When she receives her husband's letter in Act-I, Scene-iv, containing the news of his promotion and the coming of the King to their castle, she instantly begins to fantasize about the murder:

> Hie thee hither,
> That I may pour my spirits in thine ear,
> And chastise with the valour of my tongue
> All that impedes thee from the golden round,
> Which fate and metaphysical aid doth seem
> To have thee crown'd withal.
>
> (*M*, I-iv, 25–30)

It is Lady Macbeth who persuades her husband to commit the murder of King Duncan. In Act-I, Scene-v, we find her in a critical moment when she condemns the humanity in her husband's character that is too weak to carry out the murder:

> Yet do I fear thy nature:
> It is too full o'the milk of human kindness.
>
> (*M*, I-v, 15–16)

Lady Macbeth talks to herself about her husband and sees herself as a free and fearless spirit and a remedy for his weakness, and later she shows in a ruthless dramatic moment, her phallic desire, by committing crimes for her husband's sake. However, her wish to be unsexed confirms and re-enforces her rejection of femininity in the hope of becoming capable of doing things that would have been expected only from a male character in the Elizabethan era. In her soliloquy, she fantasizes about the wildness and chilling cruelty that resonate with phallic mothers in pre-Oedipal fantasy, for they are the sort of mothers who represent the so-called horror of femininity.

> Under my battlements. Come, you Spirits
> That tend on mortal thoughts, unsex me here,
> And fill me, from the crown to toe, top-full
> Of direst cruelty! Make thick my blood.
>
> (*M*, I-v, 39–42)

Then she goes further by praising and shaking her 'knife' – the phallus that always remains veiled in order to have its effect on both sexes. The phallus, as the marker of desire, makes her a phallic woman in the symbolic order, which is a masculine position that she wants to possess:

> That my keen knife see not the wound it makes,
> Nor Heaven peep through the blanket of the dark,
> To cry, 'Hold, hold!'
>
> (*M*, I-v, 51–53)

As soon as the Macbeths accomplish their mission by killing the king, we find both characters at a point where they shed their former personality traits, and Lady Macbeth is even ready to change her biological sex. Lady Macbeth is no longer the self-conscious ambitious woman while her husband becomes more cruel and a man of action. Indeed, she becomes mad when her symptom resurfaces vigorously in the real. She now has fits, sleep-walks, has uncanny feelings of guilt and sees apparitions. Her doctor understands that her illness is of an unusual kind and he seems unable to '[r]aze out the written troubles of the brain' (*M*, V-iii, 44). Up until Act-II, Scene-iii, when she faints upon hearing Macbeth talking about killing two grooms, Lady Macbeth remains a *femme à pastiche*, who like Medea will commit any crime for the love of her husband. The faint signals her gradual fall into the abyss of madness that ends in her death when her cry is heard on stage in Act-V, Scene-v. That faint and cry demarcate a peculiar space in the play in which Lady Macbeth proceeds to crossover from the symbolic to the real of *jouissance*, because as a woman, she cannot express her symptomatic femininity symbolically anymore. This is the time that she is subjected to a loss, the loss that heralds, on her part, the suspension of desire. As she says at the outset of Act-III, Scene-ii:

> Naught's had, all's spent,
> Where our desire is got without content.
> 'Tis safer to be that which we destroy
> Than by destruction dwell in doubtful joy.
>
> (*M*, III- ii, 6–9)

Thus, Lady Macbeth gives up on a phallic desire to identify with her symptom and enjoy her symptom beyond the boundaries of the symbolic. Shakespeare gives us a glimpse of her compulsive obsession, which, in clinical Lacanian psychoanalysis would be interpreted as a subject's attempt to master the Other's *jouissance.* Her obsessive hand washing, rumination on the thoughts of murdering King Duncan and the enormous guilt it generates in her, are parts of her symptom. Moreover, the sleepwalking also involves a ritual session of writing, as the Gentlewoman tells the frustrated doctor:

> I have seen her rise from her bed, throw her nightgown upon
> her, unlock her closet, take forth paper, fold it, write upon't, read it, afterwards seal it, and again return to bed.
>
> (*M,* V-i, 4–6)

This sudden shift in Lady Macbeth's thought and behaviour was interpreted by Freud as a symptom indicating the wreckage of the subject. As he writes in his essay, 'Those Wrecked by Success':

> We may take as an example of a person who collapses on reaching success, after striving for it with single-minded energy, the figure of Shakespeare's Lady Macbeth. Beforehand there is no hesitation, no sign of any internal conflict in her, any endeavor but that of overcoming the scruples of her ambitious yet tender-minded husband. She is ready to sacrifice even her womanliness to her murderous intentions. (Freud, 1988, 301)

Freud postulates that at a point when, at the ego level, conscious demand meets its ultimate satisfaction, at the level of unconscious desire, it gives rise to pathological frustration. This is a condition he terms *Versagung* (denial of the self and instinctual satisfaction). This is probably the reason why Freud and Lacan both ask analysts to prevent satisfaction of an analysand's desire by keeping the signifier of demand for love appearing and re-appearing within his/her discourse, all in all, to keep desire unsatisfied. The Freudian libidinal wish here is translated by Lacan into a demand for love, which must be preserved from satisfaction in order to preserve that pathogenic conflict between conscious and unconscious demands, or in other words, to keep the internal and external frustrations of an analysand at bay. This clears up another tangle in desire. In any structure, there remains a defensive wall, preventing a subject from falling into madness. To put it in other words, as soon as a subject ceases to desire, or when desire itself refuses its metonymic displacement, denial, death or falling into the world of the real happen in the life of the subject.

Freud's argument here, nonetheless, ends in deadlock, when he suggests that womanliness for Lady Macbeth is both a power for carrying out the crime, and a potential that she has to shun in order to achieve her goal. 'She is ready to sacrifice', Freud says, 'even her womanliness to her murderous intention, without reflecting on the decisive part which this womanliness must play when the question afterwards arises of preserving the aim of her ambition, which has been attained through a crime' (Freud, 1988, 301–302). Freud thus suggests that womanliness has to be sacrificed for the sake of womanliness. The answer to this paradox of Lady Macbeth lies in what we have termed a suspension of her own feminine desire.

Given the early Lady Macbeth's position as phallic mother, we can argue that she, no doubt, is the fourth sister of the three witches. As Janet Adelman writes in *Suffocating Mothers*, Lady Macbeth 'fuses' in many ways with the witches. The most spectacular example of this alliance lies in her perverse and inhuman pattern of mothering. Lady Macbeth embodies '[m]alignant female power both in the cosmos and in the family' (Adelman, 1992, 136). This identification with the witches intensifies when in Act-I, Scene-vii, Lady Macbeth gives us a glimpse of her cannibalistic fantasy in which we can see the pre-Oedipal image of a 'devouring' and all pervasive mother. Lady Macbeth's behaviour here is described by Adelman as '[p]erverse nursery traditionally attributed to witches' (ibid.):

> – I have given suck, and know
> How tender 'tis to love the babe that milk me:
> I would, while it was smiling in my face,
> Have pluck'd my nipple from his boneless gums,
> And dash'd the brain out, had I so sworn
> As you have done to this.
>
> (*M*, I-vii, 54–59)

A moment later in the same scene, when she has prepared her husband to carry out the crime, Macbeth begins to sense the man that his wife wants him to be. He confirms this when he begs her to bear only male children because her 'mettle' is essentially masculine:

> Bring forth man-children only:
> For thy undaunted mettle should compose
> Nothing but males.
>
> (*M*, I-vii, 73–75)

By looking at the similarity between Volumnia, Coriolanus and the Macbeths, we find infantile fantasy at work. For Coriolanus, his mother is the one who teaches, threatens and provides for the re-enactment of his infantile fantasy in the symbolic. Macbeth himself takes up the position of the son in the fantasy. Lady Macbeth teaches her husband (man)liness and ideal masculine attributes; Volumnia teaches her son to be in appearance like a 'flower' and in content like a 'serpent' (*C*, I-v, 64, 65).

In reading a literary text, we find apt illustrations of psychoanalytic themes. Thus, one may understand why for Lacan, the truth about desire is inherent in literature. Lacan insists desire is always at work in interpretation. In his soliloquy at the end of Act-II, Scene-I, after murdering Duncan, Macbeth offers a mental conceptualization of the phallus in terms of a 'dagger', an unconscious equivalent of the image of the phallus. In Lacan's teaching, the phallus signifies nothingness, emptiness and a zero ground, but it is still the signifier and marker of the desire that is grounded in this emptiness:

Is this a dagger, which I see before me,
The handle toward my hand? Come, let me clutch
Thee –
I have thee not, and yet I see thee still.
Art thou not, fatal vision, sensible . . .
To feeling, as to right? Or art thou but
A dagger of the mind, a false creation,
Proceeding from the oppressed brain?
I see thee yet, in form as palpable
As this which I now draw.
Thou marshall'st me the way that I was going;
And such an instrument I was to use –

(*M*, II-I, 32–39)

The fluidity of feminine desire in *The Merchant of Venice*

The Merchant of Venice presents a spectacle of the structure of desire as well as the plurality and fluidity of feminine desire. In Lacan, the masculine and feminine positions are not essentially static. They can cross over at any time and in any direction. The comedy draws a topological account of the structure of feminine desire in relation to the object *a*. As Lacan insists that Hamlet's desire is always at the level of the Other, his female counterpart, Portia's desire stays always at the level of an object *a*, which guarantees her status throughout the play as a desiring woman in the phallic economy.

We are introduced, at the outset, to the central concern of the play, a rich and beautiful heiress, Portia unable to choose the course of her own desire because her dead father's will (the symbol of the phallic law in the play), states that she could only marry a suitor who chose the correct casket from among three caskets, one of which hides her picture. When Portia enters in Act-I, Scene-ii, she says that her body is weary of this world, perhaps because her own essential feminine desire is foreclosed by the law of the father, for only her dead father's will can decide who she can marry:

– O me the word 'choose'! I may neither
Choose who I would, nor refuse who I dislike, so is the

will of a living daughter curb'd by the will of a dead
father: is it not hard Nerissa, that I cannot choose one,
nor refuse one.

(*MV*, I-ii, 22–26)

The casket test in the play bears out the claims of Lacanian theory about object *a*, which always remains in the dialectic of desire as the most precious treasure but is always hidden in a worthless box. The lure and the magic of the object is inherent in the fact that it can solicit, levy, and, animate desire. The object *a* that is a substitute for the missing *jouissance*, the imaginary locus of the Other, has a determining role in sustaining woman's desire. This is a desire that in the symbolic register needs to objectify something in order to be activated, for this objectification enables a subject to re-enact the primordial loss of the Other by putting object *a* in the centre of its desire.

A woman identifies with object *a* so that she can sustain herself as an object of masculine desire. Portia knows that when it comes to her desire, her picture hidden in the lead chest is more important than her own self, because this is the object *a* that guarantees her status as a desired woman. From Lacan we know that object *a* for a subject is something more than the subject itself because the subject's desire relies on it. That is why Portia metaphorically says to one of her suitors that she herself is locked up in one of the chests. Just before Bassanio attempts the test, she exclaims:

– I am lock'd in one of them –
if you love me, you will find me out.

(*MV*, III-ii, 40–41)

There are three caskets of gold, silver and lead. A suitor must select the right one in order to marry Portia. This can be understood literally as the fantasy of the dead father. Many princes come forward from all corners of the world to court Portia but all fail until Bassanio comes forward, chooses the right one and marries Portia in Act-III, Scene-ii. Each casket has an inscription. The right casket, the lead one has the apt inscription, '*Who chooseth me, must give and hazard all he hath,*' (*MV*, II-ix, 21). This conforms to the logic of the object *a*. Lacan always defines object *a* as an ineffable symbol which needs a subject's sacrifice in order to become the symbol of lack of being. This object is in the realm of the real. Thus it needs a sacrifice in order to become the witness to a subject's destruction. This is why the core meaning is hidden in the inscription of what is ostensibly the most worthless of all the caskets. This signifying effect produced by the inscription entails what Lacan terms in *Encore* an '[a]ffinity between *a* and its envelope' (Lacan, 1998a, 93). Bassanio's discovery of Portia's picture in the cheap lead, does not seem to be accidental because it highlights the love bond between Portia and Bassanio, especially Portia's desire. This 'dull lead', alongside gold and silver recalls Socrates' proverbial ugly face in which Alcibiades' desire is invested, of which Lacan writes, '[t]he inestimable treasure that Alcibiades declares is contained in the rustic box the figure of Socrates is to him' (Lacan, 2002, 309).

Lacan's theory of desire untangles the secret behind the three caskets that found their way into Shakespeare's text. For Freud this episode was problematic. In his essay 'The Theme of The Three Caskets', Freud presents an Oedipal reading of the story of the caskets, where he finally concludes that the three caskets are three women that function as primordial objects of desire. Freud attributes King Lear's three daughters and his test of their loyalty and love for the king to a similar story. Lear disinherits the youngest daughter Cordelia who refuses to compete with her sisters, and distributes his kingdom between Goneril and Regan. When ill-treated by his best loved and rewarded daughters, he ultimately returns to Cordelia, and dies while carrying her dead body. Freud concludes that the three caskets in *The Merchant* and three daughters in *King Lear* represent three figures of the mother. The lead casket is like the abandoned Cordelia who appeared the most worthless but becomes the winner.

The object *a* shows up in *The Merchant* in many shapes and fashions, however, always with a visual and an imaginary signification. As soon as Bassanio chooses the correct chest that contains Portia's picture, the object *a* persists as a knot that ties the loss in the Other to a phenomenological object outside the symbolic order. The lead casket is replaced by a ring when Bassanio marries Portia. Portia identifies with the ring as a token of her desire and she insists Bassanio not lose it in any circumstances. This re-enacts the exchange involved in the economy of desire. The ring functions now as the object-cause of Portia's desire and an assurance for her that Bassanio has to constitute her once again as his object of desire. Thus, the ring obtains its importance from the fact that if Bassanio loses it or gives it away, it would break the love bond. This has been hinted at by Portia the very minute Bassanio places the ring on his finger:

> – but when this ring
> parts from this finger, then parts life from hence –
> O then be bold to say Bassanio's dead.
>
> (*MV*, III-ii, 83–85)

This slippage along a metonymic chain is a slippage from one object to another. This is true in relation to the desire of other characters. Narissa, for instance, gives a ring to her lover Gratiano insisting he should never lose it. In a different setting, however, Jessica steals her father's chest of money and jewellery and gives it to her lover Lorenzo, before eloping with him. For Portia, however, identification with object *a* at both the level of real life and fantasy has become a source of access to *jouissance*. This is confirmed by Portia's status being reaffirmed as the semblance of the lost Other for Bassanio. As Lacan says, '[t]he subject sustains himself as desiring in relation to an ever more complex signifying ensemble' (Lacan, 1979a, 185). This idea is reinforced when Portia, succeeds in saving Antonio's life. Shylock wants a pound of Antonio's flesh, an absolute condition of the bond signed between them, for the latter has failed to repay a loan within three months:

> – let the forfeit
> Be nominated for an equal pound
> Of your fair flesh, to be cut off and taken
> In what part of your body pleaseth me.
>
> (*MV*, I-iii, 147–150)

This pound of flesh is the central object in the play which reveals a configuration in the literary text of what Lacan theorizes as the phallus, as well as object *a*. Instead of being articulated in the signifying chain, the object *a* re-appears in its crude and real shape as a pound of flesh provoking another aspect of love between Antonio and Bassanio. When the ring is lost, Bassanio himself takes the place of the phallus. He thus becomes a signifier of Antonio's desire. Shylock hints that he would cut off whichever part of Antonio's body that he likes, namely a pound of flesh from the hip or breast close to the heart. This cutting of the body or plucking an organ from it re-inforces the meaning of desire that begins with a cut and lack.

Roberto Harari takes up this notion in *Lacan's Seminar on 'Anxiety'*, and remarks that in Shakespeare's play the object *a* is 'reincarnated in the organ' (Harari, 2001, 165). As Harari emphasizes, in the case of Shylock, object *a* makes its presence more radical for it recalls the cut a subject has to inflict on its own flesh and blood. He quotes Lacan, '[i]t is always with our flesh that we must pay off the debt' (Lacan cited in Harari, 2001, 166). Elsewhere in the play, however, the price is usually paid with money, jewellery, a ring and so on. Keeping in mind Lacan's comments on *The Merchant*, we may argue that Shylock's demand of 'a pound of flesh', reveals two facts: first, the relation of object *a* to desire, the cut which he calls objectality that refers to the splitting of the subject by the signifier. Second, it shows his intention that is called objectivity that occurs in a literary text as a fantasy of the barred subject in its relation to the object *a*.

In a similar manner, but in a twist of gender transposition similar to the one we have seen between Coriolanus and Aufidius, Antonio is ready to sacrifice his life for Bassanio, because the latter occupies the status of object *a* in relation to Antonio's desire. Ironically, Portia knows about this secret love bond. She is defiant when Lorenzo, at the beginning of Act-III, disapproves of her decision to undertake a trip to Venice in order to save Antonio's life, just after she marries Bassanio:

– this Antonio
Being the bosom lover of my lord,
Must needs be like my lord. If it be so,
How little is the cost I have bestowed
In purchasing the semblance of my soul.

(*MV*, III-iv, 17–20)

Her decision to go to Venice and appear as a male lawyer at the court shows us her fantasy of *having* the phallus. She reveals this fantasy, through which she stages her desire, when she confides in Nerissa, her maid, who later poses as her male clerk in the court. In their fantasy, they indeed overcome their lack of the phallus in the court scene but ironically only when they are no more women, or to be more precise no longer wives in the eyes of their husbands. She appears all male and menacing, wearing a dagger and her talk parodies masculine demeanour.

They shall Nerissa: but in such a habit,
That they shall think we are accomplished
With that we lack; I'll hold thee any wager
When we are both accoutered like young men
I'll prove the prettier fellow of the two,
And wear my dagger with the braver grace.

(*MV*, III-iv, 60–65)

The court scene in Act-IV, Scene-i, brings us back to the ring, Lacan's object *a*, that shifts its location and function once again. Shakespeare's masterful use of dramatic irony intensifies this shift. This shift brings in another test as well, the test of loyalty that we will call the ring-test. Here Bassanio and Gratiano both fail to sustain their desires by desiring Portia and Nerissa. Bassanio hints at this when he is ready to sacrifice everything including his love for Portia in exchange for his life:

Antonio, I am married to a wife
Which is as dear to me as life itself?
But life itself, my wife, and all the world,
Are not with me esteem'd above thy life.
I would lose all, as sacrifice them all
Here to this devil, to deliver you.

(*MV*, IV-I, 280–285)

Our sympathy with Bassanio's predicament, caught between two bonds of love, is re-inforced when his double loyalty comes to light. When in court Portia insists on getting Bassanio's ring, he seems adamant to keep it in his possession at all costs. He seems to fetishize the ring exactly as Portia recommends. A little while later, when Antonio asks him to give his ring, he surprises us by succumbing to this request quite easily. Towards the end of Act-IV, he takes the ring off his finger and asks Gratiano to give it to the lawyer as a reward for her effort in saving Antonio's life:

> ANTONIO: My lord Bassanio, let him have the ring,
> Let his deservings and my love withal
> Be valued 'gainst your wife's commandment.
> BASSANIO: Go Gratiano, run and overtake him,
> Give him the ring, and bring him if thou canst.
>
> (*MV*, IV-I, 447–451)

This giving away of the ring functions exactly like the stolen handkerchief in *Othello*, as the end of a love bond. However in the latter, the object *a* – the handkerchief – has been stolen by an intruder into the intersubjective relation whereas, in *The Merchant* the ring is taken away because of an intention of the one party in the bond of desire and love, thus showing a certain one-sidedness. Like the fairytale treasures of the *Arabian Nights*, the caskets of gold, silver, lead, jewellery, money, a pound of flesh, rings and so on, as well as their circulation in a metonymic itinerary, all produce a signification with regard to the lacking signifier to which love and desire are addressed.

The last melodramatic scene, with which Shakespeare rounds off his play, presents one last exhibition of the object *a* in a bathos where Portia fantasizes making love with the lawyer (her own self) as the one who possesses the ring. Where the ring is present so also shall love be present as well as desire, for it is the object *a*, the object that causes desire. This object, in the meantime, is the symbol of lack and emptiness from which desire arises.

In contrast to the rest of the play, Portia appears in the last scene in a masculine position in the drama of desire as the imagined possessor of the phallus. This position is reinforced as soon as she, first, rescues Antonio's body and punishes the castrating father Shylock instead, and second, when she takes the ring. Possession of the ring, thus, changes her position from being an object *a* into a desiring being in fantasy. The exchange of the object *a* in *The Merchant* appears in its crude form when it is a pound of flesh, the signifier of lack; and then in a more symbolic form when it is the ring. In itself, this may sound naïve and outside any semantiç representation or semiotic reality, but as unconscious equivalents in fantasy, these two function as a compliment, marking the locus of the cut or void upon which desire stands. As a reminder of the lost Other, the object *a* always escapes language, as it is characterized often in terms of an excess and a surplus that is rooted deeply in the premature birth and fragmented body of the child in the imaginary. That is why in each scenario, Portia desperately makes attempts to place the insignia of her desire everywhere she wants to set desire in motion.

In sum, the theatricalization of feminine desire in Shakespeare's text gives credence to Lacan's claims that feminine desire can have multiple structures and may have access to dual *jouissance,* namely phallic *jouissance* and beyond the boundary of the phallic economy. Even masculine desire crosses the gender divide as Shakespeare shows in *Coriolanus* and *Macbeth.* Feminine desire is not constituted as a single category but as multiple modes of desire. Lacan's diagram of sexuation shows this in topological terms. On the feminine side, a woman functions as the object *a,* the object that causes the other's desire. On the masculine side, she is inscribed in phallic space, as in the case of Volumnia, Lady Macbeth (in the first scenes of the play), and, at times, Portia. Besides, as we saw, many of Shakespeare's male characters also position themselves on either side of the diagram. As *Macbeth* reveals, the suspension of desire pushes a woman to the excesses of the real, which remains often outside the boundaries of the symbolic and imaginary.

They are persistent pathological yearnings, and function as part of her desire. This is what Lacan emphasizes in *Television* when he argues that desire reveals itself in the persistence of demands in the matheme, d—$<> D (desire in relation to the barred subject identified as a demand). In stark contrast to her mother-in-law, Virgilia accepts her lack, as Shakespeare describes her exclusion and the exclusion of her essential femininity *per se* from the symbolic order as silence. What is the object of her desire then if she functions as an object for the motivation of other desire? The question is answered by Portia and Virgilia as, for both, the desire of the other guarantees their own desirability. Their desire is ensured in the symbolic as long as they are being loved and desired by men.

In these three Shakespeare's plays, we have revealed succinctly three vignettes of feminine desire presented in multiple and diversified structures at the core of which we find an illustration of a fixation on three unconscious choices. Some of the choices imply a diversion from femininity's inscription in masculinity, and its identification with the phallus and object *a,* an identification that positively locates a desiring woman in a place where she can function as the sole representative of the Other and the Other's desire. Far from being determined by biological sexuality, these choices characterize a process by which a subject takes up gendered positions in the unconscious. The sexed subject thus constitutes an imaginary identification in relation to the phallic function. Only by being an object *a,* or 'signifier of the One' can this entry into the Other be made possible. Apart from Lady Macbeth's experience of the real that leads to her death, one specific structure of feminine desire that Lacan describes in terms of feminine *jouissance* remains unexplored. Does this *jouissance,* have to be identified with mysticism and the transcendental space of ecstasy? Does Lacan want to feminize mysticism or mystify feminine desire? We will take up this issue in the next chapter, when we venture into the world of John Donne, the epitome of mysticism in Western literature.

Chapter 6

John Donne's Hymns to Love, Desire and *Jouissance*

The drama of desire in Donne's poetry opens with the mournful agonies of separation, and by implication, lack in being, and nostalgia for the recovery of the wholeness associated with the lost primal object. The agony over separation and the joy over the recovery of the lost object is the mystic cycle in Donne's poetry. Two mystical leitmotifs give rise to the division in Donne between love and divine poetry. The devotional religious poetry exemplifies a desire that is always on the side of the law and castration, placing limits on that desire crossing over into narcissistic masochism, or in other words, a *jouissance* of suffering. The second category constitutes a structure of a love beyond sexual affinity that calls for a *jouissance* that Lacan identifies as feminine and mystical. Donne draws on both categories in his poetry, creating an *either-or* situation for desire and *jouissance.* The following elegy points to a river of fire that runs beneath Donne's poetics: the fire rises with a rhapsodic love and the river surges with the agonies of desire and *jouissance*:

> Where is that holy fire, which verse is said
> To have? Is that enhancing force decayed?
> Verse, that draws Nature's work, from Nature's law,
> Thee, her best work, to her work cannot draw.
> Have my tears quenched my old poetic fire;
> Why quenched they not as well, that of desire?
> Thoughts, my mind's creatures, often are with thee,
> But I, their maker, want their liberty.
> . . .
> O cure me this loving madness, and restore
> Me to me; thee, my half, my all, my more.
>
> ('*Sappho Philaenis*', 1–8; 12–14; 57–58)

In these lines, the key question the poet wonders about is the eternity of desire, and its unquenchable nature. The 'holy fire' and the 'madness' represent the poet's unquenchable desire.

In this chapter, I wish to demystify mysticism by deconstructing Donne's metaphysical poetry and its theological, metaphysico-erotic and other subspecies. With late Lacan's theoretical insights as dramatized in Donne's poetry, I argue that mystical experience, as both art and *sinthome*, gives access to various kinds of *jouissance*. I will attempt to expose the vicissitudes of mystical experience in Donne's poetry, which like any other mystic literary discourse, brings desire, love and *jouissance* into play. In Donne's divine poems, repressed desire and the symbolic law co-exist side by side, and in his love poems, this bond falls apart, *jouissance* takes over his poetics. I shall also examine several paradigms of *jouissance* and their literary contexts in Donne's poetry, namely *jouis-sense*, the *sinthome* of the enigmas (where love is discussed in correlation with the erotic), a *jouissance* of ecstasy and a divine madness (feminine *jouissance* or the *jouissance* of the body), the *jouissance* of suffering, and phallic *jouissance*. Then, I will try to take on Lacan's attempt to feminize the entire mystical literary discourse by showing the paradoxes of his theory that lays down an empirical gender identity for *jouissance* beyond the phallic economy. Inferring from Lacan's various approaches to mysticism, I also argue that the essence of mystical *jouissance* is the subject's own bodily *jouissance*. As the principal proposition in this chapter, I conclude that the various forms of these ecstatic and holy enjoyments of the mystical body symbolize the *jouissance* of the Other's body.

Let us begin by looking at Donne's divine poetry, even though chronologically it comes after his love poems. We have done this because ironically his love lyrics are more mystical than his divine poems. Love poems in Donne, like every mystical poet, function as love letters which address the Other and meditate on the Other. Donne's divine poems dramatize desire in terms of the horror of the Biblical conviction of the sinfulness of the human soul that yearns for redemption in the afterlife. The love poetry presents hedonistic eroticism of the body in relation to transcendental and idealized love object. This mystical love produces an illusion of re-finding the lost object, which, in fact, has its full presence at the heart of desire as an inaccessible void. This is because desire has no object beyond an elusive one that, in mystical love, sets a subject free from the whirlpool of desire, for a desiring subject is always in touch with suffering, guilt and pain. In desire, the void of loss seems unbridgeable; and, as such, the process of desire makes the metonymic reproduction of the substitute object possible. However, this metonymic structure produces substitutes. This only defers the recovery of the primal object.

In a Lacanian way, Kristeva distinguishes this by postulating in *Tales of Love* that desire has a metonymic and love a metaphorical object. She adds that, '[t]he former controls the phantasmatic *narrative*. The latter outlines the *crystallization* of fantasy and rules the poeticalness of the discourse of love' (Kristeva, 1987, 30). Fantasy, with the practical backing of an erotic imagery and a voluptuous bodily sensuality, connects a mystical desiring subject with the assumed deity. As such, in Donne's poetry, fantasy is crystallized by means of hedonistic, profane and spiritual love. This may well be considered the defining ambience of the mystical dimension of Donne's poetry that treats the body as the real site of excessive pleasures, even transubstantiating it into the substance of *jouissance*. This theologization of bodily and spiritual sexuality very much concerns Lacan in his dealing with mysticism. Paraphrasing Lacan, Miller writes, '[t]here is a body that talks. There is a body that *jouit* in different ways. The place of *jouissance* is always the same, the body' (Miller, 2003, 44). This spells out the reason why mystic poetry in all cultures is incomprehensible without a predilection for epicurean erotomania. The eroticism of mystic discourse functions as a means of arousal, and a motive for bodily rapture – bodily *jouissance* – that is often referred to as a mystical dissipation that the mystic or some women, as Lacan insists in *Encore*, experience without understanding. The inclusion of the One, the Thing or God in this mystical game plunges the soul of the subject into *jouissance*, the eternity of being that brings a sense of cohesion and *gestalt* to the narcissistic self in which the ego and the Other are always at odds. From our theoretical exploration, we know that the ego emerges via separation from the primal object, and the Other is an unconscious construct that arises from the absence and experience of the lost object. By virtue of transference which allows for substitution of the loved object, love makes the forbidden object of desire accessible, and *jouissance* bestows upon the subject joys and suffering through the loss and imaginary rediscovery of this proto-object of desire. Donne's divine poetry thus reveals the heterogeneous pattern of mystical experience.

In his poetry, Donne presents a panorama of desire, love and *jouissance*, in correlation with each other. The lamenting and mournful mode of Donne's *Holy Sonnets* functions as a narrative of desire, a desire that yields itself to the same law that gave birth to it. What does this last statement mean? From Lacan we know that the law is an agency that promulgates a universal principle of inter-subjective exchange in the symbolic. Desire is the prototype of this exchange but it also regulates this principle. On the other hand, desire itself is a production of this law, for the law through its legislative role prohibits the association of the subject with the primary object of love. In their dialectical relationship, desire is a product of the law and the law in turn imposes limits on it. 'Divine Meditations' immerses the reader in a desire that places the subject between two deaths, the death of entry into language or logos, and the literal death of the body. In this *mis-en-abîme* of desire, Donne finds himself with 'Despaire behind, and death before.' The first death is brought about by the taboo of the law and thus by desire; and the second, by natural causes. This leads the subject towards self-deprecation and guilt in order to keep the space of desire open:

> Thou hast made me, and shall thy worke decay?
> Repaire me now, for now mine end doth haste,

I run to death, and death meets me as fast,
And all my pleasures are like yesterday,
I dare not move my dim eyes any way,
Despaire behind, and death before doth cast
Such terror, and my feeble flesh doth waste
By sin in it, which it towards hell doth weight.
('Divine Meditations', Sonnet I, 1–8)

These lines are saturated with melancholia and a feeling of the full force of a subject's desire brought about by the terror produced by the law of the tyrannical super-ego that the symbolic order has in store for the subject. Desire expresses itself through pain and suffering, making the subject conscious of his sinful guilty 'feeble flesh', as Donne says. The feeling of overwhelming guilt in the first and second rhyming couplets of the poem is part of that inexorable punishing agency in which the desiring subject is ensnared. It makes the poet seem '[b]urdened by the consciousness of his sins and aware of his need for mercy at the judgement' (Gardner, 1952, xxxvi). Pain beyond the pleasure principle is the main issue that Donne's sonnet wants to dramatize. This is reflected in words such as, 'despair', 'death', 'feeble flesh', 'sin', 'dim eyes' and 'decay'. These words present an allegory of original sin, which, in Lacanian psychoanalytical theory, makes unconscious guilt appear in terms of a moral violation. The fifth quatrain proclaims that sinfulness and blackness submerge both the body and the spirit, causing an existential feeling of suffering. The essential sinfulness, here, has been overlaid by the Biblical injunction regarding original sin. This self-reproach (or 'self-insult' to use Lacan's words), reveals a ceaseless suffering that is the ultimate goal of a desire which, on the one hand, cannot cross the boundaries of the law, and on the other, remains unable to endure the burden that this law has inflicted upon it.

That sufferance was my sin, now I repent;
Because I did suffer I must suffer pain.
Th' hydroptic drunkard, and night-scouting thief,
The itchy lecher, and self tickling proud
('Divine Meditations', Sonnet III, 7–8)

The joy of pain is the favourite topic of mystics in all traditions. Spinoza saw its source in the lost thing that we can never have. As he wrote, '[e]motional distress and unhappiness have their origin especially in excessive love towards a thing subject to considerable instability, a thing which we can never completely possess' (Spinoza, cited in Nussbaum, 2001, 505). Such a mystical pain allies itself with eroticism in Georges Bataille. Like Father Tesson, Bataille considered death to be a real spiritual unity with God. However, Bataille's literary text with its insistence on the excesses of sexual pleasure undermines the painful joy in mystical love.

Mourning and sadomasochism represent in mystical texts subjective efforts to re-experience and repeat the loss of what, following Freud, Lacan defines as 'the Thing'. The 'Divine Meditations' progress by creating image upon image, inviting the reader to see the horror of a death that separates body from soul. This estrangement is the alienation of the subject in language where all the horrors, pain and self-punishment reflect the implication of the subject's entry into the field of desire. The melancholy of the poem becomes darker and darker, displaying desire and the tyranny of the law, which develop in the last stage of the Oedipus complex. Donne shows this in Sonnet-III, and Sonnet-VI:

> O might those sighes and teares returne againe
> Into my breast and eyes, which I have spent,
> That I might in this holy discontent
> Mourne with some fruit, as I have mourn'd in vaine;
> In mine Idolatry what showres of rain
> Mine eyes did waste . . .
>
> ('Divine Meditations', Sonnet III, 1–6)

> And gluttonous death, will instantly unjoint
> My body, and soul, and I shall sleep a space,
> But my'ever-waking part shall see that face,
> Whose fear already shakes my every joint:
> Then, as my soul, to heaven her first seat, takes flight,
> And earth-born body, in the earth shall dwell,
> So, fall my sins, that all may have their right,
> To what they are bred, and would press me, to hell.
>
> (Sonnet VI, 4–7)

The mournful tone of the poem is developed here by repeating Biblical references to the divine, Jesus, and the Virgin Mary, until the last sonnet, which focuses on the poet's consciousness, is filled with a range of ideas and emotions. In the first sonnet, the poet brings guilt on himself in order to stay a desiring subject. The joy of guilt and suffering is articulated by 'mourning with fruit'. The second sonnet, in a mystical twist, creates another signifying formation linking the earthly body and the heavenly soul. The burden of desire is located in the body which is then located in a series of signifiers evoking the traditional dichotomy of body and soul. The soul will go to heaven while the body stays on earth. However, the fear of God as the fear of the Other, 'whose fear already shakes my every joint', causes the poet to relive the traumatic experience of desire at the heart of which lies the death drive. Opposite emotions such as fear, death and passionate love are part of the impulses that in Lacan's terms connect desire and its foundational lack to sadomasochistic self-destruction. This destruction marks a pathological gratification that the poet finds as an alluring imaginary annihilation in God:

As humorous in my contrition
As my profane love, and as soon forgot:
As riddlingly distempered, cold and hot,
As praying, as mute; as infinite, as none.
I durst not view heaven yesterday; and today
In prayers, and flattering speeches I court God:
Tomorrow I quake with true fear of his rod.
So my devout fits come and go away
Like a fantastic ague: save that here
Those are my best days, when I shake with fear.
('Divine Meditations', Sonnet XIX, 6–14)

Here, the poet discloses the core of his mystical desire that always calls for the repetition of the primal trauma through infinite devotion and supplication. A mystic through his obsessive devotion, prayer, contemplation and meditation, desires God in order to stay a desiring subject himself. Before the mystic desires, he or she wants to be desired by God, symbolizing the Other.

Similarly, in 'A Hymn to God the Father', the poet has recourse to his usual theme from *The Holy Sonnets* – the innate sin of the human heart – and begs God for forgiveness and redemption. He is unsure of forgiveness because his sin is always on the rise. Towards the end of the sonnet, however, he gets assurance from Jesus that he will be forgiven not for his sin *per se* but for the fear of it. For Lacan, this sin and its fear are two halves of one sphere, as he emphatically argues in *The Ethic of Psychoanalysis*, that Kant's fear and punishment of sin and Sade's cruel indulgence in sin are psychoanalytically identical. This fear of sin shows that desire is always ethical, for it enacts the fear that the moral law enshrines and which finds its reflection in scripture. In the sonnet below, in a play of the gaze, the *I* wants to see himself being seen by the Other. When Donne says, 'I fear no more,' this places himself in a transcendental position where 'thy son', 'shall shine', and the Other recognizes the subject's desire:

I have a sin of fear, that when I have spun
My last thread, I shall perish on the shore;
But swear by the self, that at my death thy son
Shall shine as he shines now, and heretofore;
And, having done that, thou hast done,
I fear no more.
('A Hymn to God the Father', Sonnet III, 1–6)

Put another way, this fear of sin, in Lacanian terms, is the source of the unconscious guilt that results from submission to the law. In this context, the fear of sin, and the endless mourning in Donne's *Divine Poems*, are part of the imaginary play of the *jouissance* of suffering. God, Jesus, the Virgin Mary, recur as empirical objects of desire here. The motive behind this horror is the effect of the absence of the object. When the poet says at his death 'thy son', 'shall shine', he wants to achieve the final goal of desire in order to die and experience the blessing of union with God. This blessing here is the blessing of the all protective and good imaginary Father, in Lacan's terms.

Donne's love lyrics show a marked shift of attention from a mysticism of Christian piety and total devotion to God to the mysticism of the demand for love. This mysticism of devotion through fear and prayer and the mysticism of love cum erotomania have at their core the *jouissance* of eroticized suffering. These two modes of mystical dissipation, guilt and erotomania, as Donne's poetry illustrates, have been living side by side in Western mysticism from the beginning of the Christian era. In Donne's poetics, nonetheless, this sensuality shows itself more fully in his divine poems with the consubstantiality of theology and eroticism. In his love poetry, on the other hand, divine and secular models of sensuous love come into a lasting alliance.

Lacan takes various theoretical positions vis-à-vis mysticism in the course of his teachings, albeit the Other (in various guises such as God, Jesus, Supreme Good and so on) constitutes their common ground. Describing mystic excesses as 'somewhat puerile' (Lacan, 1992, 187), in the *Ethic of Psychoanalysis,* Lacan seems keen to present courtly love as the exemplary structure of mysticism in which the idealized Lady represents the unknowable and unsymbolizable X that he calls 'the Thing'. In this kind of mysticism, the subject fantasizes about the object as sacred, asexual and inaccessible. He draws on Dante's Beatrice, as an example of the sublimation of the Thing, taken by the poet from real life:

> That is what made it easy subsequently for a metaphysical poet such as Dante, for example, to choose a person whom we definitely know existed – namely, little Beatrice whom he fell for when she was nine years old, and who stayed at the center of his poetry from the *Vita Nuova* to *The Divine Comedy.* (Lacan, 1992, 149)

In 'Introduction to the Name-of-the-Father Seminar', (1963), Lacan defines mysticism in terms of Freud's myth of *totem and taboo* as a demand for the erotic blessing of the Supreme Being. The desire of the Totem – primal father of the horde who, according to Freud, in the pre-cultural area, had access to unbounded *jouissance* – is replaced by the demand for erotic love. With the exception of Hebraic mysticism, mysticism for Lacan is a blissful sacramental union with God:

> Mysticism, throughout every tradition, . . . is a construction, search, *askesis*, assumption – anything you like – plunged toward the bliss of God. That is what leaves a trace in mysticism – and even more still, in Christian mysticism. (Lacan, 1990, 89)

It is in *Encore* that Lacan expresses passionate love for mysticism equating it with *feminine jouissance* or *jouissance* of the Other (JA). In all versions of mysticism, Lacan sees the Thing, the *primal father* and the Other as different names for the agency upon which mysticism grounds itself. In his *Seminar XVII: Dissolution* (1980), Lacan identifies Donne as the best poet of the metaphysical movement. Yet, in this seminar, he shows scepticism towards the name 'metaphysical', which was coined by Samuel Johnson, and fifty years after Donne's death popularized by John Dryden. Lacan says, '[t]here is no "meta" aspect to them [metaphysical] – unless, I propose to you, the meta is to stand for love – "love" as the meta-phor desire' (Lacan, cited in Sangiau, 1994, 49).

Nonetheless, the ambiguity surrounding the metaphysical poets, and the Western obsession with materialism and rationality provided incentives for literary critics to view this term with scepticism for different reasons. Samuel Johnson, for example, in his *Life of Cowley* accuses the so-called metaphysical poets of *discordia concors*, for jumbling opposite images and ideas and an occultism leading to, '[h]eterogeneous ideas . . . yoked by violence together' (Johnson, cited in Martin, 1990, 14). Another factor in this scepticism of literary critics might have been the long repression of mysticism in Western thought. Criticizing Johnson for failing in finding a definition for metaphysical poetry, T. S. Eliot takes a step farther by placing experience at the centre of metaphysical poetry, '[t]hey [the metaphysical poets] were, at best, engaged in the task of trying to find the verbal equivalent for states of mind and feeling' (Eliot, 1975, 65). Harold Bloom sees mysticism as synonymous with theosophy, shamanism, angelology and Gnosticism. In *Omens of Millennium*, he renounces the alliance of mysticism with literature.

Another aspect of mysticism that is called into question in the West is the seeming incongruity of the close alliance between the sacred and profane within mystical literary discourse. This incongruity was viewed sceptically by Simone de Beauvoir, when she noted '[i]t is sometimes piously maintained that the poverty of language compels the mystic to borrow this erotic vocabulary' (Beauvoir, 1988, 682). Likewise, Edward Fitzgerald in his translation of Omar Khayyám's *Rubáiyát* also saw Khayyám's mysticism as outside of religion. For Fitzgerald, Khayyám was '[t]he material Epicurean' but not 'a Mystic, shadowing the Deity under the figure of the Wine and Wine-bearer' (Fitzgerald, 1993, 60).

Lacan's feminization of mysticism, as we have spelt it out in previous chapters, was influenced by Freud. De Beauvoir, for example, locates the genesis of mysticism in femininity but denies that its centre is in the body. Considering the sexuality of a woman in love as platonic and mystical, she writes, '[e]cstasy mimics corporeally that abolition of the ego: the subject neither sees nor feels any longer, the body is forgotten, denied' (Beauvoir, 1988, 684). Here is a contradiction: ecstasy is mystical and is to be experienced corporeally, but by doing so, the subject goes beyond the corporeality of the body. Lacan's theory of the *jouissance* of the body and the Other, untangles this age-old paradox, as we will see below.

Donne's 'The Ecstasy', of which Lacan only mentions the title in his seminar, is a pertinent example in his love lyrics of where he offers a poetic image of desire and its correlation with love and *jouissance.* The poem introduces us to one of Donne's familiar and straightforward settings, a bed and two lovers who have become one in their union. The semantic field of the first three stanzas, together with a cluster of conceits – 'pillow on the bed', 'a pregnant bank', 'propagation' and dense visual imagery – reinforce this oneness of the two lovers, a man and a woman who are 'one another's best' (L.4). The mystic communion culminates in the fifth stanza, which declares the integration and fusion of the lover and the beloved and the imaginary interaction of the subject with the Other whom the subject desires to become a single entity: '[w]e like sepulchral statues lay/All day, the same our posture were' (Ll.18-19). The sixth and seventh stanzas surprisingly bring a third party to the lovers, *he* whom 'soul's language understands' (L.22). This third party, a witness to the fusion of the lovers, is this transcendental God, the Other where love and desire merge:

He (though he knew not which soul spake
Because both meant, both spake the same)
Might thence a new concoction take,
And part far purer than he came.

(Q. VII)

The two lovers who have become one, and the third party, now bring the poem to the climax where ecstasy emerges, and the first person narrative expands to become now the plural pronoun 'we':

This ecstasy doth unperplex
(We said) and tell us what we love,
We see by this, it was not sex,
We see, we saw not what did move.

(Q. VIII)

The Other, in the Lacanian sense, has the same function as the third party that mystics see as necessary in a dyadic love relationship. According to mysticism, a spiritual love can be eternalized only if both companions in a love-relationship find a transcendental link with God. Lacan in his seminar on transference confirms the unity of the subject with the Other when this desired object becomes an idyllic divine love object. As he stresses: '[t]he divine place of the Other gives a consecrated nature to the relationship between subjects, as long as the providence of the desire of the loved one inscribes itself in the divine place' (Lacan, cited in Salecl, 1994, 22). This means that the Other, who has a divine status, transcendentalizes the status of the loved object insofar as it occupies the absent locus of the Other. With the entry of the third party, the poem now claims the ecstasy of the asexual fusion to which the poet alluded earlier. The eighth stanza thus confirms the asexual nature of divine love in Donne's lyric.

In this lyric, ecstasy doesn't imply a rapturous intoxication, but a form of spiritual intuition and achievement. For Donne, it is through love and ecstasy that a subject finds his unity with the imaginary beloved. This is a love that dissolves 'this' [the subject] into 'that' [Other] to make a single entity. The beloved who emerges as God guarantees this oneness.

But as all several souls contain
Mixture of things, they know not what,
Love, these mixed sounds doth mix again,
And makes both one, each this and that.

(Q. IX)

Because of this 'refined' love, the two souls are joined, making a new and perfect soul. The thirteenth stanza abruptly leaves the transcendental thread of the poem as the poet takes his reader by surprise by plunging into a debate about body and soul, the first as 'sphere' and the second as 'intelligence'. Ultimately, this debate culminates in the idea that the physical union of the body takes precedence over the traditional body/soul dichotomy. This is a situation in which the beloved occupies the transcendental position, thus allowing for a mystical and asexual love. The two loving souls make a new and perfect soul, a state of being about which Lacan says '[i]n effect, as long as the soul soulloves the soul, sex is not involved' (Lacan, 1998a, 84). Here, the poet is in action not as an analysand but as a master analyst who persuades his reader of his epistemological conclusion, that in order to be felt, the soul has to descend to the level of the human senses, where the corporeal faculties function as a mediation between the soul and the body. He then justifies his view that only pure lovers are able to inscribe the soul within the body. If there were no such puritanical union the 'great prince', the soul, would be in 'prison':

So must pure lovers' souls descend
T' affection, and to faculties,

Which sense may reach and apprehend,
Else a great prince in prison lies.

(Q. XVII)

The poem's emphasis is reaffirmed when he describes the body as a site where the soul finds its inscription, the inscription introduced by the signifier to mortify the body and make it speak. The last three quatrains insert more force into the ecstatic state where love and the soul descend into the body. Now the poem reverts to the earlier divine love that emerges in the soul, to be written on the earthly body. For Lacan, mystical experience is an experience of the body proper, an experience of the *jouissance* of the Other. The poem itself reveals a psychoanalytic truth that the subject grounds the structures of his own desire in the Other, and then the Other takes one's own body as its symbol. For that reason, the enjoyment of one's body is in fact the enjoyment of the Other's body. This explains the core of Donne's mystic fantasy in 'The Ecstasy' that puts to test the notion of desire as the Other's desire, and the subject's body *jouissance* as the Other's *jouissance*:

To our bodies turn we then, that so
Weak men on love revealed may look;
Love's mysteries in souls do grow,
But yet the body is his book.

(Q. XIX)

And if some lover, such as we,
Have heard this dialogue of one,
Let him still mark us, he shall see
Small change, when we're to bodies gone.

(XX)

The last quatrains of the poem draw to a close Donne's perception of love as a sign that, by definition, represents something for someone, in Lacan's terms. This something is the body that represents the Other's body and its *jouissance*. Thus, this return to the body lays bare the bearings of mystical love (the body) through which, according to Lacan, the soul breathes. Narcissistic love arises from the body that by virtue of identification represents the Other and its *jouissance*. Desire is sublimated in a love that creates an illusion of unity.

The poem 'Epitaph of Himself: To the Countess of Bedford', superbly brings to light the play between desire and love in which the subject confirms his existence through the Other:

Madam,
That I might make your cabinet my tomb,
And for my fame which I love next my soul,

Next to my soul provide that happiest room,
Admit to that place this last funeral scroll.
Others by wills give legacies, but I
Dying, of you do beg a legacy.

('Epitaph of Himself')

There is, nevertheless, an antithesis in this poem. At first, Donne calls for the departure of the soul from the body as a precondition for divine union. Then, he preaches a descent of the soul into the body to achieve the same thing. Here we find the real ecstasy, the *jouissance* of the mystical commingling beyond the unconscious. This *jouissance* of the body that Donne stages here is a *jouissance* beyond the phallus, as Lacan says in *Encore*, '[t]here is a jouissance, since I am confining myself here to jouissance, a jouissance of the body that is, if I may express myself thus . . . a jouissance beyond the phallus' (Lacan, 1998a, 74). It is clear now that for Lacan feminine *jouissance* is in fact the pure *jouissance* of the body of the Other, or as Lacan says, '*jouir d'un corps*' [enjoying a body] (Lacan, 1998a, 23). The subject of the unconscious thinks and enjoys through the body not as an anatomical entity, but as the effect of the signifier. The mystical body is identical to the body of the hysteric, the signifying locus of a perverse *jouissance*, as a surrogate *jouissance* for the Other's *jouissance*. According to the mystic, spiritual love is, in fact, is a signifier that causes *jouissance* by attaining to the substance and materiality of the body.

> The signifier is the cause of jouissance. Without the signifier, how could we even approach that part of the body? Without the signifier, how could we center that something that is the material cause of jouissance? However fuzzy or confused it may be, it is a part of the body that is signified in this contribution. (Lacan, 1998a, 24)

Donne is even more explicit in 'The Expiration', when bodily contact has the power of making the souls of the lovers evaporate. The erotogenic zones represent the totality of the circulation of bodily *jouissance* in terms of affective spirituality:

So, so, break off this last lamenting kiss,
Which sucks two souls, and vapours both away.
. . .
Go; and if that word have not quite killed thee,
Ease me with death, by bidding me go too.
Oh, if it have, let my word work on me,
And a just office on a murderer do.

(Ll.1–2, 7–10)

This fall into the body, and then death, is a sign of pure desire that only true mystical love can put an end to. When it comes to desire, Lacan emphatically stresses, that one should learn from the poets. Donne is aware of the limit of language and the word that functions ultimately as killer of the Thing, because neither the word nor the signifier is capable of rejoining the subject with the Other in the way mystical love does. Moreover, the speaking being in this verse sees the death of the Other as simultaneously his own death. This death involves the recognition that the subject's desire comes from the Other, which Donne attempts to show by the death of the desiring subject who has internalized the Other. This death is the transgression of the pleasure principle through which the narcissistic ego takes the place of, and identifies with, the object of love. As Lacan argues in *Encore*, the body in its totality senses a *jouissance* outside the boundaries of linguistic articulation. Mystical poetry acts out this bodily *jouissance* in its painful and ecstatic rhapsodies. Donne blends the pastoral tradition of poetry with the neo-Platonic doctrine of the body's relationship to the soul. The joys of the flesh become the joys of the spirit. As always, true spirituality for Donne can exist only when the body and soul have been inextricably linked; thus, this poem seeks to bridge the void between the two. In this context, we claim that mysticism is an art made into the *sinthome*, through which the mystic experiences the real of *jouissance*.

Jakobson's theory of poetic function, which comes as a refined version of Saussure's notion of the associative function of language, further helps us to trace the logic of the repetition of the same in poetic discourse. Since poetry is essentially metaphoric, according to Jacobson, then the metonymic and metaphoric axes necessitate a parallelism or equivalence between all linguistic levels in poetry, (analogy, tropes, sound, metrics, rhythm and so on). Both selection and combination, as the two axes of language, are governed by the principle of equivalence, which aims at bringing together the various parallel and opposing semantic and syntactic elements in a sequence. In other words, this means that there is always semantic and thematic equivalence at work in poetry. For example, different syllables, metres, tropes, rhyming and stresses, as well as semantic patterns are equalized in poetry, as Jakobson writes:

> Poetic text are characterized by their setting up of equivalence relations, whether codified or not, between different points of the discourse, relations which are defined on superficial levels – where, by superficial, we mean phonetic, phonological, morphological, a/or surface syntax. (Jakobson, cited in Ruwet, 1982, 98)

Lacan translates Jakobson's parallelism into the parallelism of signifiers in poetry. This signifying parallelism helps metaphysical poets build up a repetitive pattern of eroticism, even profanity, and theological thought. We can show this parallelism of signifiers in Donne's lyric, 'The Ecstasy', where the visual imagery and semantic elements draw a parallel with one another in each line:

> Where, like a pillow on a bed,
> A pregnant bank swelled up, to rest
> The violet's reclining head,
> Sat we two, one another's best;
> Our hands were firmly cemented
>
> (Q. I, Ll. 1–6)

Here, visual imagery and the semantic field are parallel. 'Pillow', 'bed', 'pregnant bank', 'swelled up', 'reclining head', are linked words, which have a single semantic field as their referential context. In terms of analogy, the two last lines equate the signifiers above with 'we two', 'one another's best' and 'firmly cemented'. To put it another way, in the last two lines we have two persons, the lover and the beloved (the subject and the Other) paralleling the impersonalized elements of the first three lines, the elements that metaphorically refer to love-making. The subject and object nexus and inter-reflection seem pervasive in the visual game running through the poem. The second and third stanzas knot the look of the lovers together when they become an image in one another's eyes:

> Our eye-beams twisted, and did thread
> Our eyes, upon one double string . . .
>
> (Ll.7–8)

> And pictures in our eyes to get
> Was all our propagation.
>
> (11–12)

The conceit 'propagation', stages the fusion of the two divided parts into one. In the first two lines, we encounter two looks that eventually become one picture. Both passages produce parallel images. The poet is here held captive in desire in terms of the visual space of drives. Identification with the Other, also recognizes and confines desire, for desire is the desire of the Other. This narcissistic glorification of one's own image in the Other identifies a scopophilic field of desire within which the subject sees himself as a desired subject. Lacan also calls such a field *Unheimlich* in which a subject unexpectedly sees his own image in the Other.

Such visual desiring interludes are in abundance in Donne in which a desire always functions as an object for another desire; and love too turns into a demand of the subject to be loved. The gaze in 'The Ecstasy', enables the subject to see the other subject as Other-ized. Thus, a phrase 'double string', and pictures in the eyes refer to the reciprocal articulation of self and other in the imaginary. When one is looking in the mirror one is already being looked at. Donne repeats the same visual event in 'The Good Morrow'.

> My face in thine eyes, thine in mine appears,
> And true plain hearts do in the faces rest,
>
> (Ll. 15–16)

And in 'The Message':

> Which (oh) too long have dwelt on thee,
> Send home my long strayed eyes to me,
> Yet since there they have learned such ill,
> Such forced fashions,
> And false passions,
> That they be
> Made by thee
> Fit for no good sight, keep them still.
>
> ('The Message', Ll. 1–7)

In addition to poetic parallelism, verbs and nouns too have a signifying function. In 'The Ecstasy', the verbs in the poem, 'swelled up', 'cemented', 'spring', 'twisted', 'thread', 'to intergraft', 'suspends', 'mix again', 'imprints', 'flow', call for action in the fantasy and endorse the materiality of the signifier in relation to the subject. As in the clinical setting, a literary discourse reveals psychoanalytic truths through the verbs and nouns. For verbs in their double function foreground a split between the subject and the object, and the possibility of their re-union. Besides its linking function, a verb foregrounds states, actions and wants, whereas a noun encodes the name of someone or something in reference to lack. Lacan considers such verbs as closely linked with the unconscious and their use in discourse as a medium that knits the subject to the object in *jouissance.* The verb thus implies a signifier that unlike other signifiers offers '[t]he movement of a subject to his own division in jouissance' (Lacan, 1998a, 25). To take an example, the verbs 'cemented', 'swelled up', 'twisted', are signifiers, which signify the unification of two substances, or things that essentially were separated. Furthermore, in the poem the lover and the beloved, the ego and the ideal ego (in the imaginary), the body and the soul, or the subject and the Other (in the symbolic) are glued together in an imaginary fantasy with the help of verb. As Nasio comments,

> We also note that in the formal sense the verb of the sentence that designates the fantasmatic action materializes the signifier . . . The verb in the sentence of the fantasy represents, then, the cut between the subject and the object, it

> is the signifier that both separates and reunifies the subject and the object. (Nasio, 1998, 101)

That is the meaning of Donne's claim that, like every mystic poet, he uses love and speaking about love as an antidote to the overwhelming pain of desire, because love allows for an imaginary attachment to the lost object of desire, the object of love. When desire produces an impetus towards what Lacan calls the One, love makes that One out of the two. This implies that desire is always in conflict with its relation with the primordial object (the One), but love offers a union between the subject and a substitute for the object (object *a*). Lacan speaks at the beginning of *Encore* about a gap between this One and what is related to *jouissance*. The object *a* links the One and *jouissance*. In love, a subject identifies with the object *a* or is obsessed with desiring this object.

This identification, as well as the re-discovery of the object of desire in love, however, is fictive and imaginary, as Lacan spells out with the anecdote of Picasso's parakeet. The bird used to gnaw on the jackets and shirts of the painter, and took his clothes for his body. The parakeet identifies Picasso's clothes as an object *a* which is in corporeal contact with the real Picasso and is thus an object of *jouissance*. Lacan suggests that the same thing happens in love in its everyday meaning: the object, the beloved that haunts the lover isn't real. Thus, God as the supreme object of mystical love replaces the archaic object of desire with substitute objects via transference.

As Donne's poetry shows, a mystic poetics presents several paradigms of *jouissance*. One common paradigm, as we have mentioned earlier, is the imaginarization of the *jouissance* of the word and signifier (an imaginary fantasy in which talking about love is the source of enjoyment). The mystic poets articulate this paradigm by means of an erotic extravaganza. As such, mystic writing itself is an experience of *jouissance*. Another paradigm involves a *jouissance* of the body beyond the phallic economy that Lacan calls feminine *jouissance*. Marie Bonaparte closely read St Theresa's texts and concluded what Theresa saw as divine love and oneness was actually the feminine orgasm. Likewise, for Augustine, such an experience was the seventh and last step to being with God. He writes about the joy of such mystical moments:

> What its joys are, what the full enjoyment of the highest and true good is like, what serenity and eternity is in the air – How can I describe all this? It has been described by certain great and incomparable souls, insofar as they thought it ought to be described, souls whom we believe to have seen these things, and to be seeing them still. (Augustine, cited in Nussbaum, 2001, 534)

Similarly, a phallic *jouissance* in which a woman takes the place of the Other is not foreign at all to Donne. What could 'Atlanta's ball' be ['It is Atlanta who threw the golden balls to distract Hippomenes, where it was his ruse to make her turn aside in their race' (Gardner, 1972, 54)], other than the gems that function as symbols for the object *a* in the following elegy?

> Come, Madame, come, all rest my powers defie,
> Until I labour, I in labour lye.
> . . .
> Full nakedness, all joyes are due to thee
> As soules unbodied, bodies uncloth'd must bee
> To taste whole joyes. Gems which you women use
> Are as Atlanta's balls, cast in mens viewes.
>
> ('To his Mistress Going to Bed', Ll. 1–2, 33–36)

In 'A Valediction: Forbidding Mourning', we come across a topological account of the narcissistic imaginarization of the subject's relation with the Other as a locus where the demand for love arises, and a place where the subject finds its own speech. Here, the 'compass' with its two legs is the central conceit, one fixed (the Other), and another moving in a circle (the subject). The compass establishes the dependence of the subject's desire upon the Other's desire. The poem begins and ends with the same theme of the reunion of the mystic soul with its presumed origin. This circular movement links and interchanges desire, love and *jouissance.* This is a mystical circle, a circle whose centre is the lack of the Other, and the mathematician who according to Donne is '[o]ur great and good God' (Donne, 1987, 78). In his prose works, Donne also shows his love for the image of the circle. As he writes '[o]ne of the most convenient Hieroglyphicks of God is a circle; and a circle is endless; whom God loves' (221).

> If they are two, they are two so
> As stiff twin compasses are two,
> Thy soul the fixed foot, makes no show
> To move, but do, if th'other do.
>
> ('Valediction', Ll.25–28)

> . . . .
> Such wilt thou be to me, who must
> Like the' other foot, obliquely run;
> Thy firmness makes my circle just,
> And makes me end, where I begun.
>
> (Ll. 33–36)

The figurative structure of the 'Valediction' enacts the dependence of the lover on the beloved in a circular movement that, for Donne, represents the infinity of the Divine. In a very simple way, the poem displays an imaginary game of the self, its imitative gestures and identification with the image borrowed from the outside, which it internalizes:

> Our two souls therefore, which are one,
> Though I must go, endure not yet
> A breach, but an expansion,
> Like gold to aery thinness beat.
>
> (Ll. 21–24)
>
> . . .
> And though it in the centre sit,
> Yet when the other far doth roam,
> It leans, and hearkens after it,
> And grows erect, as it comes home.
>
> (Ll. 29–32)

Tropes in Donne bear upon symbolic meaning, exposing the subject to unconscious traces of love and desire. The tropes are on the side of love insofar as they transform their sensuous signification to a symbolic representation of divinity; and they are on the side of desire insofar as they open the signifying space for desire by bringing out the experience of loss and lack in being. Metaphysical conceits, like signifiers allow for an elision that signifies the lack of being in the unbridgeable gaps of the signifying chain in which desire is constituted. This structural leitmotif of Donne's figurative language has been misinterpreted by traditional literary critics from Johnson to T. S. Eliot as the emblematic feature of the language use of metaphysical poets. Traditional critics took the use of metaphor in poetry merely as a rhetorical and aesthetic device with an arbitrary meaning.

Lacan's definition of metaphor questions this traditional sense of arbitrariness in metaphor. Metaphor for Lacan always gives the illusion of signification by the slippage of a signifier into another signifier that then functions as a signified. As such, a metaphor provides the possibility of producing different meanings, from sensuality to a mystico-theological devotion. Besides, as signifiers in the symbolic, tropes call for an operation of substitution and replacement along the signifying chain. This operation causes *jouissance* by virtue of the signifiers' materiality and primacy. In this sense, Donne's conceits or as critics have called them 'black' and 'far-fetched' metaphors, allow for an identification of the subject with the object that causes desire. In a mystical discourse, this identification takes place between the desiring subject and the Supreme Being. It thus allows for the objectification of the subject and the transubstantiation of objects in love. It is in this context that Lacan insists that the signifier and tropes in a poetic language are a gift, for, through its tropic quality, poetic language enables a subject to mediate desire in the symbolic register.

By way of religious fantasy and material sensuality, Donne takes a double route to mystic union. 'The Sun Rising', celebrates the autoerotic passion of love in terms of eternal light and the rays of the sun, in contrast to the elegies: 'To his Mistress Going to Bed,' and 'On his Mistress,' which had affirmed a man's freedom in sexual union. As we have said at the outset, this sexual union is another mode of mystical discourse that links an erotic bliss with divinity.

Love, all alike, no season knows, nor clime,
Nor hours, days, months, which are the rags of time.
('The Sun Rising', Ll. 9–10)

The poem then spurns the sun as the dawn causes the lovers to part after their nocturnal dalliance. The *I* in the text proclaims the strength of the lover's love, which he deems far superior to the sun's. He can shut out the sun by the movement of a wink but can never lose the sight of his beloved. Donne describes again the idyllic status of the loved object that here is personified as a woman. The speaking subject in this poem is trapped in the lure of the scopophilic drive, establishing an imagistic relation with the Other. He loses the sight of his beloved as the Other blinds his eyes:

Thy beams, so reverend, and strong
Why shouldst thou think?
I could eclipse and cloud them with a wink
But that I would not lose her sight so long:
If her eyes have not blinded thine,
('The Sun Rising', Ll. 11–15)

In 'Love's Alchemy', Donne illustrates Lacan's theory of love, a love which is essentially a lie. It is lie because at the heart of the entire drama of any kind of love is fiction, a fiction which has a strong effect especially in mystic love. The lust a lover feels doesn't indicate real love. The same is true for desire that, at its heart, is a misunderstanding. The unconscious subject is fixated on the primal object but desire builds a conduit to it by means of object *a*. The subject exists insofar as his desire and love are based on a lie. As Bloom says, Donne, indeed, is '[d]isillusioned by the false promises of joy which lust seems to offer, he decides to embrace the source of his disillusionment rather than believing a lie' (Bloom, 1999, 43). The first stanza ridicules physical love and the second repeats this point of view with regard to spiritual love:

Some that have deeper digged love's mine than I,
Say, where his centric happiness doth lie:
I have loved, and got, and told,
But should I love, get, tell, till, I were old,

I should not find that hidden mystery;
Oh, 'tis imposture all:

(Ll. 1–6)

In sum, mystical *jouissance* remains in Donne's text at the level of the body as a signifying field for the Other. This *jouissance* is experienced in the totality of being, for this is a *jouissance* that is '[i]mplicating the entire body in a supposed divine encounter with God' (Nasio, 1998, 11). The idealized object allows no room for the presence of the ego. This is the meaning of the mystic ecstasy through which the ego dissolves in the Other, and through a psychosomatic delirium, the subject touches the Thing in the real. In other words, here desire begins to be suspended, for in these moments of ecstasy the hystericized body experiences reunion with the primordial object in a hallucinatory *jouissance*. Donne's poetry thus offers a complete picture of the actualization of desire and its suspension through *jouissance*. The motivating force in this mystical dilemma is centred on eroticism even sometimes obscenity, where love functions as evocative of unconscious pleasure through a bodily ecstasy mingled with divine ecstasy.

As said, erotic imagery is the apotheosis of mystical poetry in all cultures. Mystical union is the ultimate and only goal in Donne's poetry. It is, in fact, his symptom that he, like all mystics, believes in and identifies with. His art provides a matrix for the imaginarization of mystic *jouissance*. With Donne's poetry, we frequently find poetic truth together with psychoanalytic truth. For, in the final analysis, love coincides with hate, and Donne desires both:

Yet, love and hate me too,
So, these extremes shall neither's office do;
Love me, that I may die the gentler way;
Hate me, because thy love's too great for me;
Or let these two, themselves, not me decay;
So shall I live thy stage, not triumph be;
Lest thou thy love and hate and me undo,
To let me live, Oh love and hate me too.

('The Prohibition', Ll.17–24)

In a single stanza of 'Divine Meditation', he tells us the whole story of a desire that is caused by a primal separation from the originary object. Such a divine madness in Donne's poetry, as in all other great mystic poets, is a means of escape from the labyrinth of desire:

I am a little world made cunningly
Of elements, and an angelic sprite,
But black sin hath betrayed to endless night

My world's both parts, and, oh, both parts must die.
('Divine Meditation', Sonnet V, Ll. 1–4)

Here the 'black sin', is the black hole of desire that reveals the split in the subject's being because of his alienation in language. Besides this sinful part of the mystic's world, another part is his angelic and spiritual part that the poet wishes to annihilate in order to achieve the final goal of desire.

Donne's poetic universe is one in which the subject is lost in the slippage of signifiers: body, soul, God, woman, sun, bed and tomb, the chain can never be completed. This again unfolds Donne's *sinthome,* in the same manner as other mystics who dramatize different versions of enjoyment of the divine union – which in psychoanalysis is just an illusion. These floating signifiers are there only to underline the fundamental lack in the Other that causes a subject's desire. This explains the metonymic structure of desire and its relation to its object in terms of a constant deferral. The objects that we encounter in Donne's verses are versions of object *a,* which causes desire and kindles love. These objects are closely in touch with the Other upon whom both desire and love rely. For Lacan, the genesis of love begins with an encounter between the subject and the object in the imaginary. This encounter shifts from an imaginary register into the symbolic in terms of being, as he says, '[l]ove is also addressed to the semblance of being' (Lacan, 1998a, 92). This being is, in fact, our own being and love is aimed at '[t]he Supreme Being's *jouissance,* that is God' (70). This enigmatic *jouissance* is the Other's *jouissance,* '[t]he Other I said to be symbolized by the body' (38).

Donne's poetry bears out Lacan's theorem that '[t]o make love (*faire l'amour*), as the very expression indicates, is poetry' (Lacan, 1998a, 72). In this sense, Donne's poetry commingles sensuality with religious fantasy to address the unconscious traces of desire. This commingling is a synergy that brings narcissistic corporeal sensuality and highly utopian and subjective euphoria together, which constitute the foundation of the mystical poetic tradition. In contrast to what has been believed by critics, the core of metaphysics or mysticism is a demand for the erotic blessing of God that appears in terms of the body, the mistress and so on. This constitutes the heteronomy in mysticism in which the profane is sanctified, and sensual sexuality is evoked as spirituality. However, this heteronomy has to be accounted for in terms of Lacan's moebius-strip. The mystic poet experiences the ecstasy of this blessing within his body (not a biological body, but the psychoanalytic body as the locus of *jouissance,* and in touch with the soul). This experience is a storm of unconscious energy, which interlinks sexual orgies, divine madness, theology, the sacred, profanity and so on. Finally, in this experience, the subject falls into the real and its *jouissance,* knowledge of which remains unknown to the experiencing mystic. On the other hand, mystic literary discourse acts out the fantasy of such an experience. When Lacan assigns his *Écrits* to the mystic tradition, he acknowledges the sublime status of mystical writing, '[m]ystical jaculations are neither idle chatter nor empty verbiage; they provide, all in all, some of the best reading one can find' (Lacan, 1998a, 76).

Donne's poetry exposes the manifold vicissitudes of mystical experience. When we find the poet weeping, he is in dysphoria, in a space of desire where he enjoys his suffering in the depth of guilt, self-flagellation and lament for his sinfulness. When he desires to be an object of divine love, he is demanding to be loved in the first place. As an expression of self-love, this demand for God's love is the subject's ceaseless desire to love his own self, as Lacan says, '[b]y loving God, we love ourselves, and by first loving ourselves – "well-ordered charity," as it is put – we pay the appropriate homage to God' (Lacan, 1998a, 70–71).

Donne offers a full spectrum of this mystical experience in poetry. Such a diversity in the experience of *jouissance* implies that Donne, like any other mystic poet, enjoys his symptom but not in the way Joyce does. Joyce's *sinthome* is the pure *jouissance* of non-readable writing, but Donne's poetry unfolds the state of interplay between desire and love as that breaks up ephemerally with the mystical orgies of divine madness in the imaginary. Lacan sees the true meaning of such a love as a narcissistic autoerotic love of one's own body that represents the Other and its *jouissance*. This is a state of being-in-love that dissolves desire, because the subject and the object, whatever it may be, become one. This dissolution manifests itself in mystic ecstasy. The following chapter will deal with this eruption of the real – a break in the symbolic function of language – in Joyce's *Finnegans Wake*.

Chapter 7

Joyce's *Wakean Sinthome*

Lacan was indeed an ideal double for Joyce in many ways. He himself repeatedly noted his close bond with Joyce. From his early interest in surrealist writings which he defined as *écrits inspirés,* to his later interest in mathematics, topology and the complex system of Borromean knots, Lacan identifies with this writing tradition. In return to his *Écrits 'inspirés': Schizographie* [Inspired writings: Schizographia] (1931), Lacan writes, '[I] myself began by writing *Écrits inspirés,* so I shouldn't be too surprised when I look at Joyce' (Lacan, cited in Roudinesco, 1997, 374). With this text, Lacan inaugurates his engagement with Joyce. His reading of Joyce was, however, a landmark in his teaching, for as he admits in *Le Sinthome,* he had discovered after more than twenty-two years of searching that, in Joyce's writing, the real could be written.

Elisabeth Roudinesco, moreover, argues that Lacan's preoccupation with Joyce was partly autobiographical for he saw in Joyce his uneasy relationship with his own father: 'Lacan, the son of Alfred, was identifying with Joyce in order to speak of his own drama, obsessed as he always had been by the determination to make a name for himself' (373). Lacan's scrupulous reading of Joyce, his theoretical reveries and his recourse to the novel as a major literary and textual repository suggest that he had an exhaustive knowledge of Joyce's *Wake,* a work that for him was in the same category as an analytical discourse. It, however, seems naïve to believe the assertion of a commentator who wrote that Lacan, '[o]nly reached page fifteen', of *Finnegans Wake* (Wales, 1992, 133).

Joyce himself doesn't hide his ambivalent feelings for psychoanalysis or in his own word, 'my little psychosinology' (*FW,* 486. 13): '[I] can psyakoonaloose myself any time I want' (522.34–35). We may detect in the last pun a conglomerate of the words, *psychos, soak, loose [free], loose [immoral], lose,* with *psychoanalyse* as its denominator. Joyce thus foreshadows here Lacan's comparison of the *Wake* with an analytical discourse.

In this chapter, I return to *Le Sinthome,* Lacan's greatest contribution to literary study and criticism in relation to Joyce's *Finnegans Wake.* I wish to engage with the text of the novel in a sustained Lacanian analysis of Joyce and his writing that will explain the function and interpretation of the *sinthome.* I will attempt to answer the following key questions in relation to Joyce's text: (i) how does Joyce's art determine and constitute the structure of the *sinthome* in his writing? (ii), how does the *sinthome* as a self-made and self-serving artifact allow Joyce to play with/and enjoy his own unconscious? (iii) where in the text do we encounter the real – suspension of meaning – which is developed on the basis of one's personal *jouissance*? (iv) how is this *jouissance* unleashed when language plays with writing and by implication, when it plays havoc with the established symbolic and socio-cultural texture of literary discourse? (v) how and to what end does Joyce resort to *linguistricks* – the interplay of a multitude of rhetorical disfigurations and subversions of conventional phonetic, orthographical, morphological and semantic principles of the language-system that opens up every word in the *Wake* to multiple meanings? (vi) what does Joyce want to achieve by turning his name to a common noun? and finally (vii), how the absence of the signifier of the Name-of-the-Father, as a law promulgating formation, underpins Joyce's dissolution and fragmentation of language.

By arguing with the text and the effect of textuality, we will shift attention from the theoretical description of the *sinthome* to the practical exploration of the fundamental structure of the concept. Lacan's seminar on Joyce, fortunately, offers a set of critical formulations that enable us to catch Joyce the author in action, destroying the language system in each line of the novel. I argue that Lacan's critique of Joyce surpasses the criticism offered by Derrida's deconstruction and Eco's semiotics. In view of the fact that it is impossible to explore the whole of the novel here, I would like to select for a close investigation, chapter four of the second book entitled the 'Four Old Men', from the *fobula* of *Finnegans Wake*. This selection has been made because, like a concave mirror, the chapter structurally replicates the whole novel. Likewise, congruent with the rest of the novel, the chapter has a circular movement of narration. It begins and ends with songs in praise of the four old sailors. The whole novel too has a circular ending with '[a] last a loved a long the' (*FW*, 628. 15) which returns to the beginning of the novel to function as the definite article of 'riverrun', the first word or pun of the *Wake*. To demonstrate Lacan's point that Joyce and his text are structured in terms of a sphere and a cross, we will connect this chapter's circular structure to its representation of the four sailors as the four corners of the cross. Finally, the four tales of the sailor that holds the chapter together may symbolize Lacan's logic of the *sinthome*, which as the fourth ring, holds Joyce's chaosmos of language and Lacan's Borromean knot together.

This *amour de voyage* begins and ends in a dream, when in an erotic scene like a peepshow Isolde and Tristan are honeymooning on the deck of the ship, gazed at by four old men whose 'mouths [are] making water' (*FW*, 386.11). Joyce offers several accretions of the number *four*. The *four* could be anything as long as the adjective *four* is in front of their names. For example, in addition to the four books of the *Wake*, they can be four judges, the four provinces of Ireland, four Irish historians, 'Four Knocks' [the four knocks of Beethoven's Fifth symphony] (622.35), the four Evangelists, four waves of the sea, four seagulls and the Viconian concept of time – the cyclic recurrence of four periods. It may also refer to the Pythagorean sacred square, a square that '[i]s the emblem of moral justice and divine equity geometrically expressed' (Hart, 1962, 143). Likewise, against the narrative backdrop, this chapter looks like *The Tale of the Four Dervishes,* an allegory from the *Arabian Nights,* in which four old men tell the tales of their love affairs one by one. The *Arabian Nights* have been an important reference in Joyce's oeuvre. The only fifth element in the chapter is the donkey that the four men ride, '[a]t the carryfour with awlus plawshus, their happyass claoudius!' (*FW,* 581.22–23). The four mysterious sailors have a collective name, Mamalujo – an amalgam of Mathew, Mark, Luke and John.

The four old men are heavy drinkers at HCE's pub. This polysemic acronym stands for many things: Howth Castle and Environs, or Here Comes Everybody, for example. Like everyone in the novel the names change, as at the end of the chapter these four men become 'Mattheehew, Markeehew, Lukeehew, Johnheehewheehew!' (399.29). As the final version of their names here bears out, Joyce's elongation of the names with vowels is a familiar way of naming and renaming throughout *Finnegans Wake or ' The Phoenican Wake'* (608. 32). In the *Wake,* Joyce presents '[e]very person, place and thing in the chaosmos' (*FW,* 118.21). Even the old men change their gender, as towards the end of the chapter, they become 'four dear heladies', (386.16) 'four (up) beautiful sister misters', (393.17), and 'beautfour sisters' (22).

This shows that Joyce's characters refuse symbolic naming, as they don't seem to be premised on a unified self-identification. We can argue that the term Mamalujo resembles Lacan's puns, because of its multitude of associations. For both Joyce and Lacan, the primary purpose of making puns was to refuse to succumb to a fixed identity in a certain language, a fixed centre, reference point, name, term or a single meaning. The body of the chapter appears as songs, describing the adventures of the four mysterious men who tell the tales of their past lives between a short and repetitive introduction and conclusion. We can put the itinerary of the chapter schematically as follows:

Song → Prologue → Four Gospels → Epilogue → Song

By drawing on Clive Hart's comments on the *Wake,* Lacan emphasizes in *Le Sinthome* that Joyce's writing has the structure of a sphere and a cross. This can be represented as a circle with the mathematical sign for addition at its centre, which as we have argued above, makes four corners, representing the four sailors. Among many possible shades of meanings this sphere or circle or cross could be the Buddhist wheel and Pythagorean square. Following his Borromean logic, Lacan sees everywhere in Joyce's discourse the Borromean play of the circle that holds within itself the sign of the cross. Joyce's reading of Aquinas, according to Lacan, encouraged him to insert the cross repeatedly into his novel. Lacan concludes that Joyce's language designates a Borromean game, aimed at knotting the three registers – Imaginary, Symbolic and Real – together.

This is the starting point of Lacan's engagement with Borromean logic. Lacan rethought this notion and gave it additional resonance during the session of 8 April 1975, in *The Seminar XXII: Real, Symbolic, Imaginary,* [RSI]. Here, he argues that, like Joyce, everyone is locked up in the relationship between the sphere and the cross, as an in-built structure of subjectivity in general. As Lacan notes, '[I] have been taking a look at Joyce because I have been solicited to open a conference. Well, if Joyce is completely caught up in the sphere and the cross, it is not only because he read a lot of Aquinas thanks to his education with the Jesuits. You are all as caught up in the sphere and the cross. Here is a circle, the section of a sphere and within the cross' (Rabaté, 2001, 55–156). Lacan then argues that no one before him noticed that this cross within a sphere was itself a Borromean knot. By this Lacan means that the whole structure of the *Wake* is a circle that is crossed and a cross that is encircled. Using the circle and the cross, Lacan draws a Borromean knot symbolizing the structure of his triadic registers. This shows a crucial point in Lacan that derives its authority from the *Wake.*

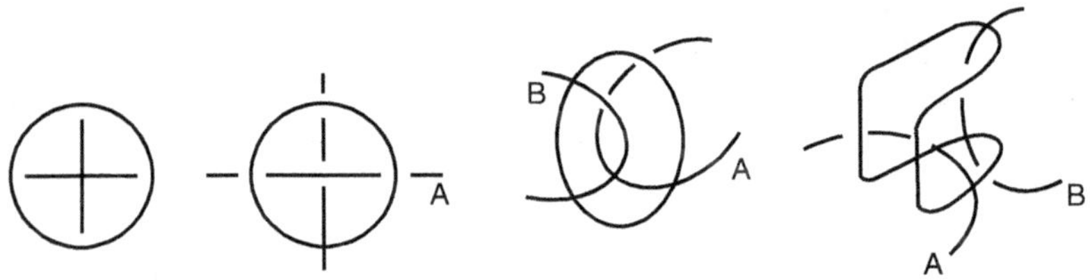

Source: Rabaté, 2001, 156

The opening song of the 'Four Old Men', begins with three 'quarks', like three knocks on the door of King Mark's fate and ends with words. The seagulls' song mocks King Mark for his unfaithful bride who will make love with the young Tristan:

Three quarks for Muster Mark!
Sure he hasn't got much of a bark
And sure any he has it's all beside the mark,
But O, Wreneagle Almighty, wouldn't un be a sky of a lark

(*FW*, 383.1–4)

Fowls, up! Tristy's the spry young spark
That'll tread her and wed her and bed her and red her.

(11–12)

Subsequent to the birds' song, the first sentence shows us: the break-down in the verbal and phonemic articulation of language when Joyce's puns 'Overhoved, shrillgleescreaming', begins the story of the four sailors. The words 'shrill' and 'screaming' signify the traumatic encounter of the subject with language because the *logos* fades away when you want to articulate the real in language. The word 'glee' gives another twist by mixing 'glee' with 'shrill' and 'screaming', recalling the ultimate joy. Joyce imposes new words, he takes away the 'r' from 'hover' and mingles both words 'over' and 'hover', and then compresses four words 'shrill', 'gulls', 'glee' and 'screaming' bringing together disparate signifiers to generate a polysemy. The homophony here and what follows: '[t]hat song sang seaswans' (*FW*, 383.15) foreground Joyce's compulsive and fetishistic infatuation with polyphonic paronomasia. The impetus behind this endless play is to subvert the traditional and symbolically prescribed interaction of signifiers. Lacan identifies Joyce's *sinthome* in this dissection, modification and breaking apart of the internal networks of the lexicon.

This perverse free play with language is a Joycean way of writing each letter and word as a material object. As he writes earlier in the *Wake*: '[s]o why pry, sign anything as long as every word, letter, penstroke, paperspace is a perfect signature of its own' (*FW*, 115.6–8). Besides, inherent in this network of paronomasia is elation and mania, which bring out their hidden *jouissance*. Joyce by adding the epithet 'glee' reinforces his delight with the sounds of the words. This ineffable elation is defined by Lacan in clinical terms as part of the latent psychotic articulation of the signifiers, wherein a subject enjoys hearing voices. Lacan even assumes that Joyce's third person narrative is a technique that allows the author to hear his own voices, as what is said is always behind what is heard, '[t]he fact that one says remains forgotten behind what is said in what is heard' (Lacan, 1998a, 15). The enjoyment involved in such wordplay is what Lacan calls *j'ouïs sens* meaning (I hear meaning), as Harari says,

> The opening implied by jouis-sens also entails another, closely related sense: *j'ouïs sens* ['I hear meaning']. With this, a fundamental element comes into play: that of the voice. Concerning Joyce, Lacan will work on the singular question of what he terms *imposed words*. There are paroles, spoken words, and not *mots*: not isolated words, but phonic structures that are articulated (even if particular types of articulation may be enigmatic, latent). The effect of these spoken words is sharply more visible in psychotics . . . as in the case of Joyce – it may be worked on with letters, making this 'hearsay' [*ouïe*] into *sinthome*. (Harari, 2002, 113–114)

Such wordplay, sometimes, is concomitant with erotic scenes or images: '[t]he winging ones. Seahawk, seagull, curlew and plover, kestrel and capercallzie. All the birds of the sea they trolled out rightbold when they smacked the big *Kuss* of Trustan with Usolde' (*FW*, 383. 16–18). We can see that the words, 'right' and 'bold', have been stitched together. And the word *kiss* has been decomposed by producing a polysemy with its German equivalent *kuss*. The word *kuss* also means female genitalia in Arabic.

Joyce shows great interest in staging erotic scenes with a far-reaching visual effect in the *Wake*. The erotic scene between Tristan and Isolde – the bride of King Mark – on the deck of the ship produces an audio-visual polarity by staging both seeing and hearing. In these semantic metamorphoses of words lies the power of the Joycean *sinthome*, '[a]llowing the unconscious and the ego to attain different degrees of signifying coherence in the fact of the asemic force of *jouissance*' (Thurston, 2004, 94). The four old men are listening and watching the love scene. They are voyeurs par excellence, as Joyce repeatedly says, 'Deepsee- peepers gazed and sazed and dazecrazemzed' (*FW*, 389. 28). The last pun condenses three signifiers: daze, craze, amaze, producing the meaning effect of a dense moment of a symptomatic voyeurism.

This reminds us of Beckett's comment who insisted that the *Wake* '[i]s not written at all. Is not to be read – or rather it is not only to be read. It is to be looked at and listened to' (Beckett, 1961, 21). Joyce tries to place as many *sememes* (meaning) as he could within each *lexeme* (word). The homophony and alliteration of words: 'trolled', 'bold', 'song', 'sang', 'seaswan' and 'seahawk' display Joyce's enormous interest in the sounds of words that mobilize the letters and rupture the materiality of the signifiers by sundering their unity. Sound is intermingled with the letter to produce phonetic ambiguity.

The *sibilance* – a repetition of the phoneme 's' – in the above passage reveals another idea of Lacan's in relation to the phallic function in a literary discourse. Elsewhere too the 's' is repeated to produce onomatopoetic effect: '[t]o me or not to me. Satis thy quest on' (*FW*, 269. 19–20). 'Oyes! Oyeses! Oyesesyeses!' (604. 22), 'spickspookspokesman of our specuturesque silentiousness' (427.33–34), and 'Kiss. Kiss Criss. Cross Criss. Kiss Cross' (11.27). This recurrence of the same phonemes is a way of repeating the foreclosure of symbolic castration, and by implication, strengthening the claim for the possession of the phallus. The homophony reveals what we have said about the inter-relation of *lalangue*, and the body that comes into play as part of Joyce's symptom. The term *lalangue* implies infantile babblings or *lallation* beyond perception and sense. The signifier in *lalangue* 'reveals itself as "enjoying substance" beyond any meaning its signification may support' (Dravers, 2002, 144). Joyce exploits this phonetic power of language masterfully to reach to the real and *jouissance*. As we have said above, this *jouissance*, in repeating the same phoneme, is related to the bodily assertion about having the phallus, for *lalangue* is connected with the body.

To simplify these various forms of phonation, let us return briefly once more to the Freudian *fort/da* game in which two phonemes *fort* (gone), *da* (here it is again) produce opposing significations. If the *da* in a subject's utterance occurs frequently, it will logically mean the reality of the *fort* is being denied.

The bobbin that is used in Freud's grandson's game is what Lacan calls object *a*. In a similar way, the letters and signifiers function in Joyce's game as object *a* with which the author's whole existence is possessed. Therefore, as soon as phonation appears, the subject denies the lack of the phallus. Lacan in *Le Sinthome*, highlights the letter *phi* or Φ [the first word of the (ph)allus] as the first word of fantasy. In addition, a *lalation*, in fact, joins the subject with the Other as the locus of its origin:

> If the symptom is an event of the body then Joyce certainly makes it sing. In his own words, it is a *songtom*, the body's song, a body resonating with the effects of speech. He thus illustrates Lacan's untranslatable definition of the symptom as '[u]n événement de corps, lié à ce que: *'l'on l'a, l'on l'a de l'air, l'on l'aire, de l'on l'a.'* Here Lacan is playing upon a having that is only the semblance of having (the phallus), while sounding out a score that supports the being of the body and the symptom. (Dravers, 2002, 167–168)

At the heart of this dissolution of the traditional system of language lies *la linguisterie* [*linguistrickery, linguistricks*] wherein, because of the default of the paternal metaphor, the symbolic structure of language cannot be supported. We may well take these *linguistricks*: paronomasia, heteroglossia, equivocality, puns, *lalangue*, ambiguities, oxymorons, polyphonies, homophonies, littering and so on, as Lacan's umbrella term for all language play that by definition is a reminder of the joyful pre-linguistic experience that finds its resurrection in a textual writing like Joyce's. By coining this term, an exploration of whose different aspects is our main concern here, Lacan, nevertheless, is endeavouring to dissociate it from structuralist literary criticism whose main concern is to bring everything in an autonomous text under the domain of linguistics or semiotics. These *linguistricks*, in fact, could be taken into account as the psychogenesis of the *sinthome* in the exploitation of which, Joyce masterfully brings into play language as an unreadable writing. Joyce's art and ego are conflated in his symptom and writing, the function of which is the knotting together of the triadic registers as well as compensation for the lack of the Name-of-the-Father.

This latter is a signifier whose foremost signification is the *no* of the father and the dereliction of his symbolic function. This *no* in the *Wakean* context is a *no* to meaning, as well as a *no* to the symbolic articulation of the real. In the intersection of the real and the symbolic, signs seem reluctant to be transformed into signifiers, because in Joyce the two registers remain incompatible and cease to collocate. That is why Lacan argues, '[w]hat happens in Joyce's writing? The signifier stuffs (*vient truffer*) the signified' (Lacan, 1998a, 37). This signified, conversely, doesn't imply a metaphysical presence, but a non-representative, non-meaning, or a lapse. This lapse opens the gap or hole of the real, beyond symbolization, and its function in Joyce's text is to reaffirm the lack and absence in the Other, the 'psychous of the Real Absence' (FW, 536. 5).

What is this absence in Joyce's discourse? The signifier of the paternal function in the symbolic, as we have suggested above, is that very absence. Towards the end of *Seminar III: Les Psychoses,* Lacan outlines the absence of this signifier of the Name-of-the-Father with an anecdote. Lacan metaphorically calls this signifier a *highway* where a traveller (in whom the paternal signifier is functioning) never loses his way nor his final destination. However, those who lack this signifier, have to travel on minor roads and lanes under the guidance of different signs, subject to losing their way. This is where the paternal signifier doesn't function, and where consequently '[t]he signifiers begin to talk, to sing on their own' (Lacan, 1993, 294). This is exactly what happens in Joyce's text where the deployment of an enormous mass of amorphous signifiers remains '[l]aden with nonmeaningfulness, the decomposition of internal discourse' (321).

This internal discourse belongs to the subject that in Joyce's case projects its decomposition onto his writing. This signifier or the phallus principally has to be passed onto the son by his father to guarantee the son's claim to carry the phallus and its signifier. Joyce's father, according to Lacan, failed to transmit the phallus to his son, because in practical terms, he didn't have a caring father himself. His *sinthome* and art are taken by Lacan as the author's compensation for this lack. Joyce's war against language constitutes a multilayered strategy in the *Wake,* showing the incompatibility of the signifier with its own content, and thus allowing for the pure *jouissance* of the meaningless signifier.

By giving the example of poetry at the beginning of *Encore,* Lacan contradicts the notion that everything that makes language belongs to the field of linguistics. There are many non-verbal expressions embedded in language beyond the grasp of linguistics. In other words, through fragmented language, equivocation, epiphanies, puns and other forms of wordplay, Joyce builds a short-cut to the domain of the real and its *jouissance.* Lacan here clarifies his theoretical position vis-à-vis his famous statement that the unconscious is structured like a language, which means that the unconscious doesn't imply language and its structure alone. He emphasizes that extra-linguistic trickery and wordplay constitute more a game the author is playing with the traces of language than the traditional metaphysical perception of language in which grammatical logic is a *priori* of writing. As he says, '[t]he fact that I say (*Mon Dire*) that the unconscious is structured like a language is not part and parcel of the field of linguistics' (Lacan,1998a,15). Joyce thus plays with words, making the whole novel, as he himself admits, a 'pouch filled with litterish fragments' (*FW,* 66. 25–26) linked with the real of the unconscious, because the unconscious is a censored knowledge that only *lalangue* articulates. This is the secret behind Joyce's writing, that is written in *d'anglas landadge,* not in conventional literary and formal English, as he himself proposes in a series of bilingual puns: '[a]re we speechin d'anglas landadge or are you sparking sea Djoytsch?' (485. 12–13).

Elsewhere, Joyce reveals the *Wake* as a writing of the night that has to be in a close bond with the unconscious:

> In writing of the night I really could not, I felt I could not, use words in their ordinary connections. Used that way they do not express how things are in the night, in the different stages – conscious, then semi-conscious, then unconscious. I found that it could not be done with words in their ordinary relations and connections. (Joyce cited in Sollers, 1983, 197)

As we have pointed out, the littering of the letter is another key device that Joyce uses to accomplish the above quest – the dissolution of language as an independent system. Joyce himself indicated that coextensive with his writing, was 'a litteringture of kidlings', (*FW*, 570. 18), which is, according to Lacan, the crux of Joyce's *sinthome*, and the author's unique way of enjoying his unconscious. Lacan identifies Joyce's littering in terms of the fragmentation and mixing up of signifiers and letters. Joyce was a real man of letters, all kind of letters swarmed in his memory, and he treated them as objects. As he writes, '[a] comedy of letters! I have them all, tame, deep and harried, in my min's I' (*FW* 425. 24–25). Puns, as fruit of this littering of the letters, constitute a great part of Joyce's translinguistic game and, according to Lacan, are the sources of unconscious play and the support of the symptom. As he says, '[I]f the unconscious is as Freud depicts it, a pun can itself be the linchpin that supports a symptom, a pun that doesn't exist in a related language' (Lacan, 1993, 119). As deployed in the *Wake*, punning and paronomasia amuse the author.

Excessive punning was a Lacanian life-long preoccupation too. Lacan investigates in the last part of 'Rome Discourse', the preoccupation of a subject with letters and words in the imaginary, '[w]ords are trapped in all the corporeal images which captivate the subject; they can make the hysteric pregnant' (Lacan 1981a, 64). In each phonetic and semantic mutilation, Joyce, in fact, is tearing up the symbolic, for words, according to Lacan, '[c]an undergo symbolic lesions and accomplish imaginary acts of which the patient is the subject' (65). Nonetheless, by the power of his symptom, he uses his *linguistricks* to artificially hold the real, the imaginary and the symbolic together. To put it concisely, the *sinthome* is a symbolic construction of a signifying field often at the intersection of the symbolic and the real. The *sinthome* functions in Joyce's case, as the chief device for a pervasive production of paralinguistic and trans-linguistic free play. Joyce's writing functions as a supplement to his symptom by way of the exclusion of an imaginary solution and with the introduction of a particular mode of his personal *jouissance.*

The real emerges with the symptom allowing access to the *jouissance* that is associated with it. The Other who speaks through the subject, whose speech, or in Joyce's case, writing is marked by the presence of the lack that reveals itself as a fragmented or dysfunctional signifier. In other words, these lapses filled with *linguistricks*, in fact, indicate one thing, the lack of the paternal signifier to which the whole novel is anchored, as Joyce himself writes, ' [w]ith stolen fruit how cutely to copy all their various styles of signature so as one day to utter an epical forged cheque' (*FW*, 181. 14–16). As Voruz says,

> Joyce's writings, therefore, harbor the opportune prospect of a way out of the self-serving enjoyment of the symptom, insofar as it is Other to the subject. Here is a writer who seems to enjoy without the Other, without being subjected to the discourse of the Master, to fantasy. (Voruz, 2002, 115)

In addition to disfiguring words and phonation, Joyce's littering frequently uses agglutination, mixing up sounds with letters and undermining conventional meaning, in order to produce an equivocation that reveals his play with the unconscious. Consider the following words and phrases from the Anna Livia chapter (Chapter VIII of Book I): 'last wik' [last week], (FW, 169. 13), 'dud-durty devil', [the dirthy devil] (16), 'And the dreepest of wet and the gangers of sin in it!' [deep, drip, dangers] (18), 'ebro at skol', [Hebrew at school] (198. 19–20), 'ten kerchiefs', [handkerchief] (213. 27) 'the honeying of the lune', [the honeymoon] (215. 3–4), 'forgivemequick, I'm going! Bubye!' [byebye] (7) 'forgetmenot' (8), 'howmulty plurators' [how manipulators], (25). Furthermore, Joyce combines letters to make allographs. For instance in the expression '[p]alpably wrong and bulbubly improper', (384. 30) Joyce uses both phonemes 'p' and 'b' as the allographs of the phoneme 'p'. This incessant non-communicative free play that we have been exploring here comes from the unconscious knowledge that knows how to play with *lalangue.* Since unconscious knowledge itself is an enigma, it often produces enigmas. Joyce and his art know what to do with *lalangue* and how to play with writing. This is what Lacan repeatedly calls in *Le Sinthome* Joyce's *savoir-faire.* Joyce's writing itself is identified as a symptom that offers suppléance, Lacan's concept of a substitute, healing and repair for the failure of phallic signification. This suppléance is, as Lacan insists, part of the *sinthome,* a defensive strategy against delusional process and falling into psychosis. In the absence of a symbolic or imaginary process, this suppléance provides a unique articulation of *jouissance* that arises from many forms of Joyce's distinctive language system.

Furthermore, Joyce's art of the word and the letter in conjunction with his encyclopedic knowledge of human history, science, literature, were all aimed at his ego's need to find a supplementary name. This naming strategy in place of the lack of the Name-of-the-Father is '[a]nother mode of remedying the absence of the phallus, *universal* marker of the subject's *particular* position in language' (Voruz, 2002, 127–128) This is manifested in the way Joyce uses the signifier that represents the subject and its symptom.

This is the core of the *sinthome*, which divides Lacanian criticism from traditional Joycean studies. For instance, Derrida's reading of Joyce outlined in his short essay, 'Two Words for Joyce', is influenced by traditional criticism. In reference to Joyce's text, he argues that writing has two greatnesses. One is the effacement of the self of the writer and the presence of an 'archive', of his memory; and the second, is the greatness of Joyce's writing that succeeds in releasing enormous energies from each fragment of his text. Derrida's deconstruction attempts to anaesthetize Joyce's discourse, for, the source of Joyce's equivocation in this context is the encyclopedic knowledge and his adaptation of Babylonian writing (Derrida's words) in *Finnegans Wake.* It seems that the undecidability that Derrida frequently talks about doesn't apply to Joyce:

> Joyce has represented for me the most gigantic attempt to gather in single work, that is, in the singularity of a work, which is irreplaceable, in a singular event – I am referring here to *Ulysses* and to *Finnegans Wake* – the presumed totality, not only of one culture but of a number of cultures, a number of languages, literatures, and religions. (Derrida, 1996, 185)

Derrida doesn't investigate Joyce's particular use of language to find its root-cause, as Lacan does. The self-containment of the language system, or non-system for Derrida, expels every presence of non-language from its web. His deconstructive reading of Joyce remains to some degree similar to structuralist and semiotic textual reading, for like the latter, he sees the conglomeration of fragments of language as an in-built dynamism of the text itself. Besides, in Joyce, according to Derrida, the rupture of 'metaphoricity' and the multiplicity of languages make his text. This rupture is what happens in deconstruction:

> To this Derrida joined a fascination with the explosion of metaphoricity and of multilingual association in Joyce. 'It is from the tension between these two interpretations of language', he says in the 'Roundtable', 'that I tried to address the question of language'. (Caputo, 1997, 182)

Joyce's text is a mirror of Derrida's deconstruction because it often deconstructs itself, and the impossibility of its meaning and of presence is the impossibility where deconstruction comes into play. Joyce, for Derrida, as he himself admits, is '[a] name for an operation, an energy, that is always at work in language, and, hence, in deconstruction' (Derrida, 1996, 184).

Derrida's deconstruction fails with *Finnegans Wake* for what Joyce writes is Derrida's ultimate goal. Whereas in Lacan, Joyce's text is caught in a double bind of the *sinthome* that conjoins the author's ego, the unconscious, and his art. In addition, Derrida excludes Joyce's subjectivity and signature from his text, by his insistence on countersignature. Joyce's *linguistrick* for Derrida will be simply linguistic articulation, seeking its own deconstruction by its internal free play.

In the narrative background of the chapter of the four sailors, Joyce's obsession with the father emerges in the image of the dead father, bearing on Lacan's notion that Joyce is stuck with the father despite his rejection of him. This is prevalent in the iteration of the episode of the drowning Pharoah in the tales of the four sailors. In John's recollection, the drowning emerges as '[a]nd there was the drowning of Pharoah and all his predestrains and they were all completely drowned into the sea, the red sea' (*FW*, 387. 26–27). Lacan relates such images, as signifiers, to the non-existence of the real father figure in Joyce's discourse. Lacan insists that the idea of the dead father appears frequently in Joyce's discourse as the insistence of the Oedipal instance in the unconscious. For Lacan, in *Finnegans Wake* as in his other novels, Joyce gives the impression of the dead father, but fails because he is stuck to his father's problem, and succeeds in dumping him only by making a name for himself or replacing his proper name with a common name.

Johnny MacDougal is then the first of the sailors who tells the tale of his adventures. Then comes a cluster of puns: '[t]ruly they were four dear old heladies and really they looked awfully pretty and so nice and bespectable,' (*FW*, 386.16–18) and, 'darkumound', (22–23) 'prostituent', (24) 'creaters', 'prumisceous', (26–27) 'Gotopoxy [God-a-mercy]', (33) 'praisers be to deeseesee! [praise be to disease]', (38) 'hopolopocattle', (38) 'confusionaries', (387. 1) 'Noord Amerikaans', 'Suid African' and so on (2). Marcus or Mark begins his story as a reverberation of the previous ones, in which drowning happens yet again. 'The Flemish Armada, all scattered, and all officially drowned, there and then, on a lovely morning, after the universal flood, at about eleven thirty two was it?' (*FW*, 388. 10–13). Thus in Joyce's text the absence of the father appears in terms of a dead father in a circular movement that doesn't reach a culmination. This also reveals Joyce's belief in the circular flow of history that Lacan relates in *Le Sinthome* to Madame Blavatsky's notion of Hindu *mahamanvantara* – a cycle that symbolizes the universe and the movement of spiritual bodies. At the end, Mark seems to have become Joyce, when he lectures '[t]o the oceanfuls of collegians green and high classes and the poor scholars and all the old trinitarian senate and saints' (388. 36) and 'sages' (389.1). Later in the chapter, Joyce offers another pun 'Mahazar ag Dod! [Mother of God]' (32). He seems obsessed with bygone eras and the past as a whole, as he says [a]nd present and absent and past the present and perfect' (389. 18–19). Thus, the past is perfect when it is absent but present. All the four old men in their anecdotes reveal their fascination with the past. Finally, the third to tell a tale is Lucas (Luke), who becomes 'kingly leer [King Lear]' (398. 23). His adventures also echo what the past three men told in their tales. In this tale, the most important thing is the image of the 'Irish prisscess' (princess) who as we mentioned above can be likened to Molly as he writes, '[t]he vivid girl, deaf with love, (ah sure, you know her, our angel being, one of romance's fadeless wonderwomen' (395. 29–30).

Considering the last line of the chapter: 'So to John for a john, johnajeams,' (*FW*, 399. 34), Michel H. Begnal argues that this scene is inspired by 'The Mousetrap', in *Hamlet*, for Hamlet calls himself, 'A dull and muddy-mettled rascal, peak,/Like John-a-dreams' (*H*, III, i, 594). He writes, '[i]t is possible to see the Tristan and Isolde action as a play within a play, a miniature drama which is meant to aid the elucidation of the themes of the larger [drama]' (Begnal, 1974, 141) find out. The erotic scene in this chapter is precisely arranged like 'The Mousetrap' in *Hamlet*, creating a visual excitation on the part of both Hamlet in Shakespeare, and here the four old men or Mamalujo. The scene however, is not primarily for the elucidation of the larger drama as Begnal asserts but it presents a play on the gaze that always emerges in Joyce's works in terms of erotic representation. This means that the essential riveting power of the erotic scene in Joyce is a trap for the gaze. The scene produces an arresting effect on Mamalujo. As we mentioned above, at the end of the four adventures, the erotic scene with Tristan and Isolde recurs. Their names are now 'Iseult la belle! Tristan, sad hero!' (*FW*, 398. 29). At the conclusion of the chapter, Joyce repeats his mention of 'The Mousetrap', from *Hamlet*:

> at the end of it all, at that time (up) always, tired and all after doing the mousework and making it up, over their community singing (up) the top loft of the voicebox, of Mamalujo like the senior follies at murther magree, squatting round two by two. (*FW*, 397. 8–12)

The 'mousework', 'murther [muder], and squatting round two by two are allusions to Hamlet who sits with Ophelia while watching the play-within-the-play. Joyce produces a plenitude of possibilities in everything he says. Repetition of signifiers, their displacement and their constant interchanging and translocation convince us that there is a surplus of something latent in the letter which the author apparently wants to distort. Shakespeare too staged the-play-within-the-play in *Hamlet* for a similar effect. Joyce himself also recalls this play-within-the-play.

> A time.
> Act: dumbshow
> Closeups. Leads.
>
> (*FW*, 559)

As the obsessive repetition in Joyce's text warns, we may argue that this erotic scene at issue here has at its heart, a replication of the theme of Molly's monologue in 'Penelope', in *Ulysses* and Joyce's memory of it. Old Mark is a reincarnation of Leopold Bloom who throughout *Ulysses* is preoccupied with

Molly's adulterous affairs with Blazes Boylan. The Isolde of Celtic mythology, in fact, is Molly whom Joyce recalls here towards the end of the chapter as '([y]s! ys!), at all hours every night' (*FW*, 393. 31) and 'Miss Yiss' (398. 17). The sound of Molly's 'jangling bed' in Bloom's ear functioned as a signifier of his obsessive fantasy of cuckoldry. Here, the same fantasy is turned into a voyeuristic scene for Mamalujo. Moreover, from *Ulysses*, we know that Bloom was interested in seagulls and that he once fed them with a piece of cake. Mark may have been reincarnated in the guise of the young and knightly Tristan. The four old men are asleep and stay witness to the dream of King Mark. This is true to Joyce's literary personae in the *Wake*, who never appear as a single identity but are always subject to renaming. Reincarnation through different names is one of the central motifs in *Finnegans Wake*. The novel begins with the resurrection of Finnegan. As one commentator writes about Mark, '[h]is body, helpless on the floor, will be the King Mark of the story; but his spirit, rejuvenated in the sonlike image of the successful lover [Tristan], will know again the joys of the youthful lover' (Campbell, 1961, 248).

This is another feature of Joyce's characterizations that always resist a unified '*I*'. Every one is metamorphosed into different names. We always come upon the question of who this or that character really is. Is he a man, is she a woman? Is he Adam, Shaun, Bloom, Boylan, Joyce himself? Or is Isolde, Molly, Anna Livia, Nora, Eve and so on? The identity of names shifts constantly, because, according to Lacan, a subject in the symbolic is always being-less, and his being is deferred in the chain of signifiers, in the chain of naming and renaming. Joyce plays with writing his own name frequently in the *Wake*. As he writes, '[l]ong suffering of longstanding, ahs ohs ouis sis jas jos gias' (184, 1–2). Thurston comments,

> The adoption and adaptation, transplantation and translation of names form a central preoccupation, almost signature, of Joyce's art . . . When in *Ulysses* Bloom's name appears amid the 'nonsensical howlers of misprints' in a newspaper report as 'L. Bloom' (U 16.1260), the disfigured name might serve as an ironic index of the semiotic explosion or over-production potentially triggered by automatic – or rather, telegraphic – accidents of language. (Thurston, 2004, 67)

Besides erotica, laughter is another feature that frequently comes into the spotlight in the *Wake*. Throughout the novel, the phonetic and semantic distortions and the images they create or destroy more often than not rely on humour. As he writes:

> They were the big four, the four maaster waves of Erin, all listening, four. There was old Matt Gregory and then besides old Matt there was old Marcus Lyons, the four waves, and oftentimes they used to be saying grace together,

> right enough, bausnabeatha, in Miracle Squeer: here now we are the four of us: old Matt Gregory and old Marcus and old Luke Tarpey: the four of us and sure, thank God, there are no more of us. (*FW*, 384. 6–12)

And the *ekphrasis* – describing images in words: '[l]istening and listening to the oceans of kissening, with their eyes glistening, all the four, when he was kiddling and cuddling and bunnyhugging scrumptious his colleen bawn' (384. 19–21).

Like Derrida's deconstruction, Umberto Eco's theory of semiotics also centres its focus on the multiplicity of voices and meanings in Joyce's text, or the possibility of a perpetual semiosis that falls short in deciphering and uncovering the unconscious being which is the condition for Joyce's play with language, as Lacan insists. By considering socially and culturally predetermined signs, codes and sub-codes, Eco undermines Lacan's emphasis on the signifier and thus subscribes to the signified in terms of Saussure's structuralism. In *The Middle Ages of James Joyce,* Eco takes on Joyce's peculiar use of puns, and claims that in Joyce, puns make present both their components, namely vehicle and tenor '[b]oth embedded, reciprocally sending back one to another' (Eco, 1989, 65). He gave the example of Joyce's multi-cum-bilingual-pun 'Jungfraud's messonge book . . . *Jung + Freud + young + fraud + Jungfrau +message + songe + mensonge*' (65–66). Eco adds that when Joyce couldn't find a phonic similarity between two English words, he borrowed freely from every language in the world. For instance, since there is no such similarity between Jung and Freud, Joyce borrows the German word *jungfrau.* For Eco, each pun is constituted by the co-presence of pre-codified words and words that they dislocate. For Lacan, by contrast, puns are associated with an unconscious elation in which the disfiguring of the signifier allows for an eruption of polymorphous pleasure. Since Joyce rejects an imaginary relation to the Other, puns are addressed to no one, inscribing unconscious enjoyment as in jokes.

Drawing on his semiotic methodology, Eco takes the different signifiers in a pun as cultural or social references, or codes. He treats these signifiers as signifieds when he says, '[t]hese signifieds are the culturally defined units that a given culture has recognized and organized into a system of relationships' (Eco, 1989, 68). Thus Eco embeds Joyce's poetics of punning in its linguistic context and its relation to cultural determination. Joyce mixes up signs with the signifier or places the sign in the latter. As such, according to Eco, different poetics are at play within Joyce's discourse that '[r]eads as a meta-linguistic discourse about itself' (82). Eco reverses Lacan's dictum that the signifiers themselves in *Finnegans Wake* function as signifieds, whereas the letter, on the other hand, functions like a thing. Eco writes, 'In *Finnegans Wake,* Joyce establishes the possibility of defining our universe in the "transcendental" form of language. He provides a laboratory in which to formulate a model of reality and, in so doing, withdraws from things to language' (84–85). If things are conveyed through words, as Eco claims, then language itself can convey things. For Lacan, however, things are revealed when the texture of language breaks up, producing equivocation, and rapturous moments of non-meaning. When Lacan says that Joyce is writing the real, he means the author's capacity to play with language and produce a peculiar text reduces the organization of language to the debris of non-meaning. Thus, Derrida by attributing Joyce's use of language to the internal dynamism of the text, and Eco by connecting Joyce's messages to the pre-determined cultural codes deny subjective investment in the text. From Lacan we know that behind the systematic metamorphosis of language in Joyce unfolds the being of the subject side by side with the void and the object *a*. In other words, the signifier reveals the alienation of the subject that primarily tries to cover up this void with a magical object, the object *a*. Each individual product of the *linguistricks* that we have explored in this chapter, functions as object *a*, in the *Wake*. The object *a*, in turn, produces *jouissance* in Joycean hieroglyphics. Despite its role as unsettling and breaking up in discourse, the *sinthome* brings the triadic registers together, like holes in the rings of a chain; the *sinthome* allows the rings to knit together.

In sum, according to Lacan, Joyce sets out to employ a set of para/trans-linguistic devices or *linguistricks* in the *Wake* in order to inscribe the real and have access to his personal *jouissance*. When he decomposes the paradigmatic and syntagmatic networking of language, he is articulating a new language of his own. This is the language, which produces pure *jouissance* for him, like the babbling of an infant that mixes and remixes phonemes beyond any articulation (*lalangue*). A child will always use puns of his or her own making for pure enjoyment. In such a constant slippage of sound and sense, Lacan locates *jouissance*. It is not surprising that a child who first struggles to know language will pronounce every word as a pun. He or she may call computer, *pukiter*, boot as *toob*, put as *tup*, letter as *rettel* and so on, when they place the second consonant letter at the start of these words, enacting a wordplay that is part of the unconscious linguistic preoccupation. Joyce's example is 'jinglish janglage' (*FW*, 275. f.6) in which 'e' is changed into 'j', and then 'j' takes the place of 'l'. Lacan also uses onomatopoeia in his writing. Further, Joyce writes, '[i]t is surely a lesser ignorance to write a word with every consonant too few than to add all too many' (115. 1–2). Joyce doesn't speak his language but the latter speaks through him. His mind is infected with myriad letters and their dissipation into littering. Sometimes, Joyce uses homophonic sounds in an array of words but in different semantic fields. Joyce's text, according to Lacan, creates an unconscious horizon of lapses, spaces of non-meaning, cut discourse and so on. Like epiphany, *lalangue* is another device that takes a subject headlong into the real of the unconscious. Joyce himself was aware of something within himself that was inexpressible in conventional language. *Finnegans Wake* as he once hinted, represents a lucubration, the night version of literary discourse, so its language should be unique. The traditional use of language for Joyce is unable to communicate what a speaking being wants. This shows Joyce's self-awareness of the limits of language that in turn put limits on symbolization. There is always something left over in the symbolic that erupts as the real.

On this basis, we can formulate that the letter in Joyce is writing in the register of the real, whereas the signifier that is always fragmented and displaced represents a speech that becomes *lalangue.* That is why Joyce's text is full of a phonographic organization always distanced from its original semantic field. The letter has become a phonogram with no meaning. These letters allow the real to invade the symbolic. This being in the real makes the letter that resists any meaning a phonogram.

What about the nonsense in Joyce's text that caused H. G. Wells to name *Finnegans Wake,* the 'gibbering of a lunatic' (Wells, cited in Wales, 1992, 133). That nonsense was what Lacan defines in terms of the littering of the letter. In *Finnegans Wake,* the letter is always reminiscent of litter. Lacan identified with Joyce and Beckett when he defined their texts as suitable for *Poubellication* – his pun on publication and 'poubelle' (dustbin). Joyce himself says in *Finnegans Wake* that it is 'usylessly unreadable Blue Book', (*FW,* 179. 26–27), and '[h]ow very many piously forged palimpsests slipped in the first place by this morbid process from his pelagiarist pen?' (182.1–2). This is one of the reasons why Lacan has compared Joyce to Thomas Aquinas. The littering is aimed at writing the real and getting access to *jouissance.* In such a writing, unconscious residues find their way into the text. When a compulsive playfulness causes communication to collapse in *Finnegans Wake,* Lacan takes it as a digging of the hole in the symbolic. We can see the subject in such holes representing himself and his *jouissance* in the littering of the letters and signifiers. This littering takes place in a writing that brings the real to the fore and the *jouissance* that is in touch with it. Joyce's art enables him to write the real. His symptom, gives rise to this *sinthome.* Joyce manages to transform the latent psychotic structure of his writing into a creative work of art. Identification with the symptom allows the author to enjoy his own symptom and knot together the triadic registers that are falling apart due to the lack of the phallic signifier in Joycean discourse. Lacan saw this operation of the symptom in Joyce's text, so instead of delving into a thematic interpretation (something he has done with all other literary texts) he chose to analyse it in terms of Borromean knots.

The crucial factor in Lacan's approach is Joyce's trouble with the symbolic order, defined by the foreclosure of the Name-of-the-Father. The symbolic without the paternal function makes his writing incommensurate with a phallic signifying operation. According to Lacan, in order to compensate for the lack of the paternal signifier or the law of the father, Joyce self-consciously makes a name for himself, as one of the great writers with one of the great novels of the century trying to put an end to literature, or as Lacan says, the dream of literature. Lacan confirms this by quoting Joyce's statement that the *Wake* will keep the university professors busy for three centuries. As Lacan writes, it is '[n]ot

Joyce's desire to be an artist in whom everyone would be interested . . . a compensation for the fact that his father had never been a real father for him' (Lacan, cited in Roudinesco, 1997, 373). The *Wake* bears witness to this. On the last page of the novel, Joyce rounds off his 'circular circulation', (*FW*, 427. 7–8). Like a prodigal son, in the last turn of self-reflexivity, he makes himself the object of the Other's desire. He accepts 'fafafather of all schemes' (45.13), 'the bad father!' (94. 34–35), the 'Dirty Daddy' (94. 34–35), of the early novel, and self-effacingly bows down before his 'taddy', 'tid' [daddy, dadd] (628. 8, 8). In the last chapter of the novel the *I* is definitely Joyce himself, and *you*, his addressees, his father, mother and daughter:

> I am passing out. O bitter ending! I'll slip away before they're up. They'll never see. Nor know. Nor miss me. And it's old and old it's sad and old it's (FW, 627. 34-36) . . . sad and weary I go back to you, my cold father, my cold mad father, my cold mad feary father, till the near sight of the mere size of him, the moyles and moyles of it, moananoaning, makes me seasilt saltsick and I rush, my only, into your arms (628. 1-4) . . . Yes, carry me along, taddy (8) . . . I skink I'd die down over his feet, humbly dumbly, only to washup. Yes, tid. (10-12)

In addition to compensation for the lack of the Name-of-the-Father, in Lacan's view, Joyce's art helped him not to fall headlong into psychosis, by binding the triadic registers in his literary discourse in a fourth ring. This is the way he deploy his art as suppléance. This is the *sinthome*, which is as creative, and as redemptive as psychoanalytic therapy. Joyce has shown this by epiphanies in his earlier writings, which were the first signs of his symptom, and completed it with writing the real in *Finnegans Wake*. The epiphanies of *Ulysses* recur in the *Wake* in what Joyce calls telepathy, which seems to come to his mind every time he reads Freud's *The Interpretation of Dreams* that he calls a 'Messonge-book': '[e]veryday, precious, while m'm'ry's leaves are falling deeply on my Jungfraud's Messonge-book I will dream telepath posts dulcets on this isinglass stream' (*FW*, 460. 19–20). His phobia about Freud's text is also symptomatic because, as he admits, reading him often fomented what he describes as telepathy in him. Moreover, Joyce defended his daughter Lucia from the diagnosis of schizophrenia. This for Lacan was an attempt to make his own writings not appear schizophrenic too.

Joyce's symptom deconstructs language by littering the letter, displacing the contextual and isotopic field of each morpheme and each word. What is left in his discourse is the real of his unconscious that produces *jouissance*. Thus, in Joyce's discourse, the *sinthome* and the subversion of language are the determinants. At the heart of this symptom is the crippling power of language over a speaking being. As Lacan says, '[l]anguage [la parole] is a parasite: it is a veneer; it is the form of cancer which afflicts the human being . . . there are some who go as far as feeling it, and Joyce gives us a taste of it' (Lacan, 1975–1976, n. p.). For Lacan, the break-up of language itself is an effect of the unconscious, when non-meaning appears in writing. As Lacan teaches whenever language refuses to communicate, we are in the midst of the unconscious. Such blind spots in communication are of crucial importance for Lacanian literary criticism in which parts of the text escape the hold of discourse. Such moments, that have invaded almost the whole of the *Wake,* are arguably those moments that Joyce calls in a pun on psychology, a 'psocoldlogical [so-cold-logical] moment' (*FW,* 396. 14).

Finally, Joyce, like Lacan, invests a lot in his puns. For instance, 'wordherfhull', 'loveleast dress' (*FW,* 624. 22) 'foraignghistan', (493. 2), 'duchtars of Iran', (358. 22). He uses this pun when he has been talking about Irish prisscess (princess), who is Molly from *Ulysses* with '[a] firstclass pair of bedroom eyes, of most unhomy blue, (how weak we are, one and all!) . . . could you blame her, we're saying, for one psocoldlogical moment? What would Ewe do? With that so tiresome old milkless a ram' (*FW,* 396. 11–15). Joyce stresses here the power of human desire that when it reaches its extremes – psychological moments – overcomes resistance. Probably he is referring to Molly's extramarital affairs. Here the fragmented words and phrases are punctuated with the memory of Molly, and Joyce underpins those moments when a subject succumbs to desire. As he asked what would 'Ewe' do?

Lacan's theory of the *sinthome* is not confined to the study of *Finnegans Wake.* It is seminal for all contemporary and avant-garde literary texts and arts. In the next and last chapter, we will move on to discuss John Ashbery's poetry, whose work exhibits a similarly *sintomatic* structure.

Chapter 8

The Function of the Specular Image and the *Littoral* in John Ashbery's Poetry

Through examining two of John Ashbery's texts, the long poem, 'Self-Portrait in a Convex Mirror' (1972), and *Hotel Lautréamont,* a collection from 1992, I wish to set two goals in this last chapter. First, to show that in Lacanian criticism, a literary discourse itself calls for an appropriate critical mode. Second, in order to consolidate this notion, I will try to apply two different modes of interpretation to the texts, which have been developed in Lacan's earliest and final phases of teaching. In the first poetic text, I will show how the subject is getting an imaginary mastery of his ego by identifying with his own mirror image or his 'fellow-being' (Roudinesco, 2003, 29). In the second text I will consider Lacan's theory of the *sinthome* and supplement this with his idea of the *littoral* from his essay '*Lituraterre*', which maps a topological account of textual writing. Lacan, in this essay, suggests that a critic has to *lituraterre* literature; thus himself developing *lituraterre* as a critical technique. This combination will redouble the exegetical power of our critique of Ashbery's poetics, especially those approximations to the real that following Lacan, we call *littorals* that have to be taken into account as the signifying localization of the *jouissance* and the unconscious knowledge in a text. The two theoretical texts, furthermore, conceive of art and poetry as a way of inventing an artifact that is produced in *jouissance* for the sake of *jouissance*; and Ashbery's first text functions as a *mise-en-acte* of Lacan's *stade du miroir* (mirror phase), and the second a site that is littered with *littorals*. Unmasking these *littorals* as residues of the real in literature offers literary studies a new mode of reading as well as an exceptional critical authority. As Leclaire states,

> The work of the psychoanalyst is defined by one imperative: *to unmask the real.* His goal is to reveal the inconceivable place in which anxiety unfolds, to shine light into the crack in which ecstasy hides. It is in this locus of the impossible that the psychoanalyst locates the object as nameless index of the real. (Leclaire, 1999, 320)

Unmasking the real here is, in fact, an exposition of the symptom of the poet. Language becomes effective in Lacan when it becomes writing. For writing is anterior to the signifier and has a power that can instantiate the real of the unconscious in a process permeated with erasures and disruptive holes. Writing, in Lacanian theory, functions as a separate register, and a *lucubration* of the signifier that has precedence over speech. In other words, the interaction of the unconscious process and the poet's symptom produces breakages in the signifying process of the symbolic. This means that in terms of Lacan's theory, in textual writing, of which poetry is the epitome, the *littoral* discloses the real, and marks out a process that allows unknown unconscious knowledge to transform into enjoyment. As the impasse of signification, the *littoral* is thus the *sinthome* of Ashbery's poetic creation. I use the *littoral* as that which Lacan describes in Encore, '[t]he textual work that comes out the spider's belly, its web . . . that show the real acceding to the symbolic' (Lacan, 1998a, 93).

As Ashbery's poetic cryptograms, the enigmas are aggregated by his prolific allusions, dense and open-ended hyper-textuality, and intentional opacities. Thus, Ashbery brings enigmas into play in his text as a response to what resists the symbolic. This, in light of late Lacan, is Ashbery's art through which the poet displays and dramatizes the core of subjectivity and enjoys his own unconscious. The source of the *jouissance* is thus non-meanings and erasures – non-perceptible *littorals*.

Like other avant-garde literary texts, in Ashbery's poetry, these indelible textual loci remain covered with excessive borrowings. Following Lacan's essay '*Lituraterre*', we have concluded in the preceding chapters that these *littorals* function as erasures that divide unconscious knowledge from *jouissance*. Thus, when we come across a *littoral* in Ashbery's verse, we are dealing with a rupture in the unconscious signifying chain, to which the poet gains access by way of the enjoyment of his symptom. As Voruz describes such a process:

> The unconscious knows the unknown of its inscription, or the unconscious is a *lucubration* of knowledge on an inscription that does not belong to the order of the knowable. The unconscious is now revealed as the conjunction of knowledge and the mark of jouissance. (Voruz, 2002, 132)

The *littorals* in Ashbery, nevertheless, function like Joyce's fragmentation of the signifiers, not at the level of the letters but at the level of words, phrases, sentences and the overall semantic network. The *littorals* mark semantic confusions in Ashbery's text as the eruptions of the inassimilable in language that ceaselessly bubbles through the poet's text in the guise of enigmas and impenetrable textual opacities. This, in other words, is the way the poet reveals his own symptom, providing an explanation for his art and for *jouissance* as well:

> The work of art as *sinthome* is a unique response that contains the enigma it corresponds to and that brings it about, an enigma that resonates with a

> lacuna of a quite different status than that of the Symbolic. It corresponds, not to a lack defined by the phallic mechanism of castration, but to what is not yet there, what is yet to come, what resists the Symbolic. (Ettinger, 2002, 96)

Such a process, however, doesn't happen as an isolated event. On the contrary, it incorporates and re-enacts a concatenation of infantile experiences that arise from the tension between the imaginary and the symbolic. The subject embarks on such activities in the period of language acquisition. Lacan argues that the first encounter of the subject with pre-existing language is itself metaphoric, because the subject receives his signifiers from the Other in reverse, so that their effect as such can be expressed only metaphorically. When an intention passes through the Other, it bends itself at the *point de capiton*, which has the structure of a metaphor in which signifiers function as symbols of absence. Considering this view, the poetry attempts to re-enact this play of the tropic encounter of one's self with language. For language functions as both a site for a subject's self-alienation, as well as a space for the subject to re-find and express this self-alienation. In this sense, a subject's unconscious language takes the form of poetry. Poetry, thus, pushes language to its limits. In such a context, Lacan argues in *Écrits* that once the tropic game or the process of concealment ceases, poetry too comes to an end. This process in poetry should not be understood as a self-conscious articulation but as a rupture between consciousness and perception, just as the insistence of affect is a response to the failure of conceptualization. Like concealment, the *littoral* makes holes in the signifying chain that give way to an absence in the discourse.

In both texts in question, Ashbery seems poised between two legendary artists, the Italian Renaissance painter, Parmigianino, and the French surrealist poet Comte de Lautréamont. He aims to draw upon them for his own projective identification. Ashbery's 'Self-Portrait in a Convex Mirror', reveals a disjointed and polymorphous signifying operation where, in the most part, a given semantic field attached to a signifier is not on a par with the underlying syntactic plane. The spread of non-meaning and non-knowledge (unconscious knowledge) produces an intentional interpellation of enigmas, elision and ambiguities. These empty spaces are filled in with allusions and a web of borrowings from any text and anyone in a dense inter-textual free play. This interpellation, as we pointed out, is indicative of the splits between the registers and a failure in the symbolization of the imaginary. The images and the visual interplay that take place in the mirror phase have to be articulated in the coherent and harmonized language of the symbolic. Because of the inherent incompatibility between the two registers (especially with the interference of the foreclosure of the master signifier), the codes and rules of the symbolic become chaotic. This symbolization, of course, is not articulated by the symbolic order and that is why it endlessly emerges as blind spots in the 'Self Portrait'. Nevertheless, whenever we come upon a resistance to signification or a persistence of non-meaning, we are in the midst of a penumbra, a textual conflict where access to the symbolic register is blocked out. In other words, the *littorals* disrupt the articulation of signifiers in the symbolic register. This is what occurs in poetry, the effect of a force that pushes the poet to the limit – subversion of meaning and intelligibility in his or her poetics.

The 'Self Portrait', starts off with a description of the anamorphic painting by Parmigianino in which a spectacular and larger than life hand frames the face of the painter. Amid borrowings from the painter's biographer and art critic, Vasari, the poem introduces us to the human 'soul', the central signifier of the self that is caught between its own self-image and its reflection in the mirror. The 'soul' represents the Lacanian subject that finds itself captured in the vortex of imaginary narcissism, where its ego is alienated from itself, in the mirror phase. This vortex later turns into the symbolic matrix for the formation of the lyric *I* of the poem that is always in a struggle to transform itself into a textual subject.

Lively and intact in a recurring wave
Of arrival. The soul establishes itself.
But how far can it swim out through the eyes
And still return safely to its nest? The surface
Of the mirror being convex, the distance increases
Significantly; that is, enough to make the point
That the soul is a captive, treated humanely, kept
In suspension, unable to advance much farther
Than your look as it intercepts the picture.

('SPCM', 68)

The images of the poem portray the soul or the self as captive in the mirror, and as something that cannot be distinguished from its own picture. For the ego identifies with the mirror image of itself from the outside. Therefore, as the poem insists, the soul is an image, and presents itself by words that are also essentially images. Ashbery's pun 'speculation' etymologically derives the mirror from the Latin '*speculum*'. The soul or the self portrays itself with images and his words are also images. The poem demonstrates that the poet is in the imaginary in which perception is only possible in terms of images not words.

. . . that the soul is not a soul,
Has no secret, is small, and it fits
Its hollow perfectly: its room, our moment of attention.
That is the tune but there are no words.
The words are only speculation
(From the Latin speculum, mirror)

('SPCM', 69)

As the poem develops, Ashbery seems to distinguish the look from the gaze, which according to Lacan, belongs to a different register. The origin of the look is not the same as the gaze. Reflection doesn't belong to the one who looks, but to the Other that already looks at the subject with its captivating and hypnotizing power, the power that Hoffmann often describes in his stories. For example, Nathaniel, the central character of the short story 'The Sandman' falls in love with the image of a wooden doll. He is fooled by this false image and its otherness. That is the reason why Hoffmann's characters are easily captivated by false images, which often take the power of reflection from them. With this void of reflection, the otherness of the image is internalized by the subject. The poet too seems to be replaced by the Otherness of the painter with whom he identifies:

> (It is the first mirror portrait),
> So that you could be fooled for a moment
> Before you realize the reflection
> Isn't yours. You feel then like one of those
> Hoffmann characters who have been deprived
> Of a reflection, except that the whole of me
> Is seen to be supplanted by the strict
> Otherness of the painter in his
> Other room.
>
> ('SPCM', 74)

The conflict between self and other, self-alienation and ambivalence towards the specular image recur throughout the poem, which is related to the *méconnaissance* of both the ego and self-knowledge in the mirror-phase. Ashbery is pondering here how there can be self-reflection and a return gaze when the subject looks at 'otherness'. He explains that in the mirror there is more than the reflection of the self. What we see in the mirror is a reflection of ourselves but also being itself as something that is not in us, what Ashbery calls 'Not-be-in-us'. Ashbery insists on self-alienation in the imaginary in which the subject remains stuck in a seesaw with his mirror image which he fails to articulate in the symbolic register. The relation of the subject to the Other, according to Lacan, is often blocked by an imaginary fixation of the subject with the mirror image.

> This otherness, this
> 'Not-be-in-us' is all there is to look at
> In the mirror, though no one can say
> How it came to be this way.
>
> ('SPCM', 81)

This mirror exchange is what in Lacanian psychoanalysis could be called homeo(heteromorphic) identification in the mirror phase. The relation of the subject to the image in the mirror, or to an object, or a person, is strange to the subject, yet provides the invisible centre of gravity of its subjectivity and its desire in the imaginary.

In *The Four Fundamental Concepts of Psychoanalysis,* Lacan draws on a figure to illustrate how the decentred ego sees itself in the mirror as a whole and unity:

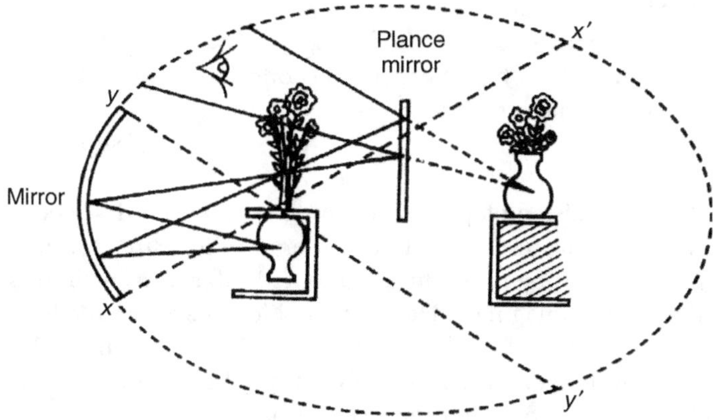

Lacan, 1979, 145.

The figure illustrates the decentred subject, $ finding the imago of his body in the mirror as a whole and united entity. This misrecognized *gestalt* and wholeness is grounded in the picture of the *ego ideal,* i(*a*), the image of the self in the mirror. The decentred subject is shown in a flowerpot in the left side where the flower is visible but the pot is hidden in a box, which remains invisible. By contrast, the flowerpot looks in the mirror on the right hand side to be a perfectly visible flowerpot. The only invisible part is the box that is hidden on the left hand side. At stake here is the subject who projects his fragmented ego on the image in the mirror which is external to him. Ashbery's personae seem lost in the mirror that in return portrays him in the uncertainty imposed by the external image. The poet dramatizes the constitutive exclusion of the elements of the self in the mirror image that amounts to a radical otherness of the subject to his own self. The poet's use of the mirror, other and otherness, self-alienation, and Hoffmann's characters moreover, suggest and confirm the otherness of the subject to itself and in relation to the Other. In the imaginary game that Ashbery is re-enacting in his long poem, the ego is shown to be other to itself. This illustrates Lacan's emphasis in his theory of the gaze on how the gaze from the outside transforms the subject's position from being-in-looking to a position of being looked at. This looking and being looked at takes place in a scopic field in which the subject is determined by the gaze from the outside. In this context, according to Lacan, a subject is a picture that wants to be looked at.

The contextual structure of the poem here as elsewhere in Ashbery's poetry indicates his interest in epistemological arguments. This is what Lacan defines as a common ground between art and psychoanalysis. The word is the murder of the thing in Lacan's teaching, and the poet is aware unconsciously of the limit of language which always fails to hold on to its contents.

Or the other notion that,
because there is in this world no one thing
to which the bramble of blackberry corresponds,
a word is elegy to what it signifies.

(Ashbery, 1995, 417)

Ashbery takes this epistemological quest further when he describes the function of the critic and art historian. His comments indicate that for him painting and poetry connect a subject and his fragmented subjectivity with the spectacular scopic field of the imaginary. He views the idea of artistic freedom in terms of 'art for art's sake' to be elusive, for the artist always remains under cultural constraints, and inner voices call for a revelation of the truth not as it is in the real world, but as an artificial and distorted product.

Plunged in the imaginary, the poet shows the intersection of the imaginary and the symbolic, where meaning arises. However, this meaning is temporarily erased when the symbolic intersects with the real and the imaginary becomes absent. These temporal moments or flashes illustrate the closure of the unconscious in which something cannot be articulated in the symbolic. These moments are what we want to explore here. In other words, when the signifier fails to signify and thus defers its signification to another signifier, we know that this failed signifier has installed within itself the lack of being, or the division of the subject. This break in signification, in turn, brings out a fracture in knowledge due to primary repression. In such moments of breakage, as in the following lines, verbal hallucination or the *littoral* gives way to the release of *jouissance*. The imaginary fails to pass into the symbolic, and the real emerges where something resists symbolization. In the following verses, the discourse breaks up and a reader is plunged into fragmented images.

The balloon pops, the attention
Turns dully away. Clouds
In the puffle stir up into sawtoothed fragments.

('SPCM', 70)

Like vapor scattered on the wind. The fertile
Thought-associations that until now came

So easily, appear no more, or rarely. Their
Colorings are less intense, washed out
By autumn rains and winds, spoiled, muddied,
Given back to you because they are worthless.

(81)

The 'Self-Portrait' is divided into six parts. The first immerses the reader in the poet's preoccupation with the present, past and future tenses which remind us of the pre-occupation of the narcissistic subject with time. The second part manifests an exceptional semantic and syntactic coherence in comparison to the other parts of the poem. Here, Ashbery asserts his belief about artistic creation as a product that comes into being as a result of a compromise between the artist and the constraints of expression. 'His (Ashbery's) poetry is reconciliation, at its best, between the human subject and the inhuman working of arbitrariness, between the fact of value and the value of fact' (Shapiro, 1979, 12). These cultural constraints are, in fact, the poet's own inner urges that he seems keen to project onto the outside. To this end, Ashbery wants his reader to believe that memories of the past, cultural injunctions, even what Lacan calls *psychasthenia* (spatial captation) push an artist's brush and a poet's pen in a direction other than what they intended in the first place.

Meanwhile Ashbery here is influenced by the Parisian Oulipo's group of poets and writers who preached inspiration through socio-cultural constraints. The Oulipo consider literature as a 'combination of inspiration and constraint, and [explore] how formal constraints can be used to generate literary text' (Macey, 2001, 286).

Ashbery parodies Parmigianino's portrait and sees it as his own self-portrait. In the painting itself, the hand that looks larger than the face and the claw-like fingers display the painter's obsession with objectifying the image. The hand seems to be amazing him. Parmigianino's painting that presents the truth in a distorted way is used by Ashbery as a template for the core of creativity in art. Ashbery identifies with Parmigianino as though the painter was his ideal-ego. Still, the poet portrays himself as a literary subject who is lost in an identity that is outside himself and that takes a thousand and one shapes. The self is depicted as fixed and lost in these polymorphous images. 'Me on all side', 'boil down to one', 'uniform substance' and 'magma of interiors', in the following passage, suggest the loss of bodily unity in the imaginary and the crisis of the primary identification of the ego. Ashbery lucidly re-stages a visual interplay of the eye with the mirror image that constitutes the ego and the specular *I* that misunderstands it. He knows the captivating and the generative force of this image in the psycho-ontological development in a subject's life. The eyes 'are empty', and 'know nothing', but after an interaction with the 'round mirror which organises everything', they visualize and comprehend a plethora of objects. Here Ashbery's revelation is what Lacan conceptualized as 'scotomisation' in which, the 'Lacanian subject is caught in a contentious struggle for mastery between the eye and the gaze' (Apter, cited in Jay, 1994, 353). This shows the function of the imago that determines the alienation of the subject in the jubilant and aggressive relationship between the body and its reality:

I see in this only the chaos
Of your round mirror which organises everything
Around the polestar of your eyes which are empty,
Know nothing, dream but reveal nothing.
I feel the carousel starting slowly
And going faster and faster: desk, papers, books,
Photographs of friends, the window and the trees
Merging in one neutral band that surrounds
Me on all sides, everywhere I look.
And I cannot explain the action of leveling,
Why it should all boil down to one
Uniform substance, a magma of interiors.

('SPCM', 71)

The present moment is Ashbery's muse. His poetics dwell on the immediacy of the now, its thought, feeling, ecstasies and melancholies. This self-confession and self-description are told in figurative mode in the last and longest part of the 'Self-Portrait'. In the following passage, he outlines his own experience with the composition of his verses during which diverse and opposing ideas and tendencies take his thought in a direction that he did not intend. Thus, Ashbery illustrates in his poem deep psychoanalytic insights:

It is the principle that makes works of art so unlike
What the artist intended. Often he finds
He has omitted the thing he started out to say
In the first place. Seduced by flowers,
Explicit pleasures, he blames himself (though
Secretly satisfied with the result), imagining
He had a say in the matter and exercised
An option of which he was hardly conscious.

('SPCM', 80)

The imagery in 'Self-Portrait' is typical of Ashbery's early poetry, and at surface, on a par with the romantic quest for natural and cultural parallelism. His intensive use of images demonstrates that the poet's early poetry is mainly settled in the imaginary, as a selection of passages show.

The soul has to stay where it is,
Even though restless, hearing raindrops at the pane,

The sighing of autumn leaves thrashed by the wind,
Longing to be free, outside, but it must stay
Posing in this place

('SPCM', 69)

A breeze like the turning of a page
Brings back your face: the moment
Takes such a big bite out of the haze
Of pleasant intuition it comes after.

(76)

Yet the 'poetic', straw-colored space
Of the long corridor that leads back to the painting,
Its darkening opposite – is this
Some figment of 'art', not to be imagined
As real, let alone special? Hasn't it too its lair?

(78)

The first passage portrays Ashbery's familiar preoccupation with self-alienation and autonomy within a poetic creation that has to be always free from constraint. The 'autumn leaves', depend for their movement on something from the outside, as leaves need wind to fall. This metaphorical use of the 'leaves' thus reveals a tendency in the self or 'soul' to look outside to gain freedom from its origin. However, the poet advises the soul to look within for its freedom. The second passage gives us the moment of poetic 'intuition' that comes like a 'breeze' and shines through 'haze'. The breeze here refers to those pleasant moments in a subject's memory related to those Lacanian infantile jubilees in the mirror whose repetition in a text is a pleasurable experience. The final passage combines poetry and painting as arts that have a 'darkening opposite' that cannot be accounted for. The images that Ashbery accumulates here are signifiers that have a signification beyond what they attempt to mean. The images create their own signifying field as a pictorial visualization but with a symbolic meaning. Yet, the images as representatives, like words, have their own *jouissance.* The images act out the imaginary preoccupation with the process of image-formation that perception is primarily dependant on. What Ashbery is concerned about is the splitting of the self. He wants to gain wholeness by keeping the 'soul' that represents the self in its place, as he says in the first line of the first passage, 'the soul has to stay where it is'. From Lacan we know that the self of the subject is not separated from the signifier, therefore, 'raindrops at the pane', and 'sighing of autumn leaves', signify that the self is torn apart and the poet wants to assemble them back into a single unifying strand. All this shows the poet's attempt to recover his alienated self and create a centre for the subject in language. The long poem, in short, seems to be an imagined seesaw between the poet and his ideal-ego, Parmigianino.

In a very bleak image that recalls *The Waste Land*, Ashbery expresses his discontent with post-modern society. The context of the poem and its analogy to T. S. Eliot suggest that the poet's grievances are in reference to the contemporary cultural milieu in which he lives.

> In the climate of sighs flung across our world
> A cloth over a birdcage.
>
> ('SPCM', 77)

> We have seen the city; it is the gibbous
> Mirrored eye of an insect. All things happen
> On its balcony and are resumed within,
> But the action is the cold, syrupy flow.
>
> (63)

In the end, Ashbery is wondering for the last time about the *I* he is representing or the subject that speaks through him. This is the *I* that functions as a literary subject and designates the subject of enunciation in relation to the unconscious. This *I*, as often in Ashbery's poetry, emerges in the silent and shadowy emptiness of the image in the mirror, vainly seeking his own image in the other. The poem ends with a despairing emptiness. This emptiness represents the void and lack of the Other and the self. Language separates the self from the other of the imaginary and marks the Other of the symbolic with absence as well. This lack in literary discourse manifests the emergence of the real as a result of the failure of the passage of the imaginary into the symbolic. This impasse causes a poet to fight with language and its conventions. This otherness of the image in the mirror, according to earlier Lacan, has a captivating and seductive power.

Ashbery demonstrates a disregard for the coherent organization of his verses. Such a semantic incoherence allows him to create a puzzling condensation of meanings in his poetry. Through such a strategy, the poet wants to create *littorals* in order to produce a polymorphous semantic field. As Jacques-Alain Miller writes in his essay 'Lacan's Later Teaching': '[t]his is what poetry exploits in order, as Lacan says, to wreak violence on the common usage of language' (Miller, 2003, 40). By means of these blind spots in the semantic field, the *sinthome* ensures its textual presence in the unconscious eruption through voids and gaps in the text. As Lacan says, '[t]he *sinthome* is situated at the place where the knot slips, where there is a lapsus of knot' (Lacan, 1975–1976, n. page). This strategy calls for widely different responses to Ashbery's poetry.

Ashbery seems more in line with French poetics and the sudden disruptions in the flow of his poems are comparable to Mallarmé and Lautréamont. Writing on Lautréamont's novel, *Les Chants de Maldoror* [*Songs of Maldoror*], Maurice Blanchot identifies a consistent discontinuity and disruption in Lautréamont's discourse. Blanchot's reference to this abrupt disruption in discourse reveals what Lacan calls the *littorals,* which, as we have pointed out earlier, connect unconscious knowledge and *jouissance*.

Ashbery's collection of poems, *Hotel Lautréamont,* draws on the legendary French poet Isidore Lucien Ducasse, who became the godfather of the surrealist movement in France.

Poets always claim they bring new metaphors to life and bring into view a hitherto unfathomable field. Ashbery shows his affiliation to this poetic tradition when he says that, unlike other poets, he respects his audience by offering it something new, something that his reader didn't know before. Like Aristotle, Lacan saw the poet as a prophet capable of saying something new. As Soler says, Lacan '[p]uts the poet beside the prophet, which means that poetry belongs to the dimension of pure saying (*le dire*)' (Soler, 2003, 96). Ashbery compulsively draws upon paradoxes and riddles in his text. Like his long poem, here too he identifies with the French poet and portrays him as his alter-ego. Although he is referring to Lautréamont's habit of disclaiming his own verses after he wrote them, he seems to show the fragmentary nature of the being that writes itself every hour anew:

> Dear ghost, what shelter
> in the noonday crowd? I'm going to write
> an hour, then read
> what someone else has written
>
> (*HL*, 3)

'Light Turnouts' is the opening poem of *Hotel Lautréamont,* a poem in rather simple and conversational language in which the poet alludes to Lautréamont, who becomes Ashbery's ideal-ego:

> You've no mansion for this to happen in.
> But your adventures are like safe houses,
> your knowing where to stop an adventure
> of another order like seizing the weather.
>
> We too are embroiled in this scene of happening,
> and when we speak the same phrase together:
> 'We used to have one of those',
> it matters like a shot in the dark.
>
> (*HL*, 3)

Ashbery refers to Lautréamont's adventurous life, and his restless soul that could not stay for a single day in the same place. The repeated phrase, 'one of us', identifies the poets with one another:

> One of us stays behind.
> One of us advances on the bridge

as on a carpet. Life – it's marvelous–
follows and falls behind.

(*HL*, 3)

'The Garden of False Civility', is another poem where Ashbery laments the loss of his alter-ego. However, it is not certain who the addressee of the poem is. Is it referring to Lautréamont or the original loss of the expulsion of humanity from the Garden of Eden? In much the same way as Donne, while he is lamenting loss as the source of his suffering, the poet desires an illusory wholeness, this lost object that he saw for the first time and the last time together. The subject of his text is anxious about this lost home, the pre-symbolic void that he describes with superb imagery.

Where are you? Where you are is the one thing I love,
Yet it always escapes me, like the lilacs in their leaves

(*HL*, 8)

The last time I see you is the first
commencing of our time to be together, as the light of the days
remains the same even as they grow shorter,
stepping into the harness of winter.

(8)

A few subtle rhyming lines punctuate the usually prosaic flow of his verse. Here, the poet's only compensation for that bygone time is the gift of his poetry or, to be more precise, his poetic style. Such a swing in poetic discourse shows Ashbery's familiar deployment of semantic emptiness and a polymorphous association of ideas:

Between watching the paint dry and the grass grow
I have nothing too tragic in tow.
I have this melting elixir for you, front row
tickets for the concert to which all go.
I ought to
chasten my style, burnish my skin, to get the glow
that is all-important . . .

(*HL*, 8)

Towards the end of the poem, Ashbery tells us that he remembers only 'sightings' of those bygone times. This confirms the connection between the past and the imaginary, which thus emerges only as holes and voids in the symbolic. The noun 'sightings' has the power to evoke a landscape in our mind. Right from the beginning, each stanza refers again to the place that is missing forever.

The iteration of the same in each line affirms what Jakobson said about a poetic text as a pursuit of the law of syntactic parallelism. In a declarative mode, each stanza stresses this lost location. The semantic unity in this poem is caused by interference in such a parallelism of signifiers in Lacanian terms, which bears on the unity of the poem as a whole.

> Measly is a good word to describe
> the running between the incoming and the outgoing tide
> as who in what narrow channels shall ever
> afterwards remember the keen sightings of those times,
> the reward and the pleasure.
> Soon it was sliding out to sea
> most naturally, as the place to be.
>
> (*HL*, 8)

Many critics blame the poet for disseminating non-sense. This accusation is addressed to the blind spots in the texture of the poem, what we call *littorals.* Phrases such as 'harness of winter' (first stanza), 'ticket for the concert' (second stanza), 'the running between the incoming and outgoing tide' (third stanza), make intrusions in the overall semantic field of the poem, and consequently make gaps that disrupt the flow of the poem and don't lend themselves to communicative significance. Such a paradox 'gives body, in its repetitive pattern, to some elementary matrix of *jouissance,* of excessive enjoyment' (Žižek, 1992a, 199). It is noteworthy that the above phrases apparently make syntactic sense, but they stand on their own without any referent. For example, we don't know what ticket and what concert the poet is referring to.

In the title poem 'Hotel Lautréamont', each quatrain repeats its second and fourth lines in the first and third lines of the next quatrain. The *pantoum* (Malayan poetic style), gives a more metonymic power to the semantic texture and the central idea of the poem. The poem is divided into four sections that each consist of four quatrains. Each section tries to deal with the idea of how the collective imagination influences the thoughts and feelings of the individual. In the first section, several works of art are presented as examples of how people in each era produce a certain artistic style by way of collective production. The poem proposes that the art of poetry serves certain roles determined by collective social demands, the demands that ultimately affect the integrity of the poetry itself. Ballads are mentioned as examples of collective production that have been handed down orally for centuries. The road to imagination was opened by collective euphoria as a sign of our 'commonality'.

In the third section, the poet seems to put this sense of 'commonality' into question as far as the empirical demands of time rule it by taking everything hostage. The imagination is a force within a poet, which transcends time. Ashbery revives the quest of Romanticism for breaking art free of any constraint.

He advocates spontaneity and lyrical experimentalism in poetry. In the last section, the poet vigorously asks his reader to join his quest for a change in this tradition, which now looks passé:

> It was their choice, after all, that spurred us to feats of the imagination.
> Now, silently as one mounts a stair we emerge into the open
> and in so doing deprive time of further hostages,
> to end the standoff that history long ago began.
>
> (*HL*, 15)

The next quatrain in this last section inaugurates an antithesis. It now seems illusory that we have reached a time when we have to abandon tradition. If we do so, we will end up in perversity:

> Now, silently as one mounts a stair we emerge into the open
> but it is shrouded, veiled: We must have made some ghastly error.
> To end the standoff that history long ago began
> Must we thrust ever onward, into perversity?
> . . .
> You mop your forehead with a rose, recommending its thorns.
> Research has shown that ballads were produced by all of society;
> Only night knows for sure. The secret is safe with her:
> the people, then, knew what they wanted and how to get it.
> (*HL*, 16)

The *Hotel Lautréamont* satirizes collective imagination and its deterministic role in the production of a work of art. In the second quatrain, the poet shows his scorn for the collective signifier.

However, towards the end of the poem, the poet rehearses his antithesis once more when he wants us to think that a quest for change culminates in perversity.

> But it is shrouded, veiled: we must have made some ghastly error
> You mop your forehead with a rose, recommending its thorns.
> Must we thrust ever onward, into perversity?
> Only night knows for sure; the secret is safe with her.
>
> (*HL*, 16)

Ashbery is a poet who knows that to undermine collective cultural signifiers and create personal ones would naturally end up in perversion and other extremes. When a poet cannot enmesh the real into a symbolic network, perversion will be the logical result.

In abstract and loose syntax, 'Another Example', displays Ashbery's taste for the avant-garde strategy of shocking the reader. Right from the opening lines, we know that the poet is busy with his illusory interlocutors; we are entangled in a web of pronouns, '*we*', '*they*', '*you*' and '*he*'. It is not certain where a reader can situate the *I* as the self-image of the poet. Who are '*we*', '*they*', '*you*'? And finally who is that 'he' who jumps into the last line of the poem. As in 'Self Portrait', here too, Ashbery seems to be wondering about the fragmentary nature of the self, through the mixing of pronouns. This mix of voices does not represent a cacophony. It rather represents a single voice raised by many individuals. The poem is permeated with broken utterances, and the emission of anaphors (words or phrases referring to their earlier use). Even the poem in its entirety doesn't seem to reveal a sequence of meaning or a linear logic:

Of our example, earth,
we know the star-shaped universe:
divisions,
somewhere,
of July streets.
Is it a bucket you sit in
Or on?
How they led us past the fence.
The one horse was mortified.

(*HL*, 49)

This poem offers a synoptic view of the function of the *littoral* in Ashbery's poetic discourse, pockmarked by erasure and absences showing that signifiers cannot signify anything. Each part of the poem violates semantic or referential equivalence. Each word and phrase in the poem functions as a hole in the real. Even if we consider the poem in its entirety, it still doesn't give us a distinct meaning. The text breaks the signifying process at every moment, accumulating an incoherent sequence of unrelated elements. This poem bears witness to our claim that in Ashbery's text, lacunae or holes, in the Lacanian sense, instead of filling themselves function as *littorals* in order to invoke *jouissance*. The non-meaning of these *littorals* and their reproduction reveal the poet's *sinthome* through which he creates his art and his name as the one who knows how to enjoy his unconscious. Ashbery's poetry is a distilled form of writing that leaves disjointed traces of the unconscious, accommodating ruptures that allow the poet to dive into the real of *jouissance*:

To be revived like paper ants
and then endure the long vacuum of pre-eternity
and still be allowed to buy something
on the station platform?

The train is turning away –
There are no familiar quotations.
Here, put some on a plate, he said. That's the way.

(*HL*, 49)

Andrew Ross in his *The Failure of Modernism: Symptom of American Poetry* enlists Ashbery along with Eliot and Olson as the symptom of American poetry. Ashbery is a reminder of a '[s]ymptom's wayward resistance to linear readings' (Ross, 1986, 217). The symptom in Ross is not like the one Lacan redefines in his final teaching. Instead, I would argue that Ashbery's poetry is a resistance to the American symptom. We may well conclude that Ashbery is a 'symptom' in American poetry for his quarrel with American ego-psychology, and his denial of the intrinsic logos that had been first identified by T. S. Eliot who claimed that ego-psychology '[p]roduces monsters; for it is attempting to produce unified individuals in a world without unity' (218). Ashbery's poetics subverts, above all, the American obsession with ego-psychology, and instead, he adapts post-structuralism and European patterns of avant-garde poetry.

Although Joycean play with unconscious rhetoric isn't a salient feature in Ashbery's poetry, he occasionally exhibits playfulness with language in *Hotel Lautréamont*. To take an example, in 'A Mourning Forbidding Valediction' he borrows the title of a John Donne poem that we commented upon in an earlier chapter. At the opening of the poem, he uses the verb 'done' as a pun for the English Renaissance poet's name. Words such as 'thee', 'squall', 'sirens', 'perfume', 'drenches', 'pall', 'scent', 'waxeth' and 'sun' mimic Donne's words.

And who, when all is said and done,
Cares for thee like me? I know. Thy name
Is known to me, and if thou sufferest like a squall
That sirens rend, I'll be confident and of the other
Persuasion. Perfume that drenches like a pall
Is the old scent, and drear, true; its fame
Waxeth with the sun
And is not like, moreover, a lost brother.

(*HL*, 114)

Drawing on tumbling syntax and a classical semantic pattern, Ashbery identifies with Donne and imagines a parallel between the latter's eternal art and his own poetry which were both composed at a time that was 'frozen' and 'flinty'. Here, we encounter the familiar Ashberian potpourri of things, ideas, images, and, above all, random borrowings. Ashbery's words as often here are caught up in several tangled threads of meaning or as he writes in his introduction to Foucault's book on Raymond Roussel, several parentheses ((((())))). Lacan also uses multiple parentheses for the similar purpose in his seminar on Poe.

As he writes, '[N]ew words suggest new parentheses; sometimes as many as five pairs of parentheses ((((()))))' (Ashbery, 1986, xxv).

Ashbery's poetics are identified with aporias that, on the one hand, foreclose meaning and, on the other, persist as the anterior of the poet's artistic creation. Ashbery seems reluctant to say a spiritual valediction to Donne and sees his own art as continuous with the Renaissance poet's. In the concluding stanza, he affirms the connection of his art with Donne and repudiates the age of modern industrialization he had called earlier in the poem a 'mere chaff', which, prevents his soul from a quintessential connection with the past. This chaff is for him 'the power which breeds stones' (*HL*, 25).

The more marbles to our monument
The more the future won't be any less real to us, enswathed
In Hyperborean conundrums – that's as may be. To bushwhack
From here to Petaluma, then chance
Failed irrigation canals, faults, in my soul's sole integument.

(*HL*, 115)

Towards the end of the poem, like Donne, Ashbery displays interest in the conceit but not in its Renaissance use where it is defined in terms of the relationship between idea and concept. He shifts focus from metaphysical meditation to a bold exposure of American social and political realities. He launches a diatribe against modern culture:

On the raised edge of a circus ring, where sawdust
Conjures belly's emptiness and the recent elections
Are commented. Men prowl
Beside the recently abandoned pier
Sprung from any concept, from reckoning, crust.

(*HL*, 115)

This poem is syncopated with clusters of heterogeneous images with different visual and emotional bearings. The poem reverberates with portmanteau images with different emotive signifiers 'glory steed pawed the ground', 'errant ptarmigan' and 'green cardigan of duckweed' with images such as 'tumescent husks', 'moulting of the season', 'fishy smell or zygote', 'burrow', 'dunce', 'stupid shit' and 'sawdust'. These images as signifiers conjure up antithetic emotions. This implies that in his poetry, due to the interference of the real or simply, through *littorals,* the symbolic shows its limits by having a loose structure which accommodates the traces of the unconscious. These *littorals* foreshadow the forbidden unconscious knowledge that makes the poet play with equivocation in order to gain access to the real. On the other hand, they unfold the alienated being who isn't usually in accord with unconscious knowledge. The subject that speaks is not a being but the one who speaks that being. As Lacan remarks in *Encore*, '[t]his is where I play with equivocation – the impossible knowledge is censored or forbidden, but it isn't if you write "inter-dit" [prohibited or unreadable]' (Lacan, 1998a, 108). In the shattered symbolic texture of these verses, Ashbery reveals his symptom that also functions as the determinant of *jouissance*, the *jouissance* of the artistic object or his poetry. That is why like any other form of art, the poetry is created at the level of *jouissance*. To take an example, in the poem, rhythmic resonances such as, 'said and done', 'Waxeth with the sun' and alliterative pairs such as, 'here; the year', 'gallons and gallons', 'negligence, our cognizance', and 'backpack, backtrack', point to the poet's playfulness that is a condition of *jouissance*.

In sum, Ashbery territorializes the unconscious in language, something that Joyce did by means of dismantling the whole system of language. Ashbery, on the contrary brings the unconscious to his text by equivocation. This innovation is important in the English language, in which Lacan saw a 'resistance . . . to the unconscious' (Lacan, 1974–1975, n. p.). As we have seen in our analysis of the two texts, Lacan insisted on the determinant role of textuality based on his argument that there is a textual knowledge in the literary text that has its own logic. To explore that knowledge and logic in light of Lacanian theoretical discourse is the most effective advice Lacan can ever give to literary critics. As Lacan says, 'Psychoanalysis derives its consistency from Freud's texts – this is an irrefutable fact. We know what texts from Shakespeare to Lewis Caroll contribute to its genius and to its practitioners' (Lacan, 1995c, 7). Ashbery's texts offer their own knowledge and logic.

In 'Self-Portrait', he makes a regression into a narcissistic play in the mirror phase in which the ego identifies with the angelic icon that Lacan calls the mirror image. In the second text, he leaves this threshold and steps into the symbolic in which the narcissistic conflict is replaced with the problematic of equivocation. In other words, the visual field installs itself in the twists of densely tropic language and images; and then, ruptures in the signifiers when the semantic fabric of the poetry breaks up. In both texts, digression in Ashbery's poetry designates a cut in the articulation of signifiers in the symbolic register, which return with their lost communicative significance as *littorals*. The *littorals*, thus, are marking the space between heterogeneous signifying formations that entrap the reader in the vertigo of a multiplicity of meanings and utterances close to non-sense. In this context, Lacan calls attention to the *littorals* as something that is non-knowledge and non-meaning but still can be written if not necessarily for reading. In the final analysis, the *littorals* – as the playground for equivocations – function as residues of the poet's particular enjoyment. As he says, '[t]hat which is written – what would that be in the end? The conditions of jouissance. And that which is counted – what would that be? The residues of jouissance' (Lacan, 1998a, 131).

In other words, the *littorals* transform this repressed knowledge into a *jouissance* that returns in the poetry as black spots of ambiguity and non-meaning, or an 'illiterature' [Joyce's pun], that prevents access to the symbolic order. In other words, the generation of this fragmented poetic rhetoric functions like the drive component or an object *a* for the poet. An interminable recurrence of this rhetoric constitutes the *sinthome* that knots the ternary registers by its mediation of access to the real of the unconscious. This *contre-sense* or counter meaning, or to be more precise, that which signifies nothing at all in his poetic discourse, therefore, is as functional and important as Ashbery's signature, his *savoir-faire,* and is above all, his way of dealing with his s*inthome.* This *sinthomatic* enclave is his identity and underlies the art through which he creates *ex nihilo,* touching the real of his unique literary symptom and subverting the conventional use of language. At the heart of such a disjunctive language lies the persistence of the signifiers that don't lend themselves to meaning. This persistence animates a compulsive repetition in Ashbery's poetry that carries with itself the poet's symptom. This compulsive repetition makes a poet the artificer of words, as Lacan aptly put it, '[t]he poet is produced (permit me to translate my friend Jakobson who showed me this) by being eaten by verses' (Lacan, 1985, 205).

Conclusion

It is generally accepted that the conceptual universe of Lacan's theories is like a vortex that pulls a reader into its empty centre. Once caught, you cannot set yourself free, for his ideas, as Lacan himself remarks to his listener, '[t]ruly pounded . . . into you like an elephant' (Lacan, 1998a, 129). Absence of a full horizon of Lacan's theoretical universe in English language multiplies such difficulties. As this book indicates, however, with patience and time, the ordeal for a loyal reader comes to an end when one ultimately finds a way to come to terms with Lacan and his unique style. The goal of this study, as we have pointed out at the outset, was to find a new pathway for a comprehensive understanding of literary Lacan, the crucial importance of his psychoanalytic theories for contemporary poststructuralist literary studies, and finally a practical use of his theories for analysing a number of important literary texts.

It is generally thought that Lacan was using literary texts to display, verify, justify and substantiate his own psychoanalytic theories. Different parts of this book have proved it otherwise. Lacan discovers the hidden truth in literature. Joyce's *Finnegans Wake* bears witness to the fact that he articulated the *sinthome* as a means of defining and identifying the essence of modernist and avant-garde literature, arts, literariness and aesthetics. In his latter teaching, Lacan emphasizes that language cannot accommodate *jouissance* unless it breaks itself down as a unified system. Joyce was there to show him *jouissance* when he breaks language into pieces by following the logic of the signifier and letter. Like New Criticism, in Lacanian literary theory the accent falls on the internal qualities of a text. However, as our analysis of literature shows internal textual qualities in Lacanian insight aren't closed unto themselves. The intrinsic textual qualities in Lacan's literary project are seen in light of their signifying function. In Shakespeare's text, he displays an already existing dramatization of his theory of desire. In Donne, we found an underlying *sinthomatic* structure of mystical *jouissance,* and in Ashbery, we saw the *littoral* as a unifying signifying process, showing both underlying textual *sinthome* and its supplementary *jouissance.*

By exploring Lacan's theories of love, *jouissance* and the *sinthome,* we synthesized and conceptualized a critical insight that helped us to detect feminine *jouissance* or what we termed mystical *jouissance* as external to gender boundaries. Moreover, the first theoretical part of the study provided us with a self-conscious intellectual basis and capacity, enough to search and identify, in topological terms, breakdowns in the thematic and structural organization of a poetic text. Lacan's theory of the *littoral* served as a theoretical lead, pretty much in the same way as the *sinthome* in Joyce's text. The latter and the theory of mystical *jouissance* have been developed by re-reading and re-examining the primary theoretical part of the book. Thus we have showed psychoanalytic theory embedded in the matrix of our literary interpretation.

Keeping these arguments in view, I try to claim to be pioneering a better understanding of Lacan and his profound literary heritage. The first theoretical part enabled us to overcome some misconceptions and misinterpretations of the complex system of Lacan's theories and then articulate and re-conceptualize them in relation to literary theory and criticism. Our bridging Chapter 4 was a testimony to the development of Lacanian literary theory and critical models by an inquiry into a vast body of Lacanian texts where he concentrates on analysing literature and lays a framework for his literary and critical methodology. This wouldn't have been possible without having the sufficient theoretical insight that the first part of the study offers. Similarly without the theoretical part, we wouldn't have been able to map out the *sinthome* in Joyce by analysing his littering of the letter, and in Ashbery by his ritualistic intertextual aporias. Joyce showed us the self-deconstruction of the text as did Ashbery by superimposing paradoxes and semantic aporias on his text. Our discovery of these sinthomatic features, in both cases, was based in Lacan's emphasis on the linguistic matrix of signification, whose emphasis, in turn, itself was grounded in Jakobson's bi-axial structure of literary discourse. The destruction of language and ambiguity in both cases retrospectively refer to the internal division of the subject with the acquisition of language and the absence of the subject in its signifying chain. Lacan's theory of the *sinthome* revealed to us the cause for writing in both cases. Mutilation of words and the littering of the letter in Joyce and an endless play with semantic ambiguities in Ashbery find their real destiny in the light of Lacanian literary criticism.

For this discovery, psychoanalysis deserves its due credit. Textual plays are misleading unless we have a profound analytical insight. The play is very much the meaning of the Freudian joke quoted by Lacan in 'The Agency of the Letter Since Freud': '[W]hy do you tell me you are going to Cracow so I'll believe you are going to Lvov, when you really are going to Cracow?' (Lacan, 2006, 26). Theory can enable us to find out where the traveller is really going.

It is clear that no theory can be developed without a practical experience of reading a text. Literature offers vast sites for such theoretical experience for psychoanalysis. In the meantime, when in his reading, a critic sees a dramatization or imaginary enactment of a psychoanalytic fact, it does not necessarily mean that the critic wants to measure his theory against the literary production. This is a tipping point in Lacan's theoretical articulations leading some of his critics to say that Lacan merely read literature to illustrate his own theories in practise.

In Western thinking, like Aristotle, Spinoza and Kant, Lacan is the most difficult thinker of his time and the key to understanding him is to precisely and distinctly perceive his concepts, and the terms he uses. As the first part of this book shows we have tried to explore major concepts in Lacan's theory as a *priori* knowledge, but a knowledge that is extendable to my overall project. In the Kantian sense, this knowledge enabled us to reach the teleology of this project which was to understand Lacan, his literary and critical heritage and use them to analyse the literature of different historical periods. In one word, the first theoretical part has to be read as the *locus classicus* of Lacanian literary study and critical praxis. The theoretical debate in the first part revolves around clarifying confused comments on Lacanian theory in today's literary theory. In order to articulate Lacan's complex strategy of reading and analysing a literary text we added an intermediary chapter to develop tools and skills for our latter use in this study.

Our argument for and practical use in this study of the combination and correlation of critical insights from Lacan's *Le Sinthome* and its adjunct, '*Lituraterre*', could be used as a model for a better analysis of contemporary literary texts. As our chapter on Ashbery has indicated, the two theoretical strands in final Lacan offer both a theoretical basis as well as practical techniques for tracking down and investigating the operation of gaps and holes in a literary text. We have begun a scrutiny of these textual blind spots, or to use Serge Leclaire's prase, the '[n]ameless index of the real', (Leclaire, 1999, 320), in Joyce and function of *littoral* in Ashbery. Joyce uses polysemy and polyphony to cover these spots in the real that burst out in the symbolic, and Ashbery by deploying ambiguity and excessive intertextuality attempts to veil them. This combination also undercuts deconstructive interpretation and broadens the analytical and explanatory horizons of poststructuralist literary theory. It means that, for Lacan, the intrinsic instability and division of the text is not unresolved, because, as this chapter shows, Lacan offers a basic explanation of such instabilities and their nodal points. One basic Lacanian lesson in this regard is that each literary text has a latent subtext which is linked to the unconscious. When a writer or a poet organizes his or her syntax, it comes from his or her preconscious, but at that level, an act or praxis in Lacanian sense takes place. This act identifies two opposing resistances of the unconscious and the discourse itself, the resistances that place their imprint on the literary text. As Lacan writes, '[W]hen the subject tells his story, something acts, in a latent way that governs this syntax and makes it more and more condensed. Condensed in relation to what? In relation to what Freud, at the beginning of his description of psychical resistance, calls a nucleus' (Lacan, 1979a, 68). This nucleus is the traumatic touch of the real. This basic lesson has expanded our claim for the importance of Lacan for interpreting literature.

Our re-examination of Ashbery's text and its sinthomatic aspect in terms of the *littoral* and specular image has a bearing on the above argument. The letters and writing produce *littorals* for whose production the *sinthome* functions as a gravitational field. This phenomenon was instituted by Joyce and Ashbery in two different ways. This is, however, not to say that Lacanian criticism leads us to a distinct extra textual universal truth or presence in terms of traditional metaphysics. In a broader critical context, Lacan reveals the genesis of textual free-play and heterogeneity. Lacanian insight seems to corroborate the argument that the very existence and operation of textual defects and gaps in a literary discourse are functional in exposing the intrusion of the unconscious signifying chain in writing. This also means that the signifier represents the subject for another signifier and the insistence of the unconscious signifying network produces the metonymy of desire. Similarly, our investigation of different modes of *jouissance* in John Donne's poetry brings into question the Lacanian feminization of mystic *jouissance* and contributes to current heated debates over whether literary mysticism is merely an ontotheological phenomenon, or part of textual enjoyment and the *sinthome* anchored in the body. Our discussion designates mystical *jouissance* as beyond the unconscious and outside gender delimitations. This exposition takes critical inquiry down a different path towards the textual revelation of a mystic autoerotic and hysterico-erogenous body which transcends the limits of desire by indulging in an imaginary union with the Other.

A mystic body emerges that represents this lacking Other. This perception has been suppressed in Western thinking since Socrates' emphasis on the logos, a disavowal that the age of Enlightenment reinforced, but that the contemporary poststructuralist project intends to dispute. By examining Donne, this book argued that mysticism can identify metaphysical poetry in all its diversity. The common ground for literary mysticism of all traditions and all cultures is a ceaseless interplay with desire, love and *jouissance*. We have shown how Donne's poetry dramatizes desire as an erotic melancholia, mystical love produces an illusion of dissolution of desire and an erotic harmony to the *corps morcelé* of the imaginary, and ultimate mystical experience of ecstasy shows *désêtre* (non-existence), and *jouissance*. We interrogated these mystical experiences in terms of the authorial *sinthome*.

Obviously, this study by no means offers a final resolution to all problems surrounding Lacan and literature. The resolution to these problems remains a dilemma, for at present we have been dealing with the tip of the iceberg when it comes to the currency of Lacan's theoretical discourse in English. This scarcity of Lacanian texts makes the incorporation of Lacanian teaching within the mainstream of literary studies problematic. Notwithstanding the inaccessibility of Lacan's text, and the existence of various interpretations of his teachings,

Lacan's seminars and writing on literature remain largely untranslated and unpublished. Besides, this little of his engagement with a range of literary texts is available. For example, his doctoral thesis, *Le Cas Aimée*, about a novel by the paranoiac patient who wanted to become a poet, and his texts on Plato, Goethe, Artaud and Joyce, remain unpublished in English.

The expansion of interest in Lacan and the debates over his teachings in today's literary scene, nevertheless, bear witness to the probability that within the next decade or so Lacan will be within the grasp of students of literature in the English-speaking world. This could increase the appeal of Lacan and his literary theory and criticism, so that his interpretative methodology would not be confined to some of his basic concepts such as the mirror phase, the phallus, object *a* and so on.

After Lacan, we indeed have a new consciousness of literature and literary theory, undermining the age-old comfort of a transcendental, supernatural status that was granted by traditional literary criticism to literature. This status of literature began to shift with Lacan who considered literature as a textual and signifying practice analysable by psychoanalysis. This demystification of literature initiated a paradigm shift in literary study and promoted a new way of reading the literary text. By discovering the secret of Joyce's art, Lacan undermined the author's utopian vision, who expected centuries would have to pass before professors of literature could find the secret of his last work. As our exposure of Lacan's treatment of different literary texts bears out, his literary criticism should not be accounted for as merely a refinement of Freudian criticism with the addition of structuralist linguistics. Nor should it be made a universal critical hermeneutic to be applied to literature.

Lacan himself had a huge stake in his teaching's relevance to literature. As we have pointed out in our previous discussions, he pioneered the renewal of literary criticism with the help of his psychoanalysis. Shortly before his death, Lacan compared the psychoanalyst to a rhetorician who 'rhetoricizes' and 'rectifies' (Lacan, 1992, 247). It is here that psychoanalysis and literature find common ground, for both try to discover, rather than to invent new realities for life. Lacan closed the gap between literature and psychoanalysis by presenting his teaching in a discourse that itself can be identified as literature for its literary values and profound literary imagination.

There is no boundary between the domains of literature and psychoanalysis. Surrealism and its free association were the first fruit of the Freudian discovery of the unconscious, and Joyce's *Finnegans Wake* was the ground for Lacan's major discovery of literature as symptom. With Lacan, psychoanalysis and literature began a new *pas de deux* and a new form of interaction. This is a discovery that shows us the destiny of literature.

Bibliography

Abraham, Nicholas, and Maria Totok, 1986, *The Wolf Man's Magic Word,* trans. Nicholas Rand, University of Minnesota Press, Minneapolis.
Adams, Hazard, 1971 (edit.) *Critical Theory since Plato,* Harcourt Brace Jovanovich, New York.
Adams, Parveen, 2002 (edit.) *Art: Sublimation or Symptom, a Lacanian Perspective,* The Other Press, New York.
Adelman, Janet, 1992, *Suffocating Mothers: Fantasies of Maternal Origin in Shakespeare's Plays, Hamlet to the Tempest,* Routledge, New York.
Althusser, Louis, 1996, *Writing on Psychoanalysis: Freud and Lacan,* trans. Jeffrey Mehlman, Columbia University Press, New York.
Altieri, Charles, 1984, *Self and Sensibility in Contemporary American Poetry,* Cambridge University Press, Cambridge.
Apollon, Willy and Richard Feldstein, 1996 (edit.) *Lacan, Politics, Aesthetics,* State University of New York Press, New York.
Armstrong, Philip, *Shakespeare in Psychoanalysis,* 2001, Routledge, London.
Ashbery, John, 1977, *Self-Portrait in a Convex Mirror,* Carcanet New Press, Manchester.
—1986, 'Introduction', *Death and the Labyrinth: The World of Raymond Roussel,* by Michel Foucault, trans. Charles Ruas, The Athlone Press, London, pp. i–xxviii.
—1992, *Hotel Lautréamont,* Carcanet Press Limited, Manchester.
Aubert Jacques, 'riverrun', *Post-structuralist Joyce: Essays from the French,* edit. Derek Attridge and Daniel Ferrer, Cambridge University Press, Cambridge, pp. 69–79.
Augustine St, 2006, *The Confessions of St Augustine,* trans. E. B. Pusey, Watkins Publishing, London.
Badiou, Alain, 2000a, 'What is Love', *Sexuation,* edit. Ranata Salecl, Duke University Press, Durham, pp. 263–281.
—2005, 'Manifesto of Affirmation', *Lacanian Ink,* Issue No. 24, 2005, pp. 92–110.
Barthes, Roland, 1967, *Elements of Semiology,* Hills and Wang, New York.
—1974, *S/Z,* trans. Richard Miller, Hill & Wang, New York.
—1992, 'To Write: An Intransitive Verb?' in *Modern Literary Theory: A Reader* (edit.) Philip Rice and Patricia Waugh, Routledge, London, pp. 42–54.
—1993a, '*from* The Pleasure of the Text', *A Roland Barthes Reader,* edit. Susan Sontag, Vintage, London, 404–415.
—1993b, '*from* Of Lover's Discourse', *A Barthes Reader,* edit. Susan Sontag, Vintage, London, pp. 426–457.
Bataille, George, 1997, *The Bataille Reader,* edit. Fred Bothing and Scott Wilson, Blackwell Publishers Ltd, Oxford.
Beauvoir, Simone de, 1988, *The Second Sex,* trans. and edit., H. M. Parshley, Pan Books Ltd, London.

Beckett, Samuel, 1961, 'Dante . . . Bruno. Vico . . . Joyce', *Our Exagmination Round His Factification of Work in Progress*, Faber and Faber, London, 1–23.

Begnal, Michael H. and Fritz Senn, 1974 (edit.) *A Conceptual Guide to Finnegans Wake*, The Pennsylvania State University Press, University Park.

Bennett, Andrew and Nicholas Royle, 2004, *Introduction to Literature, Criticism and Theory*, third ed. Pearson Education Limited, Harlow.

Benvenuto, Bice and Roger Kennedy, 1986, *The Works of Jacques Lacan: An Introduction*, Free Association Books, London.

—1994, *Concerning the Rites of Psychoanalysis, or the Villa of the Mysteries*, Polity Press, Cambridge.

Berressem, Hanjo, 1998, *Lines of Desire: Reading Gombrowicz's Fiction with Lacan*, Northwestern University Press, Evanston.

Bersini, Leo, 1986, *The Freudian Body: Psychoanalysis and Art*, Columbia University Press, New York.

Blanchot, Maurice, 1995, *The Work of Fire*, trans. Charlotte Mandell, Stanford University, Stanford.

—2001, *Faux Pas*, trans. Charlotte Mandell, Stanford University Press, Stanford.

Bloom, Harold, 1999, *John Donne: Comprehensive Research and Study Guide*, Chelsea House Publishers, Pennsylvania.

Boheemen-Saaf, Christine Van, 1999, *Joyce, Derrida, Lacan and the Trauma of History*, Cambridge University Press, Cambridge.

Boldrini, Lucia, 2001, *Joyce, Dante, and the Poetics of Literary Relations: Language and Meaning in Finnegans Wake*, Cambridge University Press, Cambridge.

Boothby, Richard, 2001, *Freud as Philosophy: Metapsychoanalysis after Lacan*, Routledge, London.

Bowie, Andrew, 1996, 'Rethinking the History of the Subject: Jacobi, Schelling, and Heidegger', *Deconstructive Subjectivities*, edit. Simon Critchley and Peter Dews, State University of New York Press, New York, pp. 105–126.

Bowie, Malcolm, 1987, *Freud, Proust, and Lacan: Theory as Fiction*, Cambridge University Press, Cambridge.

—1991, *Lacan*, Fontana Press, London.

—1993, *Psychoanalysis and the Future of Theory*, Blackwell Publishers, Oxford.

Bracher, Marc, 1993, *Lacan, Discourse and Social Change: A Psychoanalytical Cultural Criticism*, Cornell University Press, Ithaca.

—Marshall W. Alcorn, Jr., Ronald J. Corthell and Francoise Massardier-Kenney (edit.) 1994, *Lacanian Discourse: Subject, Structure and Society*, State University of New York Press, New York.

Braunstein, Néstor A., 2003, 'Desire and Jouissance in the Teaching of Lacan', *The Cambridge Companion to Lacan*, edit. Jean-Michel Rabaté, Cambridge University Press, Cambridge, pp. 102–115.

Breton, Andre, 1978, *What is Surrealism?: Selected Writings*, edit. Franklin Rosemont, Pluto Press, London.

Bretzius, Stephen, 2000, *Shakespeare in Theory: The Postmodern Academy and the Early Modern Theatre*, The University of Michigan Press, Michigan.

Brivic, Sheldon, 1991, *The Veil of Signs: Joyce, Lacan, and Perception*, University of Illinoise Press, Illinois.

Brooker, Joseph, 2004, *Joyce's Critics: Transitions in Reading and Culture*, The University of Wisconsin Press, Wisconsin.

Brooks, Cleanth, 1968, *The Well-Wrought Urn: Studies in the Structure of Poetry*, Methuen Press, London.
Burton, Mick, 1989, 'The Imperfect Librarian: Text and Discourse in *The Waste Land and Four Quartets*', *Literary Theory and Poetry: Extending the Canon*, edit. David Murray, B. T. Batsford Ltd, London, pp. 42–61.
Campbell, Jan, 2000, *Arguing With the Phallus – Feminist, Queer, and Postcolonial Theory: A Psychoanalytic Contribution*, Zed Books Ltd, London.
Campbell, Joseph and Henry Morton Robinson, 1961, *A Skeleton Key to Finnegans Wake*, Viking Press, New York.
Canningham, James, 1997, *Shakespeare's Tragedies and Modern Critical Theory*, Associated University Press, Inc, Cranbury.
Cantor, Paul A., 1998, *Shakespeare's Hamlet*, Cambridge University Press, Cambridge.
Caudill, David S., 1991, *Lacan and the Subject of the Law: Towards a Psychoanalytic Critical Legal Theory*, Cambridge University Press, Cambridge.
Chaitin, Gilbert D., 1996, *Rhetoric and Culture in Lacan*, Cambridge University Press, Cambridge.
Cixous, Hélène, 1976, 'Fiction and its Phantoms: A Reading of Freud's Das Unheimliche', in *New Literary History*, Vol. 7, No. 3 (Spring, 1976), pp. 525–547.
—1986, *The Newly Born Woman*, trans. Batsy Wing, Manchester University Press, Manchester.
—1997, 'The Laugh of the Medusa', *Feminism – An Anthology of Literary Theory and Criticism*, edit. Robyn R. Warhol and Diana Price Herndl, Macmillan Press Ltd, Hampshire, pp. 347–362.
Clément, Catherine, 1983, *The Lives and Legends of Jacques Lacan*, trans. A. Goldhammer, Columbia University Press, New York.
Copjec, Joan, 1994, *Read My Desire: Lacan Against the Historicists*, Massachusetts Institute of Technology Press (MIP), Massachusetts.
—2000, 'The Body as Viewing Instrument, or the Strut of Vision', *Lacan in America*, Other Press, New York, pp. 277–308.
Coward, Rosalind, 1984, *Female Desire: Women's Sexuality Today*, Paladin, London.
Culler, Jonathan, 1981, *The Pursuit of Sings: Semiotics, Literature, Deconstruction*, Cornell University Press, Ithaca.
—1997, *Literary Theory: A Very Short Introduction*, Oxford University Press, Oxford.
David-Menard, Monique, *Hysteria from Freud to Lacan: Body and Language in Psychoanalysis*, trans. Catherine Porter, Cornell University Press, Ithaca.
Davis, Robert Con, 1981 (edit.) *The Fictional Father: Lacanian Reading of the Text*, University of Massachusetts Press, Massachusetts.
—1983, *Lacan and Narration. The Psychoanalytic Difference in Narrative Theory*, The Johns Hopkins University Press, Baltimore.
Derrida, Jacques, 1976, *Of Grammatology*, trans. Gayatri Chakravorty Spivak, The Johns Hopkins University Press, Baltimore.
—1981a, *Positions*, trans. Alan Bass, Chicago University Press, Chicago.
—1981b, *Dissemination*, trans. Barbara Johnson, Athlone, London.
—1984, 'Two Words for Joyce', trans. Geoff Bennington, *Post-structuralist Joyce: Essays From the French*, edit. Derek Attridge and Daniel Ferrer. Cambridge University Press, Cambridge, pp. 145–158.
—1986, *Glas*, trans. John P. Leavey and Richard Rand Lincoln, University of Nebraska Press, Nebraska.

—1987, *The Postcard: From Socrates to Freud and Beyond*, trans. A. Bass, University of Chicago Press, Chicago.

Donne, John, 1987, *John Donne: Selected Prose*, edit. Neil Rhodes, Penguin Books, London.

Dor, Joël, 1996, 'The Epistemological Status of Lacan's Mathematical Paradigms', *Disseminating Lacan*, edit. David Pettigrew and François Raffoul, State University of New York Press, New York, pp. 109–122.

—1999a, *Introduction to the Reading of Lacan: The Unconscious Structured Like a Language*, trans. S. Fairfield, Other Press, New York.

—1999b, *The Clinical Lacan*, edit. Judith Feher Gurewich and Susan Fairfield, Other Press, New York.

Dostoyevsky, F., 1992, *Notes From the Underground*, Dover Publications, Inc, New York.

Drakakis, John, 1985, *Alternative Shakespeare*, Vol. I, Methuen & Co, Ltd, London.

Dravers, Philip, 2002, 'In the Wake of Interpretation: "The Letter! The Litter!" or "Where in the Waste is the Wisdom"', *Re-inventing the Symptom: Essays on the Final Lacan*, edit. Luke Thurston, Other Press LLC, New York, 141–176.

Dufresne, Todd, 1990, *The Ideology of Aesthetics*, Blackwell, Mass.

—2000, *Tales from the Freudian Crypt, The Death Drive in Text and Context*, Stanford University Press, California.

Eco, Umberto, 1984, *Semiotics, and the Philosophy of Language*, The Macmillan Press Ltd, London.

—1989, *The Middle Ages of James Joyce: The Aesthetics of Chaosmos*, trans. Ellen Esrock, Hutchinson Radius, London.

Easterlin, Nancy, Barbara Riebling, 1993 (edit.) *After Poststructuralism: Interdisciplinarity and Literary Theory*, Northwestern University Press, Illinois.

Eliot, T. S., 1975, *Selected Prose of T. S. Eliot* (edit. with an intro.) Frank Kermode, Faber & Faber Limited, London.

Ellman, Maud, 1994, *Psychoanalytic Literary Criticism*, Longman, London.

Ellmann, Richard, 1977, *The Consciousness of James Joyce*, Faber & Faber, London.

Ettinger, Bracha Lichtenberg, 2002, 'Weaving a Trans-subjective Tress or Matrixial *sinthome*', *Re-Inventing The Symptom: Essays on the Final Lacan*, Other Press, New York, pp. 83–110.

Evans, Dylan, 1996, *An Introductory Dictionary of Lacanian Psychoanalysis*, Routledge, London.

Everett, Barbara, 1989, *Young Hamlet: Essays on Shakespeare's Tragedies*, Clarendon Press, Oxford.

Feher-Gurewitch, Judith and Michel Tort, 1996, (edit.) *The Subject and the Self: Lacan and American Psychoanalysis*, Jason Aronson, Northvale.

Feldstein, Richard, Bruch Fink and Maire Jaanus, 1995 (edit.) *Reading Seminar XI: Lacan's Four Fundamental Concepts of Psychoanalysis*, State University of New York Press, Albany.

Felman, Shoshana, 1985, *Writing and Madness: Literature, Philosophy, Psychoanalysis*, trans. Martha with the assistance of Brian Massumi, Cornell University Press, Ithaca.

Fergusson, Francis, 1977, *Trope and Allegory: Themes Common to Dante and Shakespeare*, The University of Georgia Press, Athens.

Fink, Bruce, 1995a, '"There's No Such Thing as Sexual Relationship": Existence and the Formulas of Sexuation,' *Newsletter of the Freudian Field*, Spring/Fall, Vol. 5, Nos 1–2, 1995, pp. 59–85.

—1996, 'Reading Hamlet With Lacan', *Lacan, Politics, Aesthetics*, edit. Willy Apollon and Richard Feldstein, State University of New York Press. New York, pp. 181–198.

—1997, *A Clinical Introduction to Lacanian Psychoanalysis: Theory and Technique*, Princeton University Press, Princeton.

—1998, 'The Master Signifier and the Four Discourses,' *Key Concepts of Lacanian P sychoanalysis*, edit. Dany Nobus, Rebus Press, London, pp. 29–47.

—2000b, *Lacan to the Letter: Reading Écrits Closely*, University of Minnesota Press, Minneapolis.

—2002a, 'Knowledge and Jouissance', *Reading Seminar XX: Lacan's Major Work on Love, Knowledge, and Feminine Sexuality*, edit. Suzanne Barnard and Bruce Fink, State University of New York Press, New York, pp. 21–46.

Fletcher, John and Andrew Benjamin, 1990 (edit.) *Abjection, Melancholia, and Love: The Works of Julia Kristeva*, Routledge, London.

Forrester, John, 1981, 'Psychoanalysis or Literature', *French Studies, A Quarterly Review*, Vol. XXXV, April 1981, pp. 170–179.

—1990, *The Seduction of Psychoanalysis: On Freud, Lacan and Derrida*, Cambridge University Press, Cambridge.

Fredman, Stephen, 1983, *Poet's Prose: The Crisis in American Verse*, Cambridge University Press, Cambridge.

Freud, Sigmund, 1970a, 'On Hamlet and Oedipus', *The Design Within: Psychoanalytic Approaches to Shakespeare*, edit. M. D. Faber, Science House, New York, pp. 81–86.

—1970b, 'The Theme of the Three Caskets', *The Design Within: Psychoanalytic Approaches to Shakespeare*, edit. M. D. Faber, Science House, New York, pp. 195–206.

—1977, *Sigmund Freud, Case History I, Penguin Freud Library* Vol. 8, trans, Alix and James Starchey, Pelican Books, London.

—1983, 'Creative Writer and Daydreaming', *Literature and Psychoanalysis*, trans. edit. Edith Kurzweil and William Phillips, Columbia University Press, New York, pp. 24–29.

—1988, 'Those Wrecked by Success', *Sigmund Freud: Art and Literature*, Vol. 14, Pelican Books, London, pp. 299–316.

—1991, *The Interpretation of Dreams*, trans. James Starchey, Penguin Books, London.

Freyer, David Ross, 2004, *The Intervention of the Other: Ethical Subjectivity in Levinas and Lacan*, Other Press, New York.

Gallop, Jane, 1982, *Feminism and Psychoanalysis: The Daughter's Seduction*, Macmillan, London.

—1990, *Reading Lacan*, Cornell University Press, Cornel.

—2002, *Anecdotal Theory*, Duke University Press, Durham.

Garcia, L. German, 'Psychoanalysis and Literature', trans. Josefina Ayerza, *Lacanian Ink*, No. 1, 1990, pp. 52–57.

Gardiner, Muriel, 1973, *The Wolf-Man and Sigmund Freud* (edit.) Penguin Books, London.

Gardner, Helen, 1952, 'Introduction', *John Donne's Divine Poems*, Clarendon Press, Oxford, pp. xv–liv.

—1982 (edit.) *The Metaphysical Poets,* Penguin Books, London.

Gill, Richard, 1990 (edit.) *John Donne: Selected Poem,* Oxford University Press, Oxford.

Girard, René, 1965, *Deceit, Desire, and the Novel: Self and Other in Literary Structure,* trans. Yvonne Reccero, The Johns Hopkins University Press, Baltimore.

Glowinski, Huuette, Zita Marks and Sara Murphy, 2001, *A Compendium of Lacanian Terms,* Free Association Books, London.

Grigg, Russel, 1998, 'From the Mechanism of Psychosis to the Universal Condition of the Symptom: On Foreclosure', *Key Concepts of Lacanian Psychoanalysis,* edit. Dany Nobus, Rebus Press, London, pp. 48–74.

Grof, Stanislav, 1993, *Realms of the Human Unconscious: Observations from LSD Research,* A Condor Book, Souvenir Press (E & A) Ltd, London.

Grosz, Elizabeth, 1990a, *Jacques Lacan: A Feminist Introduction,* Routledge, London.

Gunn, Daniel, 1988, *Psychoanalysis and Fiction,* Cambridge University Press, Cambridge.

Harari, Roberto, 2001, *Lacan's Seminar on 'Anxiety': An Introduction,* trans. Jane C. Lamb-Ruiz, Other Press, New York.

—2002, *How James Joyce Made His Name: A Reading of Final Lacan,* trans. Luke Thurston, Other Press, New York.

Hart, Clive, 1962, *Structure and Motif in Finnegans Wake,* Northwestern University Press, Evanston.

Hartman, Geoffrey, 1978 (edit) *Psychoanalysis and the Question of the Text,* Johns Hopkins University Press, Baltimore.

Hawkes, Terence, 1988, *Structuralism and Semiotics,* Routledge, London.

—1996, *Alternative Shakespeare, Vol. II,* Routledge, London.

Hegel, G. W. F., 1975, *Aesthetics: Lectures on Fine Art,* trans. T. M. Knox. 2 vols, Clarendon Press, Oxford.

—1977, *Phenomenology of Spirit,* trans. A. V. Miller, Clarendon Press, Oxford.

Henke, Suzette A., 1990, *James Joyce and the Politics of Desire,* Routledge, New York.

Hermann, Lang, 1997, *Language and the Unconscious: Lacan's Hermeneutics of Psychoanalysis,* trans. Thomas Brockelman, Humanities Press International, Inc., New Jersey.

Hodgson, Elizabeth M. A, 1999, *Gender and the Sacred Self in John Donne,* University of Delaware Press, Newark.

Hogan, Patrick, and Lalita Pandit, 1990, *Criticism and Lacan: Essays and Dialogue on Language, Structure and the Unconscious,* University of Georgia Press, Athens.

Hyppolite, Jean, 1974, *Genesis and Structure of Hegel's Phenomenology of Spirit,* trans. John Heckman, Northwestern University Press, Evanston.

Ingersoll, Earl G., 1996, *Engendered Trope in Joyce's Dubliners,* Southern Illinois University Press, Carbondale.

Irigaray, Luce, 1985, *Speculum of the Other Woman,* trans. Gillian C. Gill, Cornell University Press, New York.

—1993, *An Ethics of Sexual Difference,* trans. Carolyn Burke and Gillian C. Gill, Cornell University Press, Ithaca.

—1997, 'This Sex Which is Not One', *Feminism – An Anthology of Literary Theory and Criticism,* edit. Robyn R. Warhol and Diana Price Herndl, Macmillan Press Ltd, Hampshire, pp. 363–369.

—2002, *To Speak is Never Neutral,* trans. Gail Schwab, Continuum, London.

Jakobson, Roman, 1987, *Language in Literature*, edit. Krystyna Pomoroska and Stephen Rudy, Harvard University Press, Mass.

Jameson, Fredric, 1977, 'Imaginary and Symbolic in Lacan: Literature and Psychoanalysis', *Yale French Studies* (55/56, 1977), pp. 338–394.

—1981, *The Political Unconscious: Narrative as a Socially Symbolic Act*, Methuen, London.

—1993, 'Periodizing the 60s', *Modern Literary Theory: A Reader* (edit.) Philip Rice & Patricia Waugh, second edition, Routledge, London, pp. 309–341.

Jay, Mark, 1994, *The Denigration of Vision in Twentieth-Century French Thought*, University of California Press, California.

Johnson, Barbara, 1980, *The Critical Difference, Essays in the Contemporary Rhetoric of Reading*, Johns Hopkins University Press, Baltimore.

—1995, 'Writing', *Critical Terms for Literary Study*, edit. Frank Lentricchia and Thomas McLaughlin, The Chicago University Press, Chicago, pp. 39–49.

Johnston, Adrian, 'Lacan's Purloined Linguistics, Lalangue and Languages in Encore', *Lacanian Ink*, Issue No. 14, 1999, New York, pp. 47–59.

Jones, Ernest,1983, 'The Death of Hamlet's Father', *Literature and Psychoanalysis*, edit. Edith Kurzweil and William Phillips, Columbia University Press, New York, pp. 34–38.

Joyce, James, 1992, *Finnegans Wake*, Minerva, London.

Julien, Philippe, 1994, *Jacques Lacan's Return to Freud: The Real, the Symbolic and Imaginary*, trans. D. Beck Simiu, New York University Press, New York.

Jung, C. G., 1972, 'Psychology and Literature', *20th Century Literary Criticism*, edit. David Lodge, Longman Group Limited, London, pp. 175–190.

Kahn, Coppélia, 1997, *Roman Shakespeare: Warriors, Wounds, and Women*, Routledge, London.

Kastan, David Scott, 1999, *Shakespeare After Theory*, Routledge, New York.

Kierkegaard, Søren, 1989, *The Concept of Irony*, trans. Lee M. Capel, Indiana University Press, Bloomington.

Kojève, Alexandre, 1969, *Introduction to the Reading of Hegel: Lectures on the Phenomenology of the Spirit*, edit. Allan Bloom, trans. Leon S. Roudiez, Columbia University Press, New York.

Kott, Jan, 1974, *Shakespeare Our Contemporary*, Norton, New York.

Kristeva, Julia, 1980, *Desire in Language: A Semiotic Approach to Literature and Art*, trans. Alice Jardine, Thomas A. Gora and Léon S. Roudiez, edit. Léon S. Roudiez, Columbia University Press, New York.

—1986, 'Revolution in Poetic Language', *The Kristeva Reader*, edit. Toril Moi, Columbia University Press, New York, pp. 89–136.

—1987, *Tales of Love*, trans. Leon S. Roudiez, Columbia University Press, New York.

—1995, *New Maladies of the Soul*, trans. Ross Guberman, Columbia University Press, New York.

Kroker, Arthur and Marilouise Kroker, 1991, *The Hysterical Male: New Feminist Theory*, Palgrave, New York.

Lacan, Jacques, 1953, 'Some Reflections on The Ego', *International Journal of Psychoanalysis*, No. 34, 1953, pp. 11–17.

—1971, '*Lituraterre*', first published in the review Littérature (Larousse, 3, 1971) pp. 5–31, Unpublished translation, Jack W. Smith.

—1972, 'Of Structure as an Inmixing of an Otherness Prerequisite to Any Subject Whatever', *The Structuralist Controversy: The Languages of Criticism and the Sciences of*

Man, edit. Richard Macksey and Eugenio Donato, The Johns Hopkins University Press, Baltimore, pp. 186–194.

—1973, 'L'etourdit', Scilicel 4 (1973), pp. 5–52. Unpublished translation, Jack W. Stone.

—*Seminar XXII: R.S.I., 1974–75*, text established by Jacques-Alain Miller, Unpublished translation. Jack W. Stone, with the assistance of Ellie Ragland, Greg Hydre, Filip Kovacevic and Zak Watson.

—1975–1976, *Seminar: XXIII, Le Sinthome*, an unauthorised and unpublished trans. Luke Thurston.

—1977, 'Desire and Interpretation of Desire in *Hamlet*', trans. James Hulbert, *Literature and Psychoanalysis. The Question of Reading: Otherwise*, in Yale French Studies, 55–6 (1977), pp. 11–52.

— 1979a, *The Four Fundamental Concepts of Psychoanalysis*, trans. Alan Sheridan, Penguin Books, London.

—1979b, 'The Neurotic's Individual Myth', trans. Martha Noel Evans, *The Psychoanalytic Quarterly*, Volume Forty-Eight, 1979, pp. 386–425.

—1981a, *Rome Discourse, Jacques Lacan, the Language of the Self, the Function of Language in Psychoanalysis*, trans. Anthony Wilden, The Johns Hopkins University Press, 1981, Baltimore.

—1981b, 'The Seminar, Paris, 10th June 1980', *Papers of the Freudian School of Melbourne*, edit. Oscar Zentner, pp. 97–101.

—1981c, 'The Seminar, Caracas, 12th July 1980', *Papers of the Freudian School of Melbourne*, edit. Oscar Zentner, pp. 103–106.

—1982, 'Seminar of 21 January 1975', *Feminine Sexuality: Jacques Lacan and the École Freudienne*, trans. Jacqueline Rose, edit. Juliet Mitchell and Jacqueline Rose, The Macmillan Press Ltd., London, pp. 162–172.

—1985, 'Sign, Symbol, and Imaginary', *The Signs*, edit. Marshall Blonsky, Basil Blackwell Ltd, Oxford, pp. 202–209.

—1988a, 'Logical Time and the Assertion of Anticipated Certainty', trans. Bruce Fink, *Newsletter of the Freudian Field*, No. 2, 1988. pp. 4–22.

—1988b, 'Seminar on "The Purloined Letter,"' trans. Jeffrey Mehlman, *The Purloined Poe: Lacan, Derrida & Psychoanalytic Reading*, edit. John P. Muller & William J. Richardson, The Johns Hopkins University, Baltimore, pp. 28–54.

—1989a, 'Science and Truth', trans. Bruce Fink, *Newsletter of the Freudian Field*, 3: 1–2 (Spring/Fall, 1989), pp. 4–29.

—1990, *Television*, trans. Denis Hollier, Rosalind Krauss and Annette Michelson, edit. Joan Copjec, Norton, New York.

—1991a, *The Seminar of Jacques Lacan, Book II: The Ego in Freud's Theory and in The Technique of Psychoanalysis (1954–1955)*, trans. Sylvana Tomascelli, edit. Jacques-Alain Miller, W. W. Norton & Company, Inc. New York.

—1991b, *The Seminar of Jacques Lacan, Book I: Freud's Papers on Technique 1953–1954*, trans. John Forrester, edit. Jacques-Alain Miller, W. W. Norton & Company, Inc. New York.

—1991c, 'Metaphor of the Subject', trans. Bruce Fink in *Newsletter of the Freudian Field*, Vol.5, Nos 1 & 2, Spring/Fall 1991, pp. 10–15.

—1992, *The Ethic of Psychoanalysis 1959–1960: The Seminar of Jacques Lacan*, trans. Dennis Porter, edit. Jacques-Alain Miller, W. W. Norton & Company, Inc., New York.

—1993, *The Psychoses: The Seminar of Jacques Lacan, Book III 1955–1956*, trans. Russell Grigg, W. W. Norton & Company, Inc. New York.

—1995a, 'Position of the Unconscious', *Reading Seminar XI: Lacan's Four Fundamental Concepts of Psychoanalysis*, trans. Bruce Fink, edit. Richard Feldstein, Bruce Fink and Mare Jaanus, State University of New York Press, New York, pp. 259–282.

—1995b, 'A Man and a Woman', trans. Carolyn Jane Henshaw, revised by Maria-Ines Rotmiler de Zentner, in *Papers of the Freudian School of Melbourne*, pp. 79–97.

—1995c, 'Proposition of 9 October 1967 on the Psychoanalyst of the School', trans. Russell Grigg, *Analysis*, No. 6, 1995, pp. 1–14.

—1995d, 'Spring Awakening', trans. Silvia Rodriguez, *Analysis, No. 6, 1995*, pp. 32–34.

—1996a, 'Homage to Marguerite Duras', *Writing and Psychoanalysis: A Reader*, edit. John Lechte, Arnold, London, pp. 136–143.

—1996b, 'The Meaning of the Phallus', *Psychoanalytic Criticism*, edit. Sue Vice, Polity Press in association with Blackwell Publishers Ltd, Oxford, pp. 120–129.

—1996c, 'Presentation of the *Memoirs of President Schreber* in French Translation', trans. Andrew J. Lewis, *Analysis, No. 7, 1996*, pp. 1–4.

—1998a, *The Seminar of Jacques Lacan, On Feminine Sexuality: The Limits of Love and Knowledge, Encore*, trans. Bruce Fink, W. W. Norton & Company, Inc., New York.

—1998b, 'The Mirror Stage as Formative of the Function of the I as Revealed in Psychoanalytic Experience', *Modern Literary Theory: A Reader*, edit. Philip Rice & Patricia Waugh, second edition, Routledge, London, pp. 122–127.

—2002, *Écrits: A Selection*, trans. Bruce Fink, W. W. Norton & Company, Inc., New York.

—2006, *Écrits – The First Complete Edition in English*, trans. Bruce Fink in collaboration with Héloïse Fink and Russell Grigg, W. W. Norton & Company, Inc., New York.

Laplanche, Jean & Pontalis, Jean-Bertrand, 1973, *The Language of Psychoanalysis*, trans. Donald Nicholson-Smith, H. Karnac Books Ltd, London.

Larrissy, Edward, 1990, *Reading Twentieth-Century Poetry: The Language of Gender and Objects*, Basil Blackwell Ltd, Oxford.

Lechte, John, 1996 (edit.) *Writing and Psychoanalysis: A Reader*, Arnold, London.

Leclaire, Serge, 1998, *Psychoanalysing: On the Order of the Unconscious and the Practice of the Letter*, Stanford University Press, California.

—1999, '*The Real in the Text', Literary Debate, Text and Context: Postwar French Thought Volume II*, The New Press, New York.

Lee, Jonathan Scott, 1990, *Jacques Lacan*, University of Massachusetts Press, Massachusetts.

Lemaire, Anika, 1991, *Jacques Lacan*, trans. David Macey, Routledge, London.

Lentricchia, Frank and Thomas McLaughlin, 1995 (edit.) *Critical Terms for Literary Study*, The University of Chicago Press, Chicago.

Leonard, Garry M., 1993, *Reading Dubliners Again: A Lacanian Perspective*, Syracuse University Press, Syracuse.

Leupin, Alexandre, 1991, *Jacques Lacan and the Human Science*, University of Nebraska Press, Lincoln.

Luepnitz, Deborah, 2003, 'Beyond the Phallus: Lacan and Feminism', *The Cambridge Companion to Lacan*, edit. Jean-Michel Rabaté, Cambridge University Press, Cambridge, pp. 221–237.

Lupton, Julia Reinhard, Reinhard, Kenneth, 1993, *After Oedipus: Shakespeare in Psychoanalysis*, Cornell University Press, New York.

Lyotard, Jean-Francois, 1989, 'The Sublime and the Avant-garde', in *The Lyotard Reader*, edit. Andrew Benjamin, Blackwell, Oxford, pp. 69–103.

MacCannel, Juliet Flower, 1986, *Figuring Lacan: Criticism and Cultural Unconscious*, Biddles Ltd, Guildford and King's Lynn, Kent.

Macey, David, 1988, *Lacan in Contexts*, Verso Press, London.

—2001, *Dictionary of Critical Theory*, Penguin Books Ltd, London.

Marini, Marcelle, 1992, *Jacques Lacan: The French Context*, trans. Anne Tomiche, Rutgers University Press, New Jersey.

Martin, Bernard, 1990, *The Poetry of John Donne*, Sydney University Press in association with Oxford University Press Australia, Sydney.

Matthews, J. H., 1982, *Surrealism, Insanity, and Poetry*, Syracuse University Press, New York.

Mazzaro, Jerome, 1980, *Postmodern American Poetry*, University of Illinois Press, Urbana.

Mellard, James, 1991, *Using Lacan Reading Fiction*, University of Illinois Press, Urbana.

Metzger, David, 1994, *The Lost Cause of Rhetoric: The Relation of Rhetoric and Geometry in Aristotle and Lacan*, Southern Illinois University Press, Carbondale.

Miller, Jacques-Alain, 1994, '*Extimité*', *Lacanian Theory of Discourse, Subject, Structure and Society*, edit. Mark Bracher, Marshall W. Alcorn, Jr, Ronald J. Corthell and Françoise Massardier-Kenney, New York University Press, New York.

—1995, 'Context and Concepts', *Reading Seminar XI: Lacan's Four Fundamental Concepts of Psychoanalysis*, trans. Bruce Fink, edit. Richard Feldstein, Bruce Fink and Mare Jaanus, State University of New York Press, New York, pp. 3–18.

—1996, Commentary on Lacan's text ['On Freud's "Trieb" and the Psychoanalyst's desire'], *Reading Seminar I and II: Lacan's Return to Freud*, edit. Richard Feldstein, Bruce Fink and Maire Jaanus, State University of New York, New York, pp. 422–427.

—1997, 'Joyce avec Lacan – Préface', in *Lacanian Ink*, No. 11, 1997. New York, pp. 5–11.

—1999, 'Lacan Clinician' *Critical Essays on Lacan*, edit. Ellie Ragland, G. K. Hall & Co, New York. 1–17.

—2000, 'On Semblances in the Relation', *Sexuation*, edit. Slavoj Žižek and Ranata Salecl, Duke University Press, Durham, pp. 13–28.

—2001, *Clear Like Day Letter: For the Twenty Years Since the Death of Jacques Lacan*, trans. Barbara P. Fulks, The Wooster Press, New York.

—2003, 'Paradigms of Jouissance', trans. Gorge Jauregui, in *Lacanian Ink*. No. 17, 2003, pp. 8–48.

—2004, 'Religion, Psychoanalysis', in *Lacanian Ink* No. 23, 2003, pp. 8–47.

—2005, 'Introduction to the Erotic Time', in *Lacanian Ink*, No. 24, 2005, pp. 8–44.

Moi, Toril, 1985, *Sexual/Textual Politics: Feminist Literary Theory*, Methuen and Co, London.

Moraze, Charles, 1972, 'Literary Invention', *The Structuralist Controversy: The Language of Criticism & the Sciences of Man*, Johns Hopkins University Press, Baltimore, pp. 22–55.

Muller, John P. and William J. Richardson, 1982 (edit.) *Lacan and Language: A Reader's Guide to Écrits*, International Universities Press, New York.

—1996, *Beyond the Psychoanalytic Dyad: Developmental Semiotics in Freud, Peirce and Lacan*, Routledge, London.

Murray, David, 1989 (edit.) *Literary Theory and Poetry: Extending the Canon*, B. T. Batsford Ltd, London.

Nancy, Jean-Luc and Philippe Lacoue-Labarthe, 1992, *The Title of the Letter: A Reading of Lacan*, trans. François Raffoul and David Pettigrew, State University of New York, New York.

—2002, *Hegel, The Restlessness of the Negative*, trans. Jason Smith and Steven Miller, University of Minnesota Press, Minneapolis.

Nasio, Jean-David, 1997, *Hysteria: The Splendid Child of Psychoanalysis*, trans. Susan Fairfield, Jason Aronson, Northvale.

Nevo, Ruth, 1987, *Shakespeare's Other Language*, Routledge, London.

Newton, K. M., 1990, *Interpreting the Text: A Critical Introduction to the Theory and Practice of Literary Interpretation*, Harvester Wheatsheaf, Hertforshire.

Nietzsche, F., 2003, *Beyond Good and Evil*, trans. R. J. Hollingdale, Penguin Classics, London.

Nobus, Dany, 2000, *Jacques Lacan and the Practice of Psychoanalysis*, Routledge, London.

—2002, 'Illiterature', *Re-inventing The Symptom: Essays on the Final Lacan*, edit. Luke Thurston, Other Press, New York, pp. 19–44.

Nussbaum, Martha C., 2001, *Upheavals of Thought: The Intelligence of Emotion*, Cambridge University Press, Cambridge.

Nuttall, A. D., 2001, *Why Does Tragedy Gives Pleasure*, Clarendon Press, Oxford.

O'Hara, Daniel T., 1985, *The Romance of Interpretation*, Columbia University Press, New York.

Oliver, Kelly, 1995, *Womanising Nietzsche: Philosophy's Relation to the 'Feminine'*, Routledge, New York.

Oliver, P. M., 1997, *Donne's Religious Writing: A Discourse of Feigned Devotion*, Addison Wesley Longman, Essex.

Parr, Adrian, 2005 (edit.) *The Deleuze Dictionary*, Edinburgh University Press, Edinburgh.

Pelt, Tamise Van, 2000, *The Other Side of Desire, Lacan's Theory of the Registers*, State University of New York, New York.

Pettigrew, David and François Raggoul, 1996 (edit.) *Disseminating Lacan*, State University of New York, New York.

Plato, 1956, *The Symposium*, trans. W. Hamilton, Penguin Books Ltd, Harmondsworth.

Rabaté, Jean-Michel, 2000 (edit.) *Lacan in America*, Other Press, New York.

—2001, *Jacques Lacan: Psychoanalysis and the Subject of Literature*, Palgrave, New York.

—2002, *The Future of Theory*, Blackwell Publishers Ltd, Oxford.

—2003, 'Lacan's Turn to Freud', *The Cambridge Companion to Lacan*, Cambridge University Press, Cambridge, pp. 1–24.

Rackin, Phyllis, 2005, *Shakespeare and Women*, Oxford University Press, Oxford.

Ragland, Ellie, 1986, *Jacques Lacan and the Philosophy of Psychoanalysis*, Croon Helm Ltd, Beckenham, London.

— and Mark Bracher, 1991, *Lacan and the Subject of Language*, Routledge, New York.

—1995a, 'The Relation Between the Voice and the Gaze', *Reading Seminar XI: Lacan's Four Fundamental Concepts of Psychoanalysis*, edit. Richard Feldstein, Bruce Fink and Maire Jaanus, State University of New York, New York, pp. 187–203.

—1995b, *Essays on the Pleasure of Death From Freud to Lacan*, Routledge, New York.

—1999, 'Lacan's Theory of Sublimation: A New Look at Sophocles's *Antigone*', *Critical Essays on Jacques Lacan*, G. K. Hall & Co., New York, pp. 102–118.

Regnault, François, 'Art After Lacan', trans. Barbara P. Fulks and Jorge Jauregui, *Lacanian Ink*, Issue No. 19, 2003, pp. 47–69.

Richardson, The Johns Hopkins University Press, Baltimore, pp. 173–212.

—1992, *Acts of Literature*, edit. Derek Attridge, Routledge, New York.

—1995a, *Points . . . Interviews, 1974–1994*, trans. Peggy Kamuf et al., edit. Elisabeth Weber, Stanford University Press, California.

—1998, *Resistance of Psychoanalysis*, trans. Peggy Kamuf, Pascale-Anne Brault, and Michael Nass, Stanford University Press, California.

—2002, *Negotiations: Interventions and Interviews*, 1971–2001, Stanford University Press, Stanford.

Richardson, William, 1996, 'The Third Generation of Desire', *Disseminating Lacan*, edit. David Pettigrew and François Raffoul, State University of New York, New York, pp. 171–188.

Rose, Jacqueline, 1985, 'Sexuality in the Reading of Shakespeare: *Hamlet* and *Measure for Measure*', *Alternative Shakespeare*, edit. John Drakakis, Methuen & Co. Ltd, London, pp. 95–118.

—1996, *Sexuality in the Field of Vision*, Verso Press, London.

Ross, Andrew, 1986, *Failure of Modernism: Symptoms of American Poetry*, Columbia University Press, New York.

Roudinesco, Elisabeth, 1990, *Jacques Lacan & Co. A History of Psychoanalysis in France, 1925–1985*, trans. Jeffrey Mehlman, The University of Chicago Press, Chicago.

—1997, *Jacques Lacan*, trans. Barbara Bray, Columbia University Press, New York.

—2002, *Why Psychoanalysis?* trans. Rachel Bowlby, Columbia University Press, New York.

—2003, 'The Mirror Stage: an Obliterated Archive', trans. Barbara Bray, *The Cambridge Companion to Lacan*, edit. Jean-Michel Rabaté, Cambridge University Press, Cambridge, pp. 25–34.

Roughley, Alan, 1991, *James Joyce and Critical Theory: An Introduction*, Harvester Wheatsheaf, Hertfordshire.

Roustang, François, 1990, *The Lacanian Delusion*, trans. G. Sims, Oxford University Press, Oxford.

Ruwet, Nicolas, 'Parallelism and Deviation in Poetry', *French Literary Theory Today: A Reader*, trans. R. Carter edit. Tzvetan Todorov, Cambridge University Press, London, pp. 92–124.

Rylance, Rick, 1994, *Modern Cultural Theories: Roland Barthes*, Harvester Wheatsheaf, Hertfordshire, Hamel Hempstead.

Safouan, Moustafa, 1996, 'Sexuality in Neurosis and Psychosis: Two Letters from Freud to Jung', *Disseminating Lacan*, edit. David Pettigrew and Francois Raffoul, State University of New York Press, New York, pp. 241–248.

—2002, *The Seminar of Moustafa Safouan*, edit. Anna Shane and Janet Mackintosh, The Other Press, New York.

—2004, *Four Lessons of Psychoanalysis*, edit. Anna Shane, Other Press, New York.

Saguaro, Shelley, 2000 (edit.) *Psychoanalysis and Woman: A Reader*, Macmillan Press Ltd, London.

Salecl, Ranata, 1994, 'Love: Providence or Despair', *Lacan and Love*, No. 23, Summer, 1994, pp. 12–24.

—2000, 'Love and Sexual Difference: Double Partners in Men and Women', *Sexuation*, Slavoj Žižek and Ranata Salecl, pp. 297–316.

Samuels, Robert, 1993, *Between Philosophy and Psychoanalysis*: Lacan's Reconstruction of Freud, Routledge, New York.

Sanders, Wilbur, 1971, *John Donne's Poetry*, Cambridge University Press, Cambridge.

Sangiau, Nati, 1994, 'Reverencing the Letter or the Stopping of the Lacanian Movement', *The Lacanian School: Papers of The Freudian School of Melbourne*, edit. David Pereira, pp. 47–54.

Sarup, Madan, 1992, *Modern Cultural Theorists: Lacan*, Harvester Wheatsheaf, Hamel Hempstead.

Saussure, Ferdinand de, 1977, *Course in General Linguistics*, edit. Charles Bally and Albert Sechehaye, trans. Wade Baskin, Fontana/ Collins, London.

Schneiderman, Stuart, 1980 (edit.) *Returning to Freud: Clinical Psychoanalysis in the School of Lacan*. Yale University Press, New Haven.

—1983, *Jacques Lacan: The Death of an Intellectual Hero*, Harvard University Press, Cambridge.

Scofield, Martin, 1980, *The Ghosts of Hamlet: the Play and Modern Writers*, Cambridge University Press, Cambridge.

Selden, Raman, 2005, *The Cambridge History of Literary Criticism, Volume VIII: From Formalism to Poststructuralism*, Cambridge University Press, Cambridge.

Sellers, Susan, 1991, *Language and Sexual Difference: Feminist Writing In France*, Macmillan Education Ltd, Hampshire.

Shakespeare, W., 1988, *The Complete Works: Compact Edition*, edit. Stanley Wells and Gary Taylor, Oxford University Press, Oxford.

Shapiro, David, 1979, *John Ashbery: An Introduction to the Poetry*, Columbia University Press, New York.

—1992, *The Tragedy of Hamlet, Prince of Denmark*, The New Folger Library Shakespeare, Washington Square Press, New York.

Shechner, Mark, 1974, *Joyce in Nighttown: A Psychoanalytic Inquiry*, University of California Press, Berkeley.

Shepherdson, Charles, 2000, *Vital Signs: Nature, Culture, Psychoanalysis*, Routledge, New York.

Shetley, Vernon, 1993, *After the Death of Poetry: Poet and Audience in Contemporary America*, Duke University Press, Durham.

Smith, A. J. and Catherine Philips, 1996, *John Donne: The Critical Heritage, Volume II*, Routledge, London.

Smith, Grover, 1965, *T.S. Eliot's Poetry & Plays: A Study in Sources & Meaning*, The University of Chicago Press, Chicago.

Smith, Joseph, H. and William Kerrigan, 1987 (edit.) *Taking Chances: Derrida, Psychoanalysis and Literature*, John Hopkins University Press, Baltimore.

Soler, Colette, 1999, 'Literature as Symptom', *Critical Essays on Jacques Lacan*, edit. Ellie Ragland, G. K. Hall & Co. New York, 69–75.

—2000, 'The Curse on Sex' *Sexuation*, edit. Ranata Salecl, Duke University Press, Durham, pp. 39–53.

—2002, 'What Does the Unconscious Knows about Women?' *Reading Seminar XX: Lacan's Major Work on Love, Knowledge, and Feminine Sexuality* (edit.) State University of New York, New York, pp. 47–56.

—2003, 'The Paradoxes of the Symptom in Psychoanalysis', *The Cambridge Companion to Lacan*, edit. Jean-Michel Rabaté, Cambridge University Press, Cambridge, pp. 86–101.

Sollers, Philippe, 1983, *Writing and the Experience of Limits*, trans. Philip Barnard with David Hayman, edit. David Hayman, Columbia University Press, New York.

Stanton, Martin, 1983, *Outside the Dream: Lacan and French Styles of Psychoanalysis*, Routledge & Kegan Paul, London.

Staten, Henry, 2002, *Eros in Mourning: Homer to Lacan*, Johns Hopkins University Press, Baltimore.

Stoltzfus, Ben, 1996, *Lacan and Literature*, State University of New York, Albany.

Taylor, Victor E., and Charles E. Winquist, 1998, *Postmodernism-Critical Concepts*, Routledge, London.

Thurston, Luke, 1998, 'Ineluctable Nodalities: On the Borromean Knot', *Key Concepts of Lacanian Psychoanalysis*, edit. Dany Nobus, Rebus Press, London, pp. 139–163.

—2002, 'Introduction: Lacan's *pas-à-lire*', *Re-Inventing the Symptom, Essays on the Final Lacan*, Other Press, New York, pp. xiii–xx.

—2004, *James Joyce and the Problem of Psychoanalysis*, Cambridge University Press, Cambridge.

Todorov, Tzvetan, 1982 (edit.) *French Literary Theory Today*, Cambridge University Press, Cambridge.

Traub, Valerie, 'Positioning Psychoanalysis and the Female Reproductive Body', *Postmodern Shakespeare*, edit. Stephen Orgel and Sean Keilen, Garland Publishing, Inc, New York, pp. 202–221.

Turkle, Sherry, 1978, *Psychoanalytic Politics*, The Guilford Press, London.

Turve, Rosemond, 1974, *Elizabethan and Metaphysical Imagery: Renaissance Poetic and Twentieth-Century Critics*, University of Chicago Press, Chicago.

Valéry, Paul, 1972, 'Poetry and Abstract Thought: Dancing and Walking', *20th Century Literary Criticism*, edit. David Lodge, Longman Group Limited, London, pp. 254–263.

Van Boheemen-Saaf, Christine, 1999, Joyce, *Derrida, Lacan and the Trauma of History*, Cambridge University Press, Cambridge.

Vanier, Alain, 2000, *Lacan*, trans. Susan Fairfield, Other Press, New York.

Verhaeghe, Paul, 1999, *Does the Woman Exist? From Freud's Hysteric to Lacan's Feminine*, trans. Marc du Ry, The Other Press, New York.

—2001, *Beyond Gender: From Subject to Drive*, Other Press, New York.

Vice, Sue, 1996 (edit.) *Psychoanalytic Criticism: A Reader*, Polity Press, Oxford.

Voruz, Véronique, 2002, 'Acephalic Litter as Phallic letter', *Re-Inventing the Symptom: Essays on the Final Lacan,* edit. Luke Thurston, Other Press, New York, pp. 111–141.

Watson, Robert I., 1963, *The Great Psychologists: From Aristotle to Freud,* second edition, University of New Hampshire Press, Philadelphia.

Webb, Eugene, 1993, *The Self Between: From Freud to the New Social Psychology in France,* University of Washington Press, Washington.

Wellek, René and Austin Warren, 1956, *Theory of Literature: A Seminar Study of Nature and Function of Literature in all its Contexts,* Peregine Books, Harmondsworth.

William, Linda Ruth, 1995, *Critical Desire: Psychoanalysis and the Literary Subject,* Edward Arnold, London.

Wright, Elizabeth, 1984, *Psychoanalytic Criticism: Theory and Practice,* Methuen & Co. Ltd, London.

—1999, *Speaking of Desires Can be Dangerous: The Poetics of the Unconscious,* Polity Press in association with Blackwell Publishers Ltd, Cambridge.

Young, Robert, 1981 (edit.) *Untying the Text: A Poststructuralist Reader,* Routledge and Kegan Paul, London.

Žižek, Slavoj, 1989, *The Sublime Object of Ideology,* Verso, London.

—1992a, *Enjoy Your Symptom: Jacques Lacan in Hollywood and Out,* Routledge, London.

—1992b, *Looking Awry: An Introduction to Jacques Lacan Through Popular Culture,* MIT Press, Cambridge.

—1995, 'The Lamella of David Lynch', *Reading Seminar XI: Lacan's Four Fundamental Concepts of Psychoanalysis,* trans. Bruce Fink edit. Richard Feldstein, Bruce Fink and Mare Jaanus, State University of New York Press, New York, pp. 205–222.

—1997, 'From Joyce-the-Symptom to the Symptom of Power', *Lacanian Ink,* Issue No. 11, 1997, pp. 12–25.

—1998, 'The Seven Veils of Fantasy', *Key Concepts of Psychoanalysis,* edit. Dany Nobus, Rebus Press, London, pp. 190–218.

—2002, 'The Real of Sexual Difference', *Reading Seminar XX: Lacan's Major Work on Love, Knowledge, and Feminine Sexuality,* State University of New York, New York, pp. 57–76.

Zupančič, Alenka, 2000, *Ethics of the Real: Kant and Lacan,* Verso, London.

Index

www.ingramcontent.com/pod-product-compliance
Lightning Source LLC
LaVergne TN
LVHW052320200926
848481LV00002B/625

* 9 7 8 1 4 4 1 1 4 9 3 0 5 *